JAVA PROGRAMMING

By

PIYUSH CHOUDHARY

B.E. (Hons), M.Tech.

Deptt. of Computer Science & Engg.

Prestige Institute of Engg. & Science

Indore (M.P.)

S.K. KATARIA & SONS®

Educational Publishers

4885/109, Prakash Mahal, Dr. Subhash Bhargav Lane,
Opposite Delhi Medical Association, Daryaganj, New Delhi-110002 (INDIA)
Phone : +91-11-43551243; Mobile: +91-9871775858, 7678425209
e-mail: katariabook@gmail.com, katariabooks@yahoo.com
Website: www.skkatariaandsons.com

(e-books, subscriptions and bulk buying also available on our website)

Published by:

S.K. Kataria & Sons®

4885/109, Prakash Mahal, Dr. Subhash Bhargav Lane,
Opposite Delhi Medical Association, Daryaganj, New Delhi-110002 (INDIA)
Phone: +91-11-43551243; Mobile: +91-9871775858, 7678425209
e-mail: katariabook@gmail.com, katariabooks@yahoo.com
Website: www.skkatariaandsons.com

First Edition: 2012, Reprint: 2026

Laser Typesetting by :
AISA Enterprises, Delhi-110092

Printed at:
ARORA ENTERPRISES, Laxmi Nagar Delhi-92

Preface

Dear Students,

It gives us a great pleasure and an opportunity to present this book on "JAVA Programming", specially for you.

This text book has been written strictly as per revised syllabus prescribed by Rajiv Gandhi Technical University for B.E. third year Information Technology students. This book is also useful for B.E. second year (All branches students), MCA students and other B.E. students affiliating to different universities.

It is also useful for the programmers, who wish to know about the JAVA Technologies. This book uses simple and easy way to understand the basic concept of JAVA Programming.

This book has been divided into six parts. The first five parts contains the five units of the syllabus of R.G.P.V. and the sixth part contains the practical implementation of all the theoretical approaches that we had studied in above five parts. The sixth part is more important from the practical point of view.

Unit-I consists of two chapters which refers to introduction to JAVA programming.

Unit-II deals with the use of GUI, *i.e.*, Graphical User Interface, which tells us about the features of AWT, JAVA event handling, Applets and Swings.

Unit-III provides the information about the concept of multithreading and exception handling.

Unit-IV deals with exploring I/O in JAVA and Java data base connectivity.

Unit-V contains two chapters based on the concept of JAVA Networking and Remote Method Invocation.

Unit-VI consists of one chapter entitled "Programming Approach" which contains numerous of programs for beginners to experts. This chapter also contains the complete web application development process using JSP.

Efforts are made to make the book easy to understand the subject. However, I will be highly obliged to receive any suggestion in this regard that will help me for further improvement of this book.

Finally, I wish all the readers of this book a very good luck......

AUTHOR

Acknowledgement

This book would have never been a success without the help of some people, whom I would like to give my sincere thanks.

First of all, I pay my sincere thanks to **Dr. Dilip R. Pangavhane**, Director of **Prestige Institute of Engineering and Science,** Indore for their kind co-operation and encouragement.

Special thanks to **Dr. D.P.S. Chauhan** (Former Director of PIES, Indore). My Sincere thanks to Advisor **Prof. H.S. Mehta** and Vice-Principal **Dr. Atul Upadhyay** of PIES for their co-operation and moral support during development of this book.

I express the deep sense of gratitude for the encouragement received from **Ms. Jaya Thomas** and also thanks to **Ms. Rupali Pathak** for their valuable suggestions.

I would like to thank **Mr. Sanjeev Kataria** proprietor of M/s S.K. Kataria and Sons who have been taken considerable pains and shown extreme cooperation during making of this book.

I extend my thanks to my colleagues **Mr. Naveen Kumar Joshi**, **Mr. Mahavir Jain**, **Mrs. Tina Gupta** and all staff members of Prestige Institute of Engineering and Science, Indore for their console and guidance during the making of this book.

Last but not least I want to thank my sister **Ms. Harsha Choudhary** and all my family members giving me warm wishes for completing this book.

AUTHOR

This book is Dedicated to....

MY PARENTS

(Mrs. Vidhya and Mr. Subhash Choudhary)

FOR MAKING ME WHAT I AM TODAY

—Piyush Choudhary

Contents

UNIT- I

➤ Introduction to Java
➤ Object Oriented Programming in Java

SYLLABUS

The Java Environment : Java Development Kit (JDK), Java virtual machine, Java programming environment (compiler, interpreter, applet viewer, debugger), Java Applications Programming Interface (API), Basic idea of application and applet.

Java as an Object Oriented Language : Objects, classes, encapsulation, inheritance, and software reuse, polymorphism, abstract classes and abstract methods : defining an interface, implementing and applying interfaces, variables in interfaces, extending interfaces, Packages, scope and lifetime; Access specifies; Constructors; Copy constructor; this pointer; finalize () method; arrays; Memory allocation and garbage collection.

CHAPTER 1

Introduction to Java

INSIDE THIS CHAPTER

Well friends, when the chronicle of computer languages is written, the following will be said: B led to C, C evolved with C++ and C++ set the stage for Java. To understand Java is to understand the reasons that why it was created, how it works and where its scope lies. The answer to all these questions lies in this chapter. So read the chapter and have fun with JAVA programming.

1.1. INTRODUCTION TO JAVA

In 1991, Sun Micro System wants to develop a software to control electronic devices. This software is developed under the act of **Green Project**. An electronic device known as **Star-7**, for which an operating system has to be developed. The language they used to develop the software was C++. But one of the team member, **James Gosling**, was not comfortable with the performance of C++. Hence, he developed a new language for Star-7. He named it "**OAK**", as he used to see oak tree outside his office. The members other than James Gosling involve in the development process of OAK are **Patrik Naughton, Chris Warth, Ed Frank and Mike Sheridan**. But later they found that the name "OAK" was being used by some other language, sun renamed this language as "Java" in 1995.

1.1.1. What is Java?

Java is a platform independent object oriented programming language developed by Sun Micro System in the duration of 1991-1995.

Java is a Platform Independent Programming Language.

Over a period of time Java has gained a huge popularity because of its very nature of platform independence. Java has established itself as a high performance cross platform language. Java programs can run on any kind of client machine on the internet without actually making any changes to the source code. This is achieved through JVM (*i.e.,* Java Virtual Machine). JVM doesn't allow your program to directly interact with the hardware and acts as an interface between the hardware and the code. So as Java program reaches the client side, it helps in the execution of the program specific to the local processor. The following description is about how a Java program is executed:

The Java program *i.e.,* .java file executes as :

It is compiled at the developers end, uploaded on the internet server, then it is interpreted again and executed.

Java programs are compiled and converted to something called byte code (.class file). Byte code is nothing but a series of instructions in the form of bytes. These instructions are not machine specific, but are written in JVM. JVM is a software for virtual machine, *i.e.,* the machine which really doesn't exist, but in reality is a simulated environment. The byte code or the .class file is not capable of running on its own, and it has to resides in the web pages. We can develop the web pages through HTML and call the .class file inside it. The page is then transported over the internet by uploading it at a specific website.

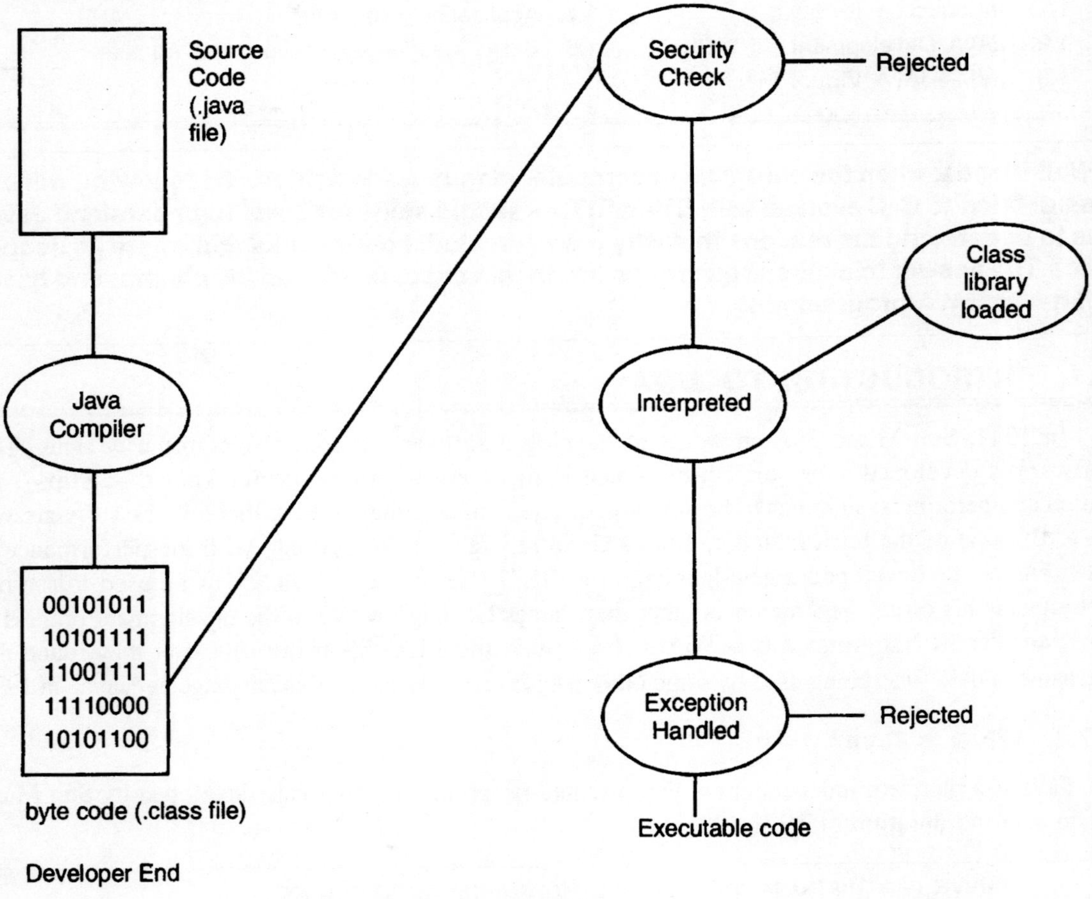

Fig. 1.1.

At the client side the web page is accessed using a browser. The browser should have a java component inside it, *i.e.,* it should be java enabled otherwise it should not recognize the applet and take it as ordinary HTML Text.

When the web page is accessed by the client, the java program embedded inside the html document begins to run.

1 At the beginning, a security check is applied on the incoming java code in-order to find out it is true java code or not.

2 It would then be linked and finally interpreted according to the current machines architecture.

3 In the meantime, if any errors or exceptions occurs, they would be handled and the program runs.

Java is object oriented programming language.

Unlike C++, java is totally an object oriented language. Everything in Java can only be written inside the classes. Though one may think that the program would some what become rigid by confining everything only inside the classes, but it is certainly has a profound effect on the programming style. In C++, we have a total flexibility of writing our programs by combining the object oriented or structured oriented programming style. But this mixed approach has a side effect, as the program tends to be less object oriented. Moreover, it becomes easier for the designer to design if the approach is totally object oriented than mixed one.

1.1.2. Features of Java

Apart, from being platform independent and object oriented java contains the following basic features :

1. Compile and Interpreted

Usually, a computer language is either compiled or interpreted. Java combines both these approaches thus making java a **two stage system.**

First, Java compiler translates source code into what is known as **Byte code** instructions. Byte codes are not the machine instructions and hence in the second step, Java interpreter generates machine code that can be directly executed by the machine that is running the java program.

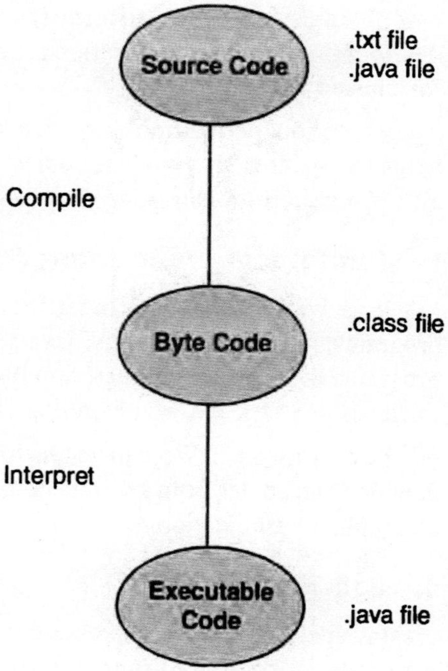

Fig. 1.2.

2. Java is Freeware Language

Java is freeware means it can be downloaded from internet absolutely free of cost, from website www.sun.com/product/jdk.

3. Easiness

Java was designed to be easy for the professional programmer to learn and use effectively. Java inherits the C/C++ syntax and many of the object oriented features of C++, hence it is easy to learn Java.

4. Robust

The multiplatformed environment of the web places extraordinary demands on a program, because the program must execute reliably in a variety of systems. Thus, the ability to create robust program was given a high priority in the design of java. To gain reliability, java restricts you in a few key areas, to find your mistakes early in program development. At the same time, Java frees us from having to worry about many of the most common causes of programming errors. Because Java is strictly **typed language**, it checks our code

1. At Compile time as well as
2. At run time.

Hence, many hard-to-track down bugs that are produced at run-time situations are simply impossible to create in Java.

For example: To better understand how Java is robust, consider two of the main reasons for the program failure :

- Memory management mistakes.
- Mishandled exceptional conditions (*i.e.,* run-time error).

Memory management can be difficult, tedious task in traditional programming environments. For example, in C/C++, the programmer must manually allocate and free all dynamic memory. This sometimes leads to problems, because programmer will either forget to free memory that has been previously allocated or, worse try to free some memory that another part of their code is still using. **Java virtually eliminates these problems by managing memory allocation and deallocation.** Infact, deallocation is completely automatic, because Java provides garbage collection for unused objects.

Exceptional condition may arise in situation such as **division by zero** or **file not found**. Java helps in this area by providing object oriented exception handling. In a well written Java program, all run-time errors can—and should—be managed by your program.

5. Multithreaded and Interactive

Java was designed to meet the real world requirement of creating interactive, networked programs. To accomplish this, java supports multithreaded programming which allows us to write programs that do many things simultaneously. This means that we need not wait for the application to finish one task before beginning another.

For example : We can listen to an audio clip while scrolling a page and at the same time download an applet from a distant computer. This feature greatly improves the interactive performance of graphical application.

6. High Performance

Java performance is impressive for an interpreted language, mainly due to the use of intermediate byte code. According to sun, java speed is comparable to the native C/C++. Java architecture is also designed to reduce overheads during runtime. Further, the incorporation of multithreading enhances overall execution speed of Java program.

7. Safe and Secure

Security becomes an important issue for a language that is used for programming on the internet. Threat of viruses and abuse of resources is every where. Java system not only verifies all memory access but also ensures that no viruses are communicated with an applet. **The absence of Pointer in java ensures that programs cannot get memory locations without proper authorization**.

8. Distributed

Java is designed for the distributed environment of the internet, because it handles TCP/IP protocols. Infact, accessing a resources using URL is not much different from accessing a file. The original version of Java (Oak) included features for intra-address-space messaging. This allowed objects on two different computers to executes procedures remotely. Java revived these interfaces in a package called **Remote Method Invocation (RMI)**. This feature brings an unparalleled level of abstraction to client/server programming.

1.1.3. Difference between C++ and Java

C++ and Java both are object oriented programming language. However, both the languages are different in both design and philosophy. The difference between both the languages is given below in table as :

S.No.	C++	Java
1.	C++ was developed by Bjarne Stroutsup in the duration of 1979 to 1983.	Java was developed by James Gosling in the duration of 1991-1995.
2.	C++ support classes, Structure and Unions.	Java Support Classes but doesn't support Structure or Unions.
3.	Global Function and Global data is allowed in C++	Global Function and Global data are not allowed in Java.
4.	C++ supports multiple inheritance.	Java doesn't support Multiple inheritance.
5.	C++ supports the concept of Pointers.	Java doesn't support the concept of Pointers. This make Java program to be very safe.
6.	C++ supports all data types like integer, character, float etc., but it doesn't support Boolean type.	Java supports all data types including Boolean type which provide true or false value.
7.	C++ requires that classes and functions be declared before they are used	It is not necessary in Java to declare classes and functions before they used.
8.	C++ support Constructor as well as Destructor.	Java support Constructor, but there is no destructor in Java.
9.	Data Structure classes are not their.	Several "data structure" classes are contained in the "standard" version of Java. More specifically, they are contained in the standard class library that is distributed with the Java Development Kit (JDK).
10.	It doesn't support concept of Multi-threading	Multithreading is a standard feature of the Java language.
11.	It doesn't support concept of Exception Handling.	It support concept of Exception handling.
12.	C++ support operator overloading	Java does not support operator overloading
13.	C++ doesn't have built-in support for program documentation.	Java has built-in support for program documentation.

1.1.4. Data Types in Java

Java defines eight basic data types, which are given below :

Data Types	Width	Range	Usage
Numbers and Floating point numbers Bytes	8	–128 to 127	Useful when working with stream of data
Short Int	16 32	–32,768 to 32,767 –2,147,483,648 to 2,147,483,647	short s; int x=200;
Long	64	-2^{63} to $2^{63} - 1$	long seconds;
Double	64	$1.7e^{-308}$ to $1.7e^{+308}$	Used when more precision is needed double speed;
Float	32	$3.4e^{-038}$ to $3.4e^{+038}$	Used when lesser level of precision is needed float sinResult;
Characters Char	16	0 to 65,536	Java uses Unicode to define characters *Character can assigned character values or codes equivalent to some character.* Char choice = 'y' Char trap = 27;
Boolean		True / false	Boolean flag = true

1.1.5. Operators in JAVA

Java classifies operators as :

S.No.	Type	Description	Symbol	Usage
1.	Arithmetic	Addition	+	int no =1+1
		Subtraction	–	int no=1–1
		Multiplication	*	int no=1*1
		Division	/	int no=1/1
		Modulus	%	int no=1%1
		Increment	++	no++ or ++no
2.	Bitwise	Not	~	a =2 Binary Representation a = 10 ~a=01

<table>
<tr><th>S.No.</th><th>Type</th><th>Description</th><th>Symbol</th><th>Usage</th></tr>
<tr><td rowspan="3"></td><td rowspan="3"></td><td>AND</td><td>&</td><td>a=2, b=3
Binary Representation
a=10
b=11
a & b=10</td></tr>
<tr><td>OR</td><td>|</td><td>a=2, b=3
Binary Representation
a=10
b=11
a | b=11</td></tr>
<tr><td>Exclusive-OR</td><td>^</td><td>a=2, b=3
Binary Representation
a=10
b=11
a^ b=01</td></tr>
<tr><td rowspan="6">3.</td><td rowspan="6">Relational</td><td>Equal to</td><td>= =</td><td>a==b</td></tr>
<tr><td>Not Equal to</td><td>! =</td><td>a!=b</td></tr>
<tr><td>Greater than</td><td>></td><td>a>b</td></tr>
<tr><td>Less than</td><td><</td><td>a<b</td></tr>
<tr><td>Greater than or equal to</td><td>>=</td><td>a>=b</td></tr>
<tr><td>Less than or equal to</td><td><=</td><td>a<=b</td></tr>
</table>

1.1.6. Versions of JAVA

Till date, JAVA has come up with various versions. JAVA was first launched as JAVA 1.0, and then came JAVA 1.1 with some additional features. After that JAVA 1.2 was launched, this was also referred to as JAVA 2. JAVA 1.4, 1.5 are the famous JAVA versions. The latest version of JAVA, *i.e.*, JAVA 1.6 supports various new built in classes and collection framework.

1.1.7. Comments in JAVA

In JAVA comments can be given to any statement by using two styles, these styles are:

1. "//" Style
2. "/*   */" Style

1. **"// " Style: "//"** Style is used to comment a single line. It can be placed anywhere in line and the compiler would ignore anything following it.
2. **"/*   */" Style: "/*   */"** used to mark a block as comment entry. This is very Useful when the comment entry extends several lines.

1.1.8. Scope of JAVA

JAVA programming enables secure and high performance software development on multiple platforms. Many companies in India have well-qualified software engineers having expertise in Java, Java Script, J2SE, JSP, and J2ME, JAVA Programming Services help your businesses to do better. They provide variety of Java development services including project solutions.

1.2. JAVA DEVELOPMENT KIT (JDK)

A Java Development Kit (JDK) is a program development environment for writing Java applets and applications. It consists of a runtime environment that "sits on top" of the operating system layer as well as the tools and programming that developers need to compile, debug, and run applets and applications written in the Java language.

JAVA development kit comes with the collection of tools that are used for developing and running JAVA programs.

It includes:

1. **applet viewer :** The applet viewer enables us to run java applets without actually using a java compatible browser.
2. **java :** JAVA Interpreter which runs java applet and application by reading and interpreting byte code files.
3. **javac :** The JAVA Compiler, which translates java source code to byte code files that the interpreter can understand.
4. **javadoc :** Creates HTML format documentation from java source code file.
5. **javah :** Produces header files for use with native methods.
6. **javap :** Java disassembler, which enable us to convert byte code files into program description.
7. **jdb :** Java debugger, which helps us to find error in our program.
8. **jps :** The process status tool, which displays process information for current Java processes.
9. **javaws :** The Java Web Start launcher for JNLP applications.
10. **jar :** The archiver, which packages related class libraries into a single JAR file. This tool also helps manage JAR files.
11. **extcheck :** A utility which can detect JAR-file conflicts.
12. **apt :** The annotation-processing tool.
13. **jhat :** Java heap analysis tool.
14. **jstack :** Utility which prints Java stack traces of Java threads.
15. **jstat :** Java Virtual Machine statistics monitoring tool.
16. **jstatd :** Jstat daemon.
17. **jinfo :** This utility gets configuration information from a running Java process or crash dump.
18. **jmap :** This utility outputs the memory map for Java and can print shared object memory maps or heap memory details of a given process or core dump.
19. **idlj :** the IDL-to-Java compiler. This utility generates Java bindings from a given Java IDL file.
20. **policytool :** The policy creation and management tool, which can determine policy for a Java runtime, specifying which permissions are available for code from various sources.
21. **VisualVM :** Visual tool integrating several command-line JDK tools and lightweight performance and memory profiling capabilities.
22. **jrunscript :** Java command-line script shell.

Hence we can says that JDK is a program development environment for writing a JAVA applets and applications. It consist of runtime environment that "sits on top" of operating system layers as well as the tools and programming that developer needs to compile, debug and run applets and application written in JAVA language.

The way these tools are applied to build and run application programs is illustrated in Fig. 1.3.

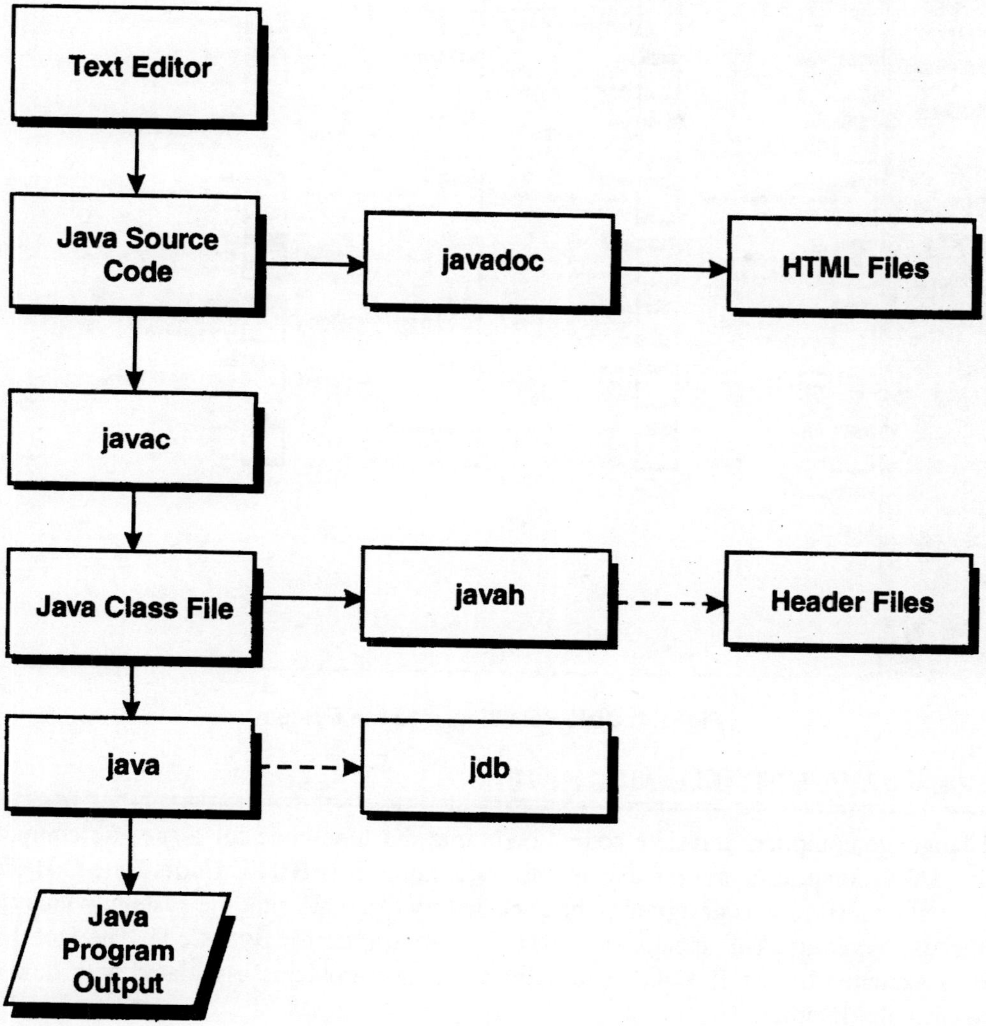

Fig. 1.3. Java Development Kit

To create a JAVA program we need to create a source code file using a text editor. The source code is then compiled using java compiler javac and executed using java interpreter java. The java debugger jdb is used to find errors, if any in the source code. A compiled java program can be converted into a source code with the help of java disassembler javap.

Note: Well friends we can see the JDK tools in our system if JAVA is installed in it by following the path as:

C:\Program Files\Java\jdk1.5.0_08\bin

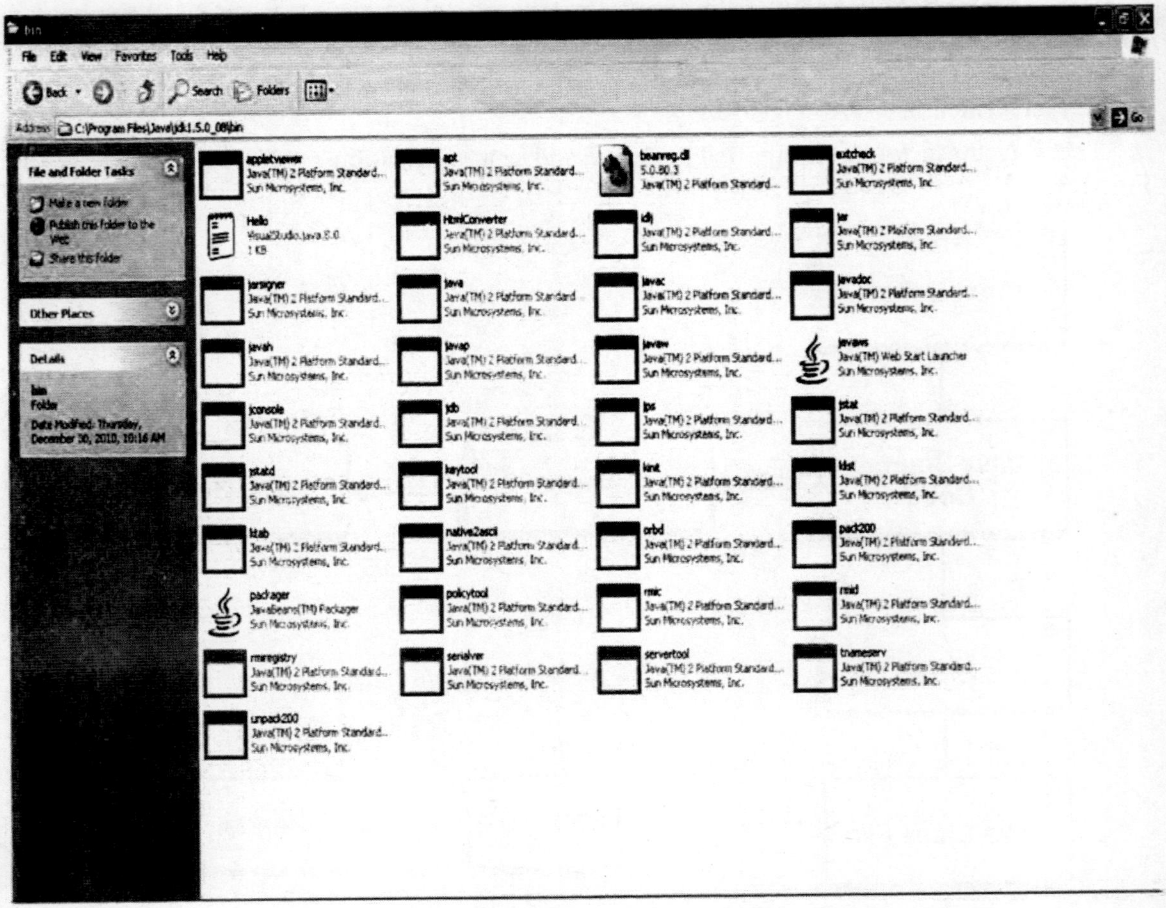

Fig. 1.4. JDK Real View Into the System

1.3. JVM—JAVA VIRTUAL MACHINE

All language compilers translate source code into machine code for a specific computer. The output of JAVA compiler is not the executable code, rather it is **BYTE Code.** Byte Code is highly optimized set of instructions designed to be executed by the JAVA runtime system, which is called **JAVA Virtual Machine.** This means that JVM is an interpreter for Byte Code. The fact that JAVA program is executed by the JVM helps to solve the major problems associated with downloading program over the internet.

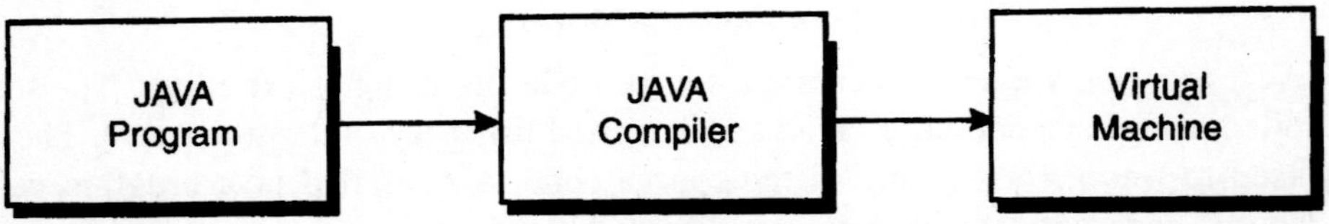

Fig. 1.5. Process of Compilation

The Virtual machine code is not a machine specific. The machine specific code (known as Machine Code) is generated by JAVA interpreter by acting as an intermediary between the virtual machine and the real machine.

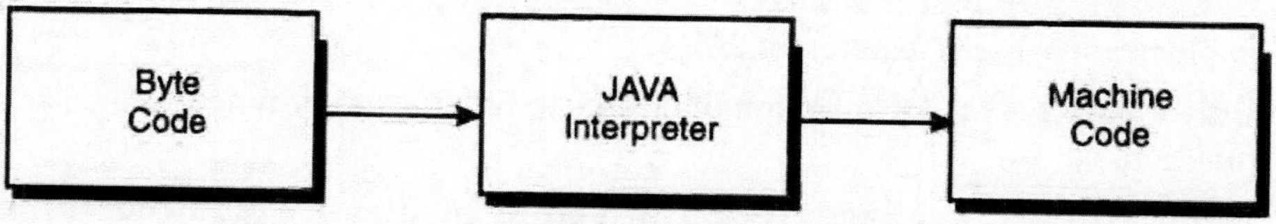

Fig. 1.6. Process of Interpretation

The fact that a JAVA program is interpreted also helps to make it secure. Because the execution of every JAVA program is under the control of the JVM, the JVM can contain the program and prevent it from generating side effect outside of the system.

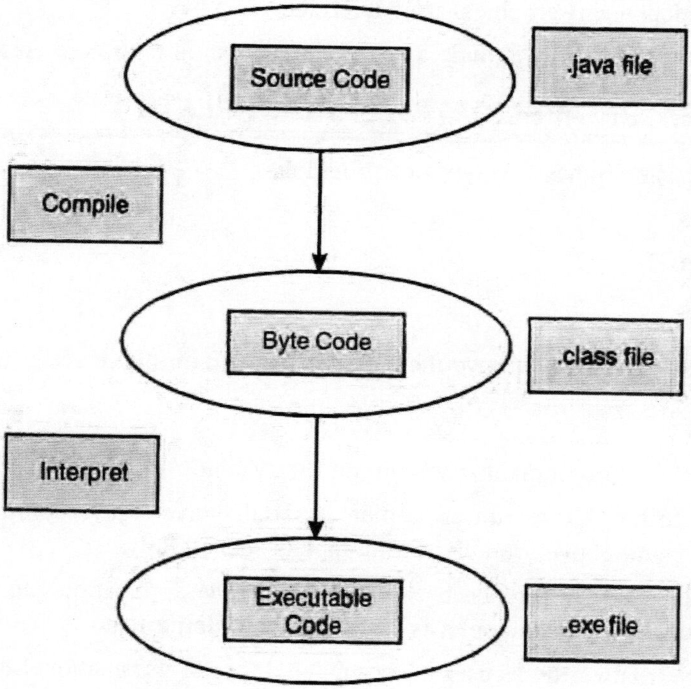

Fig. 1.7.

The figure illustrates how Java works on a typical computer. The JAVA object framework (JAVA API) act as an intermediary between the user programs and virtual machine which in turn acts as an intermediary between the operating system and JAVA Object.

1.4. APPLICATION PROGRAMMING INTERFACE (API)

The JAVA standard library (or API) includes hundreds of classes and methods grouped into several functional packages, like :

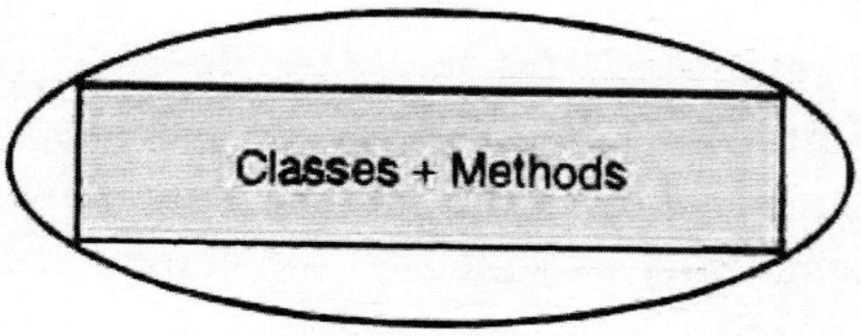

Fig. 1.8. Packages

1. **Language Support Packages :** A Collection of classes and methods required for implementing basic features of JAVA.
2. **Utility Packages :** A Collection of classes to provide utility function such as date and time function.
3. **Input/Output Packages :** A Collection of classes required for input/output manipulation.
4. **Networking Packages :** A Collection of classes for communicating with other computers via internet.
5. **Awt Packages :** The abstract windows Toolkit package contain classes that implements platform independent graphical user interface.
6. **Applet Packages :** This include a set of classes that allows us to create JAVA applet.

1.5. BASIC IDEA OF APPLICATION AND APPLETS

Java language basically has two types of programs-

1. Applets and
2. Application.

1. Applets

Applets are the programs that have the capability to run on the internet, through a browser.

2. Applications

Applications are the programs that we run on the system.

For a browser to be able to run an applet, it should have a java component inside it. The internet explorer 3.1 and above are able to run applets successfully.

There is another major difference between the two. The application can access the local file system and the resources, but the applet is restricted from doing that.

Applications are trustworthy as user is very much aware of its functionality and user knows the developer who has handed over the program to the user. But, in case of applets user do not know who is the author of the program or program is safe enough or not. Keeping this in mind, the applets are allowed to access the file system or anything else of only that machine, from where they came (*i.e.,* server hosting the applet), rather than local or client machine on which they will run.

1.5.1. Application

The applications and the applets are written completely in the form of classes as everything in java has to be present inside the class. There cannot be anything written outside a class, unlike C++, where we define the functions etc. outside a class. The class names should be following the naming conventions and it is case sensitive.

While executing an application, the JVM looks for the class with the same name as the file name. This class is called the **Initiating Class**. The public access specifier is given with the class so that the class is visible from outside, *i.e.,* to the JVM. It must have a method called the **'main( )'** which is the first method automatically executed by the compiler. From this method all the other classes and their methods are linked.

For example, A simple example of an application is given below :

```
class SimpleApplication
{
 public static void main(String args[])
{
   System.out.println("You have created your first application");
}
}
```

Save as : SimpleApplication.java

Compile as : javac SimpleApplication.java

Run as : java SimpleApplication

Output : You have created your first application

There is no inbuilt development environment in JDK. The programs can be written in the Dos editor- edit, or notepad.

Now, let us aware with the terms used in the program:

1. Public Keyword

The keyword 'public' is given which is an access specifier so as to make main( ) method visible outside the program, *i.e.,* the compiler is capable of seeing the main( ) method.

2. Static

Next appears the keyword 'static' which declares this method as one that belongs to the entire class and not a part of any object the class. The main( ) must always be declared as static since the interpreter uses this method before any object are created.

3. Void

The type modifier 'void' states that the main method doesn't return any value to the runtime environment from where it is originated.

4. Println

Print a line and move to the next line.

5. Output Line

The 'system.out.println("")' is a method to print on the output stream.

6. String args[]

String args[] declares a parameter named args, which is an array of instances of the class String. Here args[] receives any command-line arguments present when the program is executed.

1.5.2. Applets

Similar to applications, we starts writing an applet with a class having the same name as the filename. There is no main method, unlike the application. There are various other methods present in an applet.

Let us now look at how an applet runs:

```
import java.applet.*;
import java.awt.*;
public class Apple extends Applet
{
public void paint(Graphics g)
{
g.drawString("An Applet a day keeps a doctor away",50,50);
}
}
```

The first two statements are for importing or including the packages in the applet. A package is a set of classes categorized under a specific name and kept in the library. This program has included the java.awt package as it is using the method paint() and program also include the java.applet package as the main class must be inherited from the applet class. The 'extends' keyword is used for inheritance.

The paint(Graphics g) is a method used to draw a picture or text on the applet. It gets the applets graphics context automatically as the parameter. The graphics context is nothing but an area to write or draw something. So, the 'Graphics g' in the paint( ) function gets the applets graphics context, area where drawing etc. would happen. We are using the function draw String (String text, int position X, int position Y) in order to write some text on the applet.

The above applet must be saved as the same class name, *i.e.*, Apple.java and compiled as :

```
javac Apple.java.
```

This makes the .class file which contains the byte code. Since this is an applet, the .class file now have to be embedded inside an HTML document and run through a browser.

A very basic HTML document may be written as:

```
<html>
<head>
<title>"The Applet is Running"</title>
</head>
<body>
<applet code="Apple" height=200 width=200>
</applet>
</html>
```

The description of the above will be :

<html></html> tag specifies the beginning and the end of the HTML document

<head></head>tag specifies the header in which title section has been specified through**<title></title>**

<body></body>tag specifies the document region where text can be written and in which we want our applet to appear.

Finally, the applet is called through the <applet></applet>tag. The code specifies the .class filename, height and width determine the size of the applet. Now we can call the HTML document in the browser. As soon as the file is opened, the applet enveloped inside the HTML file also starts running.

SUMMARY

1. Java was developed by Sun Microsystems in the duration of 1991, originally called Oak.
2. Java is platform independent, object oriented language.
3. Java compiles and interpret, robust, simple and easy to learn, reliable, safe, secure, powerful and distributed.
4. Java supports two types of programs, application and applet. Applications do not run on the internet, whereas applets run on the internet.
5. Comments in java are with // or /* */
6. The java language has various data types like int, char, float and it support one special data type known as Boolean data type, which support only true or false values.
7. Java supports various operators like arithmetic, relational and bitwise operators.
8. Java was widely used for developing mobile applications and to develop programs that run on internet.

REVIEW QUESTIONS

1. What is JAVA? Explain the basic features of JAVA. Also explain its application area.
2. Write short note on :
   (*i*) Java Development Kit (JDK)
   (*ii*) Java Virtual Machine (JVM)
   (*iii*) Java Standard Library (JSL)
3. Write at least six differences between :
   (*i*) Compiler and Interpreter
   (*ii*) Application and Applets
   (*iii*) C++ and JAVA
4. Comment on the followings :
   (*i*) "Java language compiles as well as interprets".
   (*ii*) "Java is a platform independent language".

❑❑❑

CHAPTER 2

Object Oriented Programming in Java

INSIDE THIS CHAPTER

Well friends, in the previous chapter we found that—"object oriented programming is the core of Java Technology." But before implementing these core concepts let us learn about the OOP-methodology. This chapter tells us about the principles of OOPs methodology as it is so integral to Java.

2.1. OBJECT ORIENTED PROGRAMMING

The major objective of object-oriented approach is to eliminate some of the flaws encountered in the procedural approach. Before object oriented approach, programmers used the traditional approach of procedural programming. In procedural programming, the programmer gives a list of instructions to the computer system and the computer carries them out. As the code became large, there was a need felt to break the code into blocks called **Procedures** and **Functions**. This is known as **Structured Programming**.

Structured programming did help in maintaining manageable chunks of code but at the same time it had many drawbacks. Many time functions and procedures have to use outside their boundary. As a result of this, testing a module become more difficult, since each module has to be checked to see if it is working properly and the value that it changes isn't corrupted as a result. This problem is aggravated as a program size increase.

Another problem with the procedural programming was that data was given a secondary importance. Data is the most important thing in any application. Infact, data is the primary reason why the application exists. But in procedural programming more emphasis was laid on how data is going to be manipulated with the help of functions and procedures.

These problems are solved by the object oriented methodology. Data is given the primary importance in object oriented methodology. The core of object oriented technology is the **object,** then builds data and function around these objects.

Some of the features of object oriented paradigm are :

1. Emphasis on data rather than procedure.
2. Programs are divided into what are known as Objects.
3. Data structures are designed such that they characterized the objects.
4. Methods that operate on the data of an object are tied together in data structure.
5. Data is hidden and cannot be accessed by external functions.
6. Objects may communicate with each other through methods.
7. New data and methods can be easily added whenever necessary.
8. Follows bottom up approach is program design.

From the above discussion, we can define object oriented programming as :

Object-oriented programming is an approach that provides a way of modularizing programs by creating partitioned memory area for both data and function that can be used as templates for creating copies of such modules on demand.

2.2. BASIC CONCEPT OF OBJECT ORIENTED PROGRAMMING

The general concepts of object oriented programming which form the heart of JAVA programming are.

2.3. OBJECTS

Objects are the basic runtime entities in an object oriented system. It may represent a person, a place, a bank account, a table of data or any item that the program may handle. They may also represent user-defined data types such as vectors and list.

Definition : An instance of class is known as Objects.

An object encorporates both data and method that act upon that data.

For example : Let us take a real life example of Pen.

A Pen is an object that has characteristics (Colour, nib, body of pen etc.) and behaviour (a pen writes).

Similarly, in an object oriented technology an object comprises of characteristics (data) and behaviours (methods that operates on data).

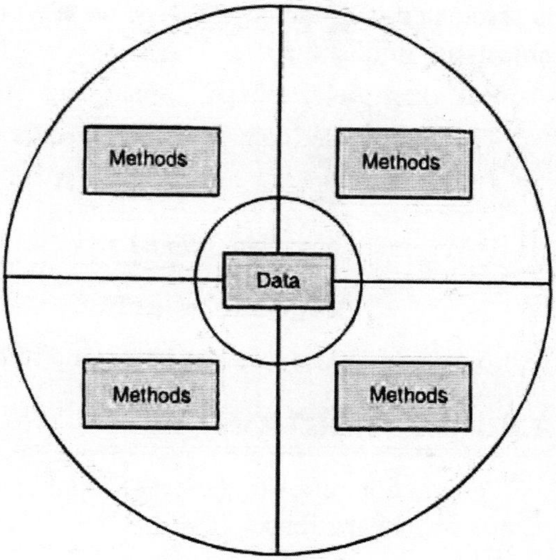

Fig. 2.1. Object = Data + Methods

When a program is executed, the objects interact by sending messages to one another.

For example : "Customer" and "account" are two objects in a banking program, then the customer object may send a message to the account object requesting for the bank balance.

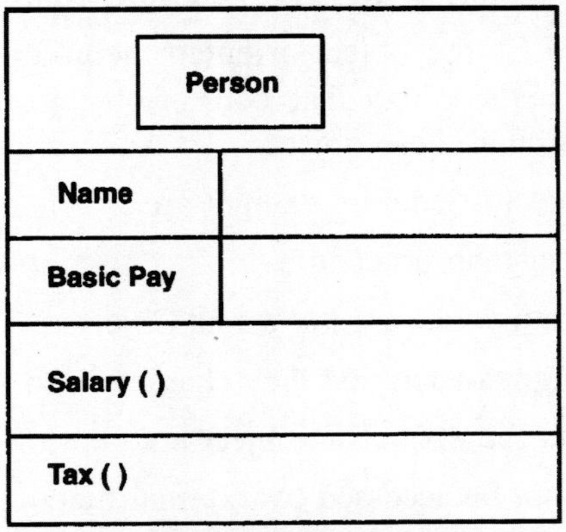

Fig. 2.2. Representation of Object

2.4. CLASSES

We know that Objects contain data and code to manipulate that data. The entire set of data and code of an object can be made user defined data-type using the concept of **class**.

A class is nothing but a collection of similar objects. These objects must have the same data structure and behaviour or method.

Definition : A Class is a user defined data type which is a collection of similar types of object.

For example, Sparrow, parrot and robin all belong to the class **bird,** since they all have same attributes and behaviour.

A class may be consider as a '**data type**' and an object as a '**variable**' of that data type. Once a class has been defined, we can create any number of objects belonging to that class. Each object is associated with the data of type class with which they are created. A class is thus a collection of objects of similar type.

For example, Cabbage, Tomato and Chilies are members of class Vegetable.

The syntax used to create an objects is similar to the syntax used to create an integer object.

```
int x;
```

If Vegetable has been defined as a class, then the statement

```
Vegetable cabbage;
```

will create an object cabbage belonging to class Vegetable.

2.5. ABSTRACTION

Abstraction refers to the act of representing essential features without including the background details or explanations.

In other words, we can says that Abstraction is the process of identifying the items of interest to a programmer from an application domain perspective and leaving out the details that are not relevant to programmer.

For example : Let us consider the example of order processing system. In this system, each item is given a unique item number by which it is identified. This item will have a description, rate, quantity on hand and reorder level status. Therefore the identity Item can have attributes as item number, description of the item, rate, quantity on hand and reorder level. Here it is noted that, we can take some more features like colour of the item, its dimensions etc.. But these attributes are not really important in order processing system so we omitted them from our design. This process of keeping the relevant details and discarding the irrelevant ones is known as **Abstraction**.

2.6. ENCAPSULATION

As we know that, an object incorporates both data and methods that act upon that data. This process of bundling data and methods together is known as **Encapsulation**.

Hence, we can define it as—

Definition : The wrapping up of data into a single unit is known as **Encapsulation**.

For example : Let us take the same example of Order Processing System again. We have decided on the data aspect of an object item *i.e.,* Item No., Description, Rate, Quantity in hand and Reorder level. Let us now identify the methods for the object item. The method could be :

- Printing the item details.
- Accepting the item details.
- Changing Quantity on hand.
- Displaying value of the stock.
- Displaying status whether an item has to be reorder or not.

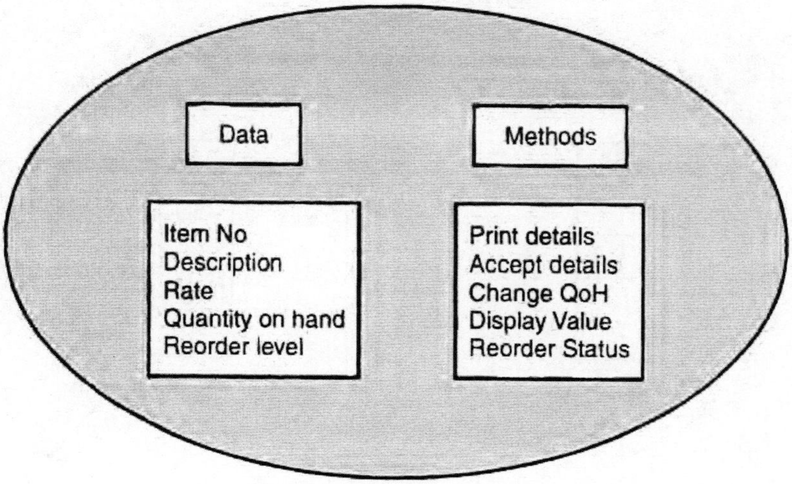

Fig. 2.3. Encapsulation

This process of bunding data and methods together (as shown in Fig. 2.3) is known as **Encapsulation**. The data is not accessible to the outside world and only those methods, which are wrapped in the class can access it. These methods provide the interface between the object's data and the program. This insulation of the data from the direct access by the program is called **Data Hiding**, and encapsulation achieve data hiding because on the outside it just presents the interfaces and the inner attributes remain hidden.

2.7. INHERITANCE AND SOFTWARE REUSE

Inheritance is the process by which objects of one class acquire the properties of objects of another class. It is the sharing of attributes and operations among classes based on hierarchical relationship.

For example : The animal dog is a part of the class Mammal, which is again a part of the class Animal. The principle behind this sort of division is that each derived class shares common characteristics with the class from which it is derived. The class dog has their own characteristics but share features of mammal class also, while mammal class have their own characteristics and share features of class Animals.

In OOP, the concept of inheritance provides the idea of reusability. This means that we can add additional features to an existing class without modifying it. This is possible by deriving a new class from the existing one. The new class will have the combined features of both the classes. Thus the real appeal and power of the inheritance mechanism is that it allows the programmer to reuse a class that is almost, but not exactly, what he wants and to tailor the class in such a way that it doesn't introduce any undesirable side effects into the rest of the classes. In Java, the derived class is known as '**Subclass**'.

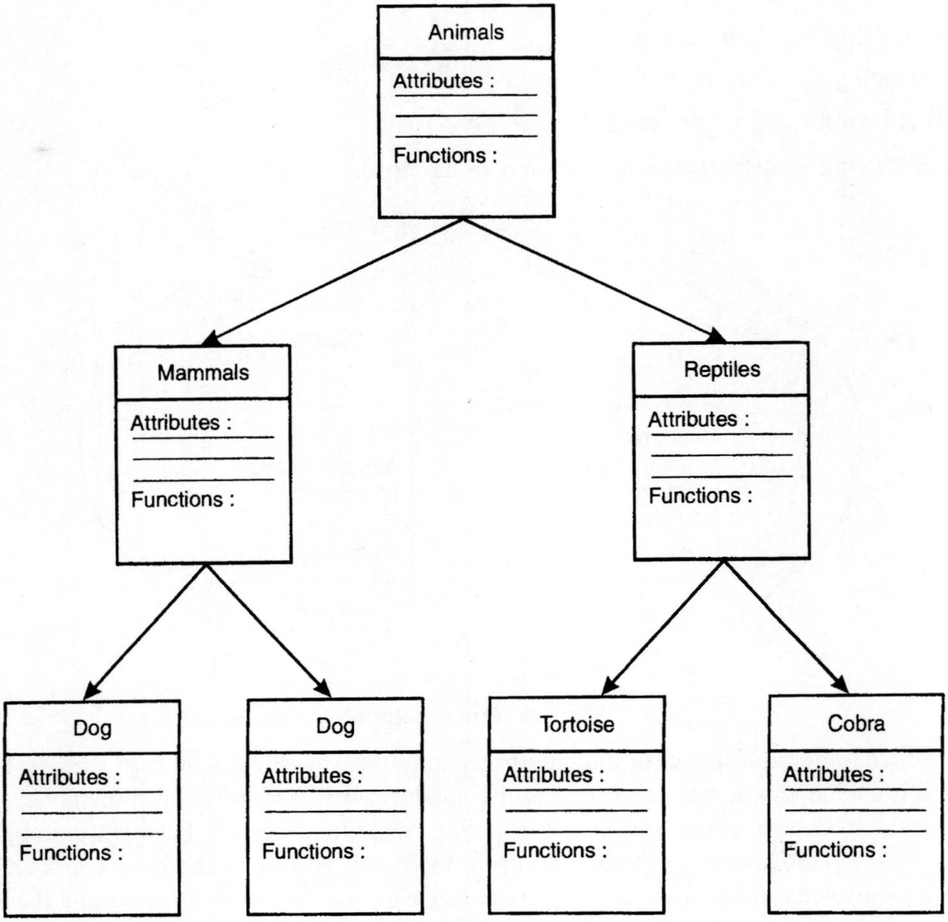

Fig. 2.4.

Note that each subclass defines only those features that are unique to it. Without the use of inheritance, each class would have to explicitly include all of its features.

2.8. POLYMORPHISM

The term 'polymorphism' is derived from a Greek word 'Poly' means many and 'morphism' means forms. Hence, we can define polymorphism as :

Definition : The ability to take more than one form is known as **Polymorphism**.

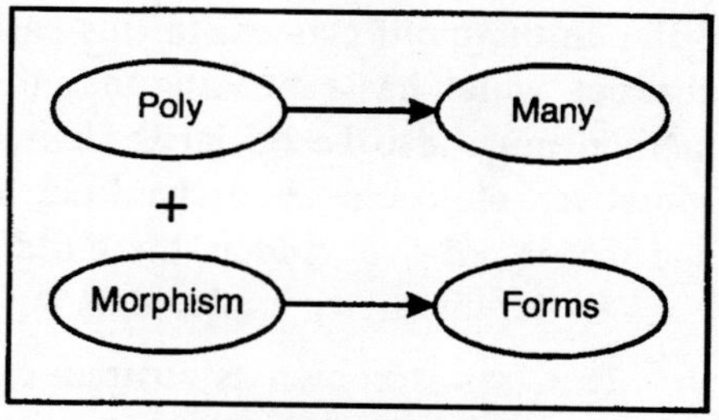

Fig. 2.5. Polymorphism

For example : An operation may exhibit different behaviour in different instances. The behaviour depends upon the types of data used in the operation. Let us consider the operation of addition. For two numbers the operation will generate a sum. If the operands are strings, then the operation will generate a third string by concatenation.

The Fig. 2.6 illustrate a single function name that can be used to handle different types of arguments.

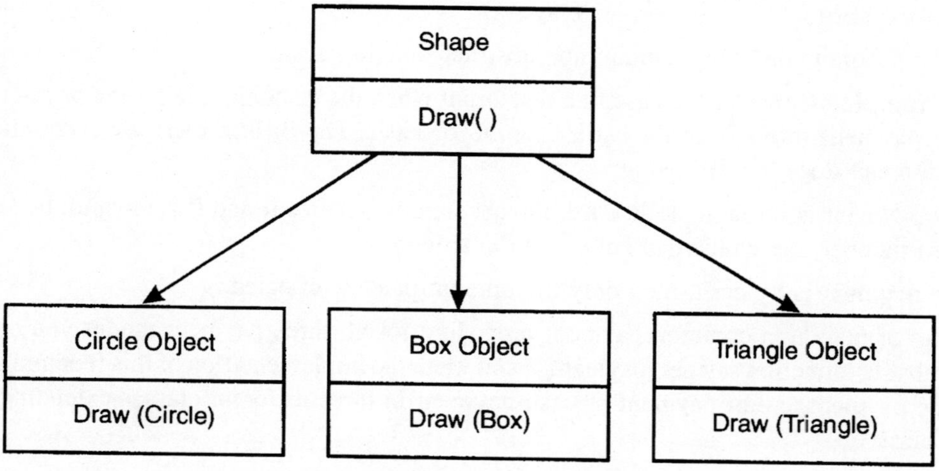

Fig. 2.6. Polymorphism

Polymorphism plays an important role in allowing objects having different internal structure to share the same external interface. This means that general class of operations may be accessed in the same manner even though specific actions associated with each operation may differ.

For example : Let us take an example of stack (Last In First Out) to understand the concept of polymorphism. Consider a stack program that takes three values. Hence normally, we require three stacks. One stack is used for integer values, one for floating point value and one for characters. The algorithm that implements each stack is the same, even though the data being stored is differ. In a non-object oriented language, we would be required to create three different sets of stack routines, with each stack using different names. However, because of polymorphism, in Java we can specify a general set of stack routine that all shares a same name.

Hence, the concept of polymorphism is often expressed by the phrase "one interface, multiple methods."

2.9. ABSTRACT CLASSES AND METHODS

The concept of inheritance is basically implemented to enhance the capability of a class without breaking or restructuring it. This is generally achieved by either over-riding the existing methods or including the new ones by introducing new child classes.

However, there may be a situation, which is very different from these. You may come across a method that is merely existing in the base class as a place-holder, and it's actual implementation differ in the child classes. In this case we can make the place holder method in the base class as abstract, which has a meaning that, this method cannot have any code. The class having an abstract method must also be declared abstract, which has the implication that it cannot be instantiated. Moreover, child classes derived out of abstract base class must override this method in particular and if it is not over-ridden, the child class must also be declared abstract until any other the child class in the hierarchy implements it.

1. Class is known as abstract class whose object can't be created but only referenced object can be created.
2. A class which contain any abstract method must also be treated as abstract class.
3. A method which is abstract can't show body.
4. If any class is derived from an abstract class then it is necessary to over-ride all the methods of the abstract class in derived class.
5. An abstract class may contain non-abstract function also.

For example : Consider the case in a restaurant when the customer makes the payment. He can make the payment through credit card, Cheque or cash. The billing clerk or accountant for an organization can does the following:

If the payment is through credit card, the accountant verifies it and if it is valid, he keys in the credit card number, the concerned bank and the amount.

If the payment is by cash, then only the amount paid is reflected.

Instead of making a common payment procedure for all three payment modes you can make a common abstract function say get_payment( ) and write the implementation of this function separately for cheque payment, credit payment or cash payment in three different classes extending from the payment class.

Program : The program for the above is implemented as—

```
abstract class Payment
{
    int bill_number;
    String customer_Name;
    String Customer_Address;

    Void accept_cust_details( )
    {
    ___________________
    ___________________
    }
```

```
    Payment( )
    {
        //Initialinzing the member variables with appropriate values
    }

    abstract void get-payment( );          //abstract method declared

}

Class Cc_payment() extends Payment
{
    void get_payment()
    {
        // Accept the cc number
        // Accept the name of the concerned bank
        //Accept the amount paid
    }
}

Class Chq_payment() extends Payment
{
    void get_payment()
    {
        // Accept the cheque number
        // Accept the drawee bank and the payment
    }
}

Class Cash_payment() extends Payment
{
    void get_payment()
    {
        //Accept the amount paid
    }
}

public class Restaurent
{
    public static void main(String arg[])
    {
```

```
            Payment p_cc = new cc_payment( );
            p_cc.accept_cust_Details( );
            p_cc.get_payment( );


            Payment p_chq = new Chq_Payment( );
            p_chq.accept_cust_Details( );
            p_chq.get_payment( );

            Payment p_cash = new Cash_payment( );
            p_cash.accept_cust_Details( );
            p_cash.get_Payment( );
        }
    }
```

In the main method, three objects of the base class Payment are created, which depending upon the mode of payment, refer to an appropriate child class and access the get_payment( ) method.

Another Example: The another example of abstract class is of book class. There are three classes, namely, the Book class, the PhoneBook class and the Novel class.

The Book class is acting as a generalized class, which is storing the details like the title, year of publication etc..

The phonebook class is a specialized class which is storing the specific details like the location, type etc..

The Novel class again is a specialized class, which is storing the details like the author, style and the language.

The above discussion is depicted in the Fig. 2.7 given below:

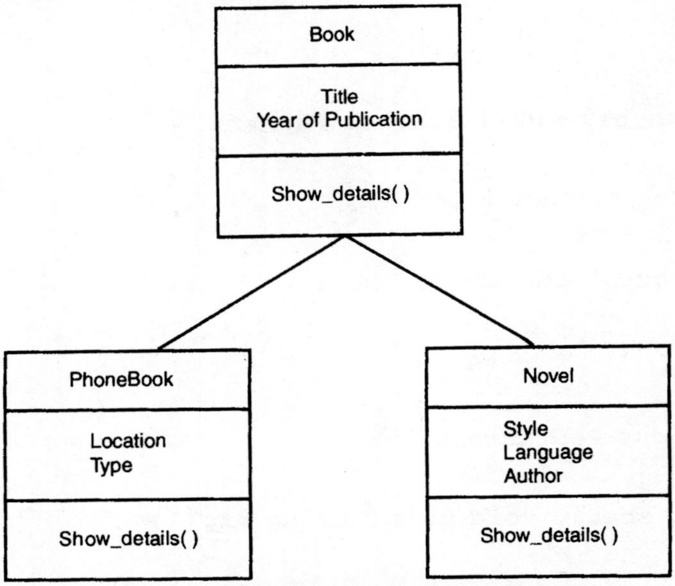

Fig. 2.7. Understanding Abstract Class

All these classes above have one method in common *i.e.,* the show_details(), which depending upon the class reference shows the details specific to a particular type of book. The program is given below:

```
Abstract class Book
{
String title;
int year;

Book(String bname, int yr)
{
    title=bname;
    year=yr;
}

abstract void show_details();

}

class Phone_Book extends Book
{
 String location;
 String type;

Phone_Book(String bname, int yr,String loc, String typ)
{
    super(bname,yr);
   location=loc;
    type=typ;
}

void show_details()
{
    System.out.println("The name of the book is:"+title);
    System.out.println("The year of publication is:"+year);
    System.out.println("The location is:"+location);
    System.out.println("The type is:"+type);
}
}

class Novel extends Book
```

```
{
String style;
String language;
String author;

Novel(String bname,int yr, String st, String lng, String aur)
{
    super(bname,yr);
    style=st;
    language=lng;
   author=aut;
}

void show_details()
{
    System.out.println("The name of the book is:"+title);
    System.out.println("The year of publication is:"+year);
    System.out.println("The Style is:"+style);
    System.out.println("The Language is:"+language);
    System.out.println("The Author is:"+author);
}
}

public class Library
{
public static void main(String args[])
{
Book book_ph= new Phone_Book("Tata Yellow Pages",1991,"Delhi",
"Business");
book_ph.show_details();

Book book_nov= new Novel("Chandrakanta", 1878,"Story","Hindi","
Devkinandan Khatri");

book_nov.show_details();
}
}
```

Output: The output of the program will be:

```
The name of the book is: Tata Yellow Pages
The year of publication is : 1991
The location is: Delhi
```

```
The type is: Business

The name of the book is: Chandrakanta
The year of publication is:1878
The style is: Story
The language is: English
The author is: Devkinandan Khatri
```

2.10. INTERFACES : MULTIPLE INHERITANCE

Java doesn't support the concept of multiple inheritance since multiple inheritance is an important concept in object oriented paradigm, java provides an alternate way of implementing this concept, that alternate approach is known as **Interfaces**, which are used to support the concept of multiple inheritance. Although, a java class cannot be a subclass of more than one superclass, it can implement more than one interface, therby enabling us to create classes that build upon other classes without the problems created by multiple inheritance.

1. An interface is little bit extension of abstract class whose object can't be created but reference object can be created.
2. In interface each method can't show body.
3. In interface each method is public and abstract implicitly.
4. In interface each variable is public static and final.
5. Interface always to be implemented by class but an interface can extend another interface.
6. Multiple classes can't be extended but multiple interfaces can be implemented.
7. If any class implement an interface then it is necessary to override all the methods of an interface body in derived classes, and while overriding access level must be public.

2.10.1. Defining Interfaces

An interface is basically a special kind of class. Like classes, interfaces contain methods and variables but with a major difference. The difference is that interfaces defines only abstract methods and final fields. This means that interfaces do not specify any code to implement these methods and datafields contain only constants.

Therefore, it is the responsibility of the class that implements an interface to define the code for implementation of these methods.

Syntax:

The syntax for defining an interface is very similar to that for defining a class. The general form of an interface definition is:

```
Interface InterfaceName
{
   variable declaration;
methods declaration;
}
```

In the above syntax the interface is the keyword and Interface name is any java variable (just like class name).

The variables are declared as :

```
static final type VariableName =  Value;
```

Note that all variables are declared as constants. Methods declaration will contain only a list of methods without any body statements.

```
return-type methodName1(parameter_list);
```

For example : Here is an example of an interface definition that contains two variables and one method.

```
interface Item
{
    static final int code=1001;
    static final String name="Fan";
    void display( );
}
```

Here it is noted that the code for the method is not included in the interface and the method declaration simply ends with a semicolon. The class that implements this interfaces must define the code for the method.

```
interface Area
{
final static float pi=3.142F;
float compute(float X, float Y);
void show( );
}
```

2.10.2. Extending Interfaces

Like classes, interfaces can also be extended. That is, an interface can be subinterfaced from other interfaces. The new subinterface will inherit all the members of the superinterface in the manner similar to subclasses. This is achieved using the keyword **extends** as shown below :

```
Interface name2 extends name1
{
    body of name2
}
```

For example: We can put all the constants in one interface and the methods in the other. This will enable us to use the constants in classes where methods are not required

```
interface ItemConstants
```

```
{
    int code=1001;
    String name="Fan";
}

Interface Item extends ItemConstants
{
void display();
}
```

The interface Item would inherit both the constant code and name into it. Note that variable name and code are declared like simple variables. It is allowed because all the variables in an interface are treated as constants although the keyword final and static are not present. We can also combine several interfaces together into a single interface.

While interfaces are allowed to extend to other interfaces, subinterfaces cannot define the methods declared in the superinterfaces cannot define the methods declared in the superinterfaces, not classes. Instead, it is the responsibility of any class that implements the derived interface to define all the methods. Note that,when an interface extends two or more interfaces, they are separated by commas.

```
Interface Itemconstants
{
    int code=1001;
    String name="fan";
}

Interface Itemmethods
{
void display( );
}

Interface Item extends Itemconstants,Itemmethods
{
________________________________
________________________________
}
```

It is important to remember that an interface cannot extend classes. This would violate the rule that an interface can have only abstract methods and constants.

2.10.3. Implementing Interfaces

Interfaces are used as superclasses whose properties are inherited by classes. It is therefore necessary to create a class that inherits the given interface. This is done as follows:

```
class classname implements interfacename
{
   Body of classname
}
```

Here, the class classname "implements" the interface interfacename. A more general form of implementation may look like this:

```
class classname extends superclass implements interface1,
interface2,...
{
      Body of classname
}
```

This shows that class can extend another class while implementing interfaces.

Program : The program for implementing the concept of interfaces is given below:

```
interface Area
{
 final static float pi=3.14F;
 float compute(float x, float y)
}

class Rectangle implements Area
{
public float compute(float x, float y)
{
   return(x*y);
}}

Class Circle implements Area
{
Public float compute(float x, float y)
{
   return(pi*x*y);
}
}

class InterfaceTest
{
public static void main(String args[])
{
```

```
        Rectangle rect=new Rectangle();
        Circle cir=new Circle();
        Area area;

        area=rect;
        System.out.println("Area of Rectangle is"+area.compute(10,20));
        area=cir;
        System.out.println("Area of Circle is"+area.compute(10,0));
    }
    }
```

Output: The output of program will be :

```
Area of Rectangle=200
Area of Circle =314
```

2.11. PACKAGES

Package is basically a name provided to a group of classes so that they can be managed in a better way. This is almost the similar concept to "Class Libraries" in other languages. Packages are used to achieve the reusability in Java.

Packages are Java's way of grouping a variety of classes and/or interfaces together. The grouping is done according to the functionality. In fact, packages act as "Container" for classes.

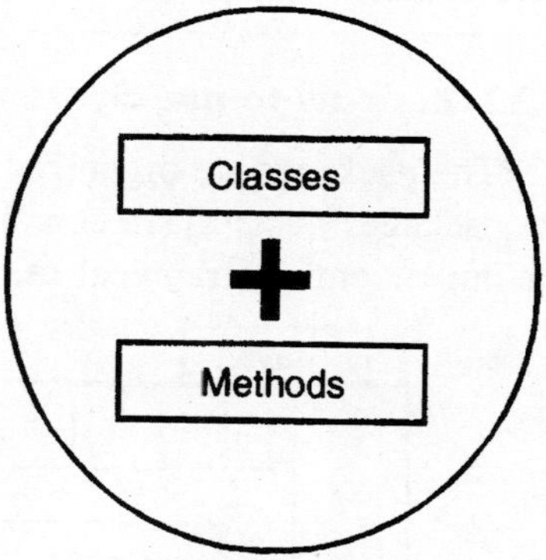

Fig. 2.8. Package

By organizing our classes into packages we achieve the following benefits:

1. The classes contained in the packages of other programs can be easily reused.
2. In packages, classes can be unique compared with classes in other packages. That is, two classes in two different packages can have the same name. They may be referred by their fully qualified name, comprising the package name and the class name.
3. Packages provide a way to "hide" classes thus preventing other programs or packages from accessing classes that are meant for internal use only.
4. Packages also provide a way for separating "design" from "coding". First we can design classes and decides their relationships, and then we can implement the Java code needed for the methods. It is possible to change the implementation of any method without affecting the rest of the design.

For most applications, we will need to use two different set of classes, one for the internal representation of our program's data, and the other for the external presentation purpose. We may have to build our own classes for handling our data and use existing class libraries for designing use interfaces. Java packages are therefore classified into two types. The first category is known as **Java API packages** and the second is known as **User defined packages**.

2.11.1. Java API Packages

Java API provides a large number of classes grouped into different packages according to functionality. Most of the time we use the packages available with the JAVA API.

Package Name	Contents
java.lang	Language support classes. These are classes that java compiler itself uses and therefore they are automatically imported. They include classes for primitive types, strings, math functions, threads and Exceptions.
java.util	Language Utility classes such as Vectors, Hash tables, random numbers, date etc.
java.io	Input/Output Support classes. They provide facilities for input and output of data.
java.awt	Set of classes for implementing graphical user interface. They include classes for windows, buttons, lists, menus and so on.
java.net	Classes for networking. They include classes for communicating with local computers as well as with internet servers.
java.applet	Classes for creating and implementing applets.

2.11.2. How to use System Packages?

The packages are organized in a hierarchical structure as shown below. This Fig. 2.9 shows that the packages named java contain the package awt, which in turn contains various classes required for implementing graphical user interface.

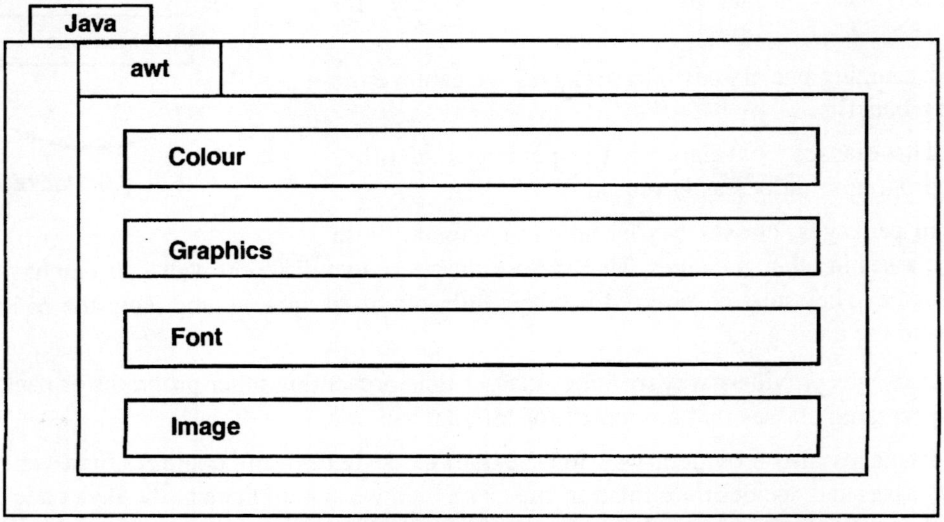

Fig. 2.9. Hierarchical Representation of Java.awt packages

There are two ways of accessing the classes stored in a package.

1. The first approach is to use the fully qualified classname of the class that we want to use.

```
import java.awt.Colour;
```

2. The second statement imports every class contained in the specified packages

```
import java.awt.*;
```

2.11.3. Creating Packages or User Defined Packages

To create our own packages we need to follow the following steps:

1. Declare the package at the beginning of file using the form

```
package packagename;
```

2. Define the class that is to be put in the package and declare its public.
3. Create a subdirectory under the directory where the main source file are stored.
4. Store the listing as the classname.java file in the subdirectory created.
5. Compile the file. This creates .class file in the subdirectory.

For example:

```
package firstpackage;
public class Firstclass
{
___________________
___________________
}
```

Here, the package name is FirstPackage. The class FirstClass is now considered a part of this package. This listing would be saved as file called FirstClass.java and located in a directory name Firstpackage. When the source file is compiled,java will create a .class file and store it in the same directory.

2.11.4. Accessing a Package

Java system package can be accessed either using a fully qualified class name or using a shortcut approach through the import statements. We use import statement when there are many references to a particular package or the package name is too long and unwieldy.

The import statement can be used to search a list of packages for a particular class. The general form of import statement for searching a class is as follows:

```
import package1[.package2][.package2][.package3].classname;
```

Here, package1 is the name of the top level package, package2 is the name of the package that is inside the package1 and so on. We can have any number of packages in packages hierarchy. Finally, the explicit class name is specified.

We can also use another approach as follows:

```
import  packagename.*;
```

Here, package may denote a single package or a hierarchy of packages as mentioned earlier. The star(*) indicates that the compiler should search this entire package hierarchy when it encounters a class name. This implies that we can access all classes contained in the above package directly.

2.11.5. Practical Usage of Package

```
//creating a new package1

package package1;
public class ClassA
{
   public void displayA( )
   {
      System.out.println("Class A");
}
}

//usage of Package

import package1.ClassA;
class PackageTest1
{
   public static void main(String arg[])
   {
      classA  objectA = new ClassA();
      objectA.displayA( );
}
}

//creating another package

package package2;
public class ClassB
{
   protected int m=10;
   public void display()
   {
      System.out.println("Class B");
      System.out.println("m="+m);
   }
}
//Usage of Both the packages

import package1.ClassA;
```

```
import package2.*;

class PackageTest2
{
    public static void main(String args[])
    {
        ClassA objectA=new ClassA( );
        ClassB objectB=new ClassB( );

        objectA.displayA( );
        objectB.displayB( );

    }
}
```

Output:

```
ClassA
ClassB
M=10
```

Save As: PackageTest2.java

Compile As: javac PackageTest2.java

Run As: java PackageTest2

2.11.6. Adding a Class to a Package

It is simple to add a class to an existing package.

1. Define the class and make it public.
2. Place the package statement before the class definition.

```
package p1;
public classB
{
    //body
}
```

3. Store this as B.java file under the directory P1
4. Compile B.java. This will create a B.class file and place it in the directory P1.

2.11.7. Hiding Classes

```
package p1;
public class X              //public class,available outside
{
```

```
    //Body of X
}

class Y                    //not public hidden
{
    //Body of Y
}
```

2.12. ACCESS SPECIFIER IN JAVA

A way to restrict access to classes, variables and methods is known Access Control.

We know that variables and methods of a class are visible everywhere in the program. However, it may be necessary in some situations to restrict the access to certain variables and methods from outside the classes. We can achieve this in Java by applying visibility modifiers to the instance variables and methods from outside the classes. We can achieve this in java by applying visibility modifiers to the instance variables and methods. The visibility modifiers are also known as Access Modifier or Access Specifier.

Java provides three types of visibility modifiers, they are:

- Public
- Private
- Protected
- Default or Friendly Access

2.12.1. Default and Friendly Access

In many of cases, we have not used public modifier, yet they were still accessible in other classes in the program. When no access modifier is specified, the member defaults to limited versions of public accessibility known as "Friendly" level of access.

The difference between the "public access" and the "friendly" access is that the public modifier makes fields visible in all classes, regardless of their packages while the friendly access makes fields visible only in the same package, but not in other packages.

Access modifier→	Public	Protected	Friendly (default)	Private Protected	Private
Same Class	Yes	Yes	Yes	Yes	Yes
Subclass in Same Package	Yes	Yes	Yes	Yes	No
Other classes in Same Packages	Yes	Yes	Yes	No	No
Subclasses in other packages	Yes	Yes	No	Yes	No
Non Subclasses in other Package	Yes	No	No	No	No

2.12.2. Some Rules

Given below are some rules for applying appropriate access modifiers.

1. Use "**public**" if field is to be visible everywhere

2. Use "**protected**" if the field is to be visible everywhere in the current package and also subclasses in other package
3. Use "**default**" if the field is to be visible everywhere in the current package only.
4. Use "**private protected**" if the field is to be visible only in subclasses, regardless of packages.
5. Use "**private**" if the field is not to be visible anywhere except in its own class.

2.13. CONSTRUCTORS

We know that all objects that are created must be given initial values. We have done this earlier using two approaches.

1. The first approach uses the dot operator to access the instance variables and then assigns values to them individually. It can be a tedious approach to initialize all the variables of all the objects.

```
Classname  objectname = new classname(Parameters);

    rect1.rectArea( );
```

2. The second approach takes the help of method like getData to initialize each object individually using statements like,

```
rect1.getData(15,10);
```

It would be simpler and more consise to initialize an object when it is first created. Java supports a special type of method, called a Constructor, that enables an object to initialize itself when it is created.

1. Constructors have the same name as the class itself.
2. They do not specify a return type, not even void. This is because they return the instance of the class itself.
3. Instance concrete representation of class itself.

```
class Rectangle
{
   int length,width;

   Rectangle(int x,int y)                    //Defining Constructor
   {
      length = x;
      width= y;
}

   int rectArea( )
   {
      return(length * width)

   }
```

```
}
class  RectangleArea
{
public static void main(String args[])
{
   Rectangle rect1 = new Rectangle(15,10);// Calling Constructor
   int area1= rect1.rectArea();
System.out.println("Area1="+area1);
}
}
```

Output : Output of program will be :

```
Area1=150
```

2.14. THIS KEYWORD

Sometimes a method will need to refer to the object that involved it. To allow this, java defines the **This** keyword."this" can be used inside any method to refer to the current objects. That is, this is always a reference to the object on which the method was invoked. You can use "this" anywhere a reference to an object of the current class type is permitted.

```
Box(double w, double h, double d)
{
   this.width = w;
   this.height=h;
   this.depth=d;
}
```

2.15. FINALIZE( ) METHOD

We have seen that constructor method is used to initialize an object when it is declared. This process is known as **Initialization**. Similarly, java supports a concept called **Finalization**, which is just opposite to initialization. We know that Java-Runtime is an automatic garbage collecting system. It automatically frees up the memory resources used by the objects. But objects may hold other non-object resources such as file descriptors or windows system fonts. The garbage collector cannot free these resources. In order to free these resources we must use a **finalizer method**. This is similar to destructor in C++.

The finalizer method is simply **finalize**( ) and can be added to any class. Java calls that method whenever it is about to reclaim the space for that object. The **finalize method** should explicitly define the tasks to be performed.

The finalize( ) method has this general form:

```
Protected void finalize()
{
   //finalization code Here
}
```

2.16. ARRAY

An array is a group of contigous or related data items that share a common name.

For example : We can define an array name salary to represents set of salaries of a group of employess.

A particular value is indicated by writing a number called **index number** or **subscript** in brackets after the array name.

For example : salary[10]

2.16.1. Types of Arrays

1. One-Dimensional Array
2. Multi-Dimensional Array

One Dimensional Array

A list of items can be given one variable name using one subscript and such a variable is called a **Single Subscripted Variable** or **One Dimensional Array**.

For example : x[n]

Which contains values as :

```
X[0],X[1],X[2],X[3],..........................................X[n]
```

2.16.2. Creating an Array

Creation of array involves three steps :

1. Declare the array
2. Create memory locations
3. Put values into the m/m location
4. Declare the array: Array in Java may be declared in two forms:

```
type arrayname[];
```

For example :

```
int number[];
float average[];

type [] arrayname;
```

For example :

```
int[] number;
foat[] number;
```

Create Memory Locations

After declaring an array, we need to create it in memory. Java allows us to create arrays using new operators only, as shown above.

For example :

```
number = new int[5]
Average=new float[10]
```

Putting values to memory location

The final step is to put values into the array created. This process is known as **initialization.** This is done as :

```
Arrayname[subscript]=value;
```

For example :

```
number[0]=35;
number[1]=5;
number[2]=25;
number[3]=15;
number[4]=1;
```

or

```
type arrayname[]={list of values};
```

For example :

```
int number[]={35,5,25,15,1};
```

2.16.3. Array Length

In java all arrays store the allocated size in a variable named length we can access the length of array using

```
a.length
```

For example :

```
int assize = a.length
```

This information is useful in the manipulation of array when their sizes are not known.

2.16.4. Two Dimensional Array

So far we have discussed the array variables that can store a list of values. There will be situations where a table of values will have to be stored.

For example : The value of 3 Items by Four sales man.

	Item1	Item2	Item3
Salesman1	310	275	365
Salesman2	210	190	325
Salesman3	405	235	240
Salesman4	260	300	380

The table contains a total of 12 values three in each line, or we can assume it as **Matrix** consisting of four rows and three columns.

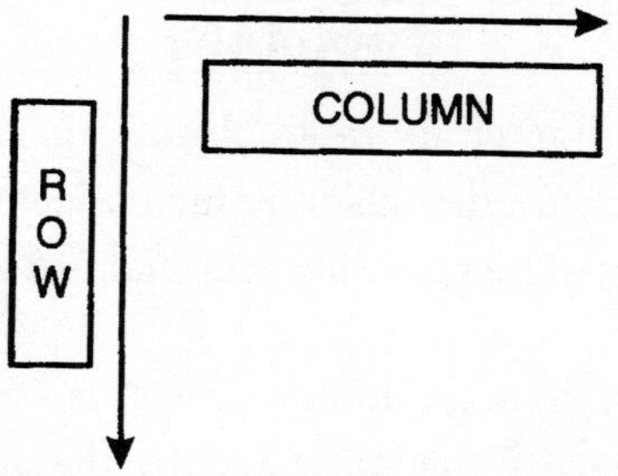

1. Each row represents the values of sales by salesman.
2. Each column represents the value of particular items.

Java allows us to define such tables of items by using **Two Dimensional Array**.

Two dimensional arrays are stored in memory as :

	Column0	Column1	Column2
Row0	310	275	365
Row1	210	190	325
Row2	405	235	240
Row3	260	300	380

Creating a multidimensional array

Defining the array: type arrayname[][]

Create memory location

```
Arrayname=new type[size][size]
```

Put values into m/m location

```
int myarray[3][4]={0,1,2,3,4,5,6,7,8,9,10,11,12};
```

2.17. GARBAGE COLLECTION

Since objects are dynamically allocated by using the **new** operator, you might be wondering how such objects are destroyed and their memory released for later reallocation. In some languages, such as C++, dynamically allocated objects must be manually released by use of a delete operator. Java takes a different approach;

"It handles deallocation for you automatically"

This technique that accomplishes this is called **Garbage Collection**.

It works like this;

When no references to an object exist, that object is assumed to be no longer needed, and the memory occupied by the object can be reclaimed. There is no explicit need to destroy objects as in C++.

Garbage collection only occurs sporadically (if at all) during the execution of your program. It will not occur simply because one or more objects exist that are no longer used. Furthermore, different Java runtime implementations will take varying approaches to garbage collection, but for the most part, we should not have to think about it while writing program.

SUMMARY

1. Objects are the basic run time entity in an object oriented system. It is instance of class.
2. Class is the user defined data type which is the collection of similar type of objects.
3. Abstraction refers to the act of representing essential feature without including the background details and explaination.
4. The wrapping up of data into a single unit (class) is known as Encapsulation.
5. The process by which object of one class acquire the property of object of another class is known as Inheritance
6. The ability to modify more than one form is known as Polymorphism.
7. Abstract class is the class which may or may not contain abstract methods.
8. Java doesnot support the concept of multiple inheritance although it support the similar concept reffered to as interfaces.
9. This keyword is used to refer to object of that class.
10. Constructor is used to initialize the object of the class.
11. Java doesn't support the concept of destructor, although it deallocate memory automatically through the concept of Garbage collection.
12. Package is the collection of classes and method.

REVIEW QUESTIONS

1. Define the following with example :
   (*i*) Objects
   (*ii*) Classes
   (*iii*) Encapsulation
   (*iv*) Inheritance and Software Reuse
   (*v*) Polymorphism
   (*vi*) Constructor
2. Write short note on :
   (*i*) Access Specifier
   (*ii*) Copy Constructor
   (*iii*) This pointer
   (*iv*) Finalize method
   (*v*) Memory Allocation and Garbage Collection
3. What are Abstract Methods and Abstract Classes? Explain using example.
4. What are Interfaces? Explain how to define, implement and applying interfaces. Also explain how to extend interfaces.
5. What are packages? Explain its scope and lifetime.

❑❑❑

UNIT–II

- Abstract Window Toolkit
- Event Handling in AWT
- Applets
- Introduction to Swing

SYLLABUS

AWT : Containers and components, AWT classes, window fundamentals: Component, Container, Panel, Window, Frame, Canvas, AWT Controls, Layout Managers and Menus:adding and removing control, Labels, Button, Check Box, Radio Button, Choice, Menu, Text area, Scroll list, Scroll bar; Frame; Layout managers—flow layout, Grid layout, Border layout, Card layout.

Java Event Handling Model : Java's event delegation model—Ignoring the event, Self contained events, Delegating events; The event class hierarchy; The relationship between interface, methods called, parameters and event source; Adapter classes; Event classes action Event, Adjustment Event, Container Event, Focus Event, Item Event, Eye Event, Mouse Event, Text Event, Window Event.

Applets : Applet security restrictions; the class hierarchy for applets; Life cycle of applet; HTML Tags for applet.

Introduction to Swing : Swing library, Building applications using Swings.

CHAPTER 3

Abstract Window Toolkit

INSIDE THIS CHAPTER

Well friends, now the time has come to make the programming approach more interesting with the help of graphical user interface in Java. This chapter introduces a new concept of AWT which makes the programming approach intresting and easy to learn.

3.1. INTRODUCTION TO AWT

3.1.1. Graphical User Interface

The java programming language provides a class library called the **abstract window Toolkit,** that contains a number of common graphical widgets. We can add these widgets to our display area and position them with layout manager.

3.1.2. AWT Basic

All graphical user interface objects stem from a common superclass, Component. To create a graphical user interface (GUI), we add components to container object. Because a container is also a component, container may be nested arbitrarily.

Each AWT component uses native code to display itself on your screen. When you run a java application under Microsoft windows, buttons are really Microsoft windows button. When we run the same application on a Macintosh, buttons are really Macintosh buttons. When we run on a unix machine that uses Motif, buttons are really Motif buttons.

3.1.3. Application V/s Applets

Recall that an applet is a java program that runs in a web page, while an application is one that runs from the command line. An applet is a Panel that is automatically inserted into a web page. The browser displaying the web page instantiates and adds the applets to the proper part of the web page. The browser tells the applet when to create its GUI (by calling the init( ) method of applet) and when to start( ) and stop( ) any special processing.

Application run from a command prompt. When you executes an application from the command prompt, the interpreter starts by calling the application's main( ) method.

3.1.4. Basic GUI Logic

There are three steps we take to create any GUI application or applets :

1. Compose your GUI by adding components to container objects.
2. Set up event handlers to respond to user interaction with the GUI.
3. Display the GUI (automatically done for applets, you must explicitly do this for application).

For example : The following simple example shows some GUI code. This example creates an applet that contain just a button.

```
import java.awt.Button;
import java.applet.Applet;

public class Abutton extends Applet
{
public void init( )
{
//Step1 : Compose the GUI

Button beepButton= new Button("Beep");
add(beepButton);

//Step 2 : Set up Event Handlers

beepButton.addActionListener(new Beeper( ));

//Step3 : Display the GUI(automatic — this is an applet)
}
}
```

In step 2 from above, event handling is set up by adding an instance of listener class, to the button. When the button is pressed, a certain method in the listener class is called. In this example, the listener class implements ActionListener (because button requires it). When the button is pressed, the button calls the actionPerformed( ) method of the listener class.

```
import java.awt.event.ActionListener;
import java.awt.event.ActionEvent;
import java.awt.Componet;

public class Beeper implements ActionListener
{
   public void actionPerformed(ActionEvent event)
   {
      Component c=(component)event.getSource( );
      c.getToolkit( ).beep( );
   }
}
```

To try this applet, create a simple HTML page as follows:

```
<html>
<applet code=Abutton.class width=100 height=100>
</applet>
</html>
```

3.2. UNDERSTANDING AWT

The abstract window toolkit or awt provides you with numerous classes and interfaces to facilitate the creation of a rich user interface. These classes range from the creation of simple GUI components, like the buttons and text boxes, containers like frames and panels, to the classes dealing with their event handling.

3.3. AWT CLASSES

The AWT classes are contained in the java.awt package. It is one of java's largest packages. Fortunately, because it is logically organized in a top down, hierarchical fashion, it is easier to understand and use than you might at first believe. Table 3.1 shown below lists some of the many AWT classes.

Table 3.1.

Class	Description
AWTEvent	Encapsulates AWT events
AWTEventMulticaster	Dispatches events to multiple listeners
BorderLayout	The border layout manager, Border layout use five components: North, South, East, West and Center.
Button	Creates a push button control

Class	Description
Canvas	A blank, semantics-free window.
CardLayout	The card layout manager. Card layouts emulate index cards. Only the one on top is showing.
Checkbox	Creates a check box control.
CheckboxGroup	Creates a group of check box controls.
CheckboxMenuItem	Creates an on/off menu item.
Choice	Create a pop-up list.
Color	Manages colours in a portable, platform independent fashion.
Component	An abstract super class for various AWT components.
Container	A subclass of **Component** that can hold other components.
Cursor	Encapsulates a bitmapped cursor.
Dialog	Creates a dialog window.
Dimension	Specifies the dimensions of an object. The width is stored in **width** and the height is stored in **height**.
Event	Encapsulates events.
EventQueue	Queues events.
FileDialog	Creates a window from which a file can be selected.
FlowLayout	The flow layout manager. Flow layout positions components left to right, top to bottom.
Font	Encapsulates events.
Font Metrics	Encapsulates various information related to a font. This information helps you display text in window.
Frame	Creates a standard window that has a title bar, resize corners, and menu bar.
Graphics	Encapsulates the graphics context. This context is used by the various output methods to display output in a window.
GraphicsDevice	Describes a graphics device such as screen or printer.
GraphicsEnvironment	Describes the collection of available **Font** and **Graphics Device** objects.
GridBagConstraints GridBagLayout	Defines various constraints relating to the **GridBagLayout** class. The grid bag layout manager. Grid bag layout displays components subject to the constraints specified by **GridBagConstraints**.
Image	Encapsulates the borders of a container.
Insets	Encapsulates the border of container.
Label	Creates a label that display that display a string.
Media Tracker	Manages Media objects.
Menu	Creates a pull-down menu.
Menu-Bar	Creates a menu bar.
Menu Component	An abstract class implemented by various menu classes.
MenuItem	Creates a menu Item.
MenuShortcut	Encapsulates a keyboard shortcut for a menu item.
Panel	The simplest concrete subclass of **Container**.

Class	Description
Point	Encapsulates a Cartesian coordinate pair,stored in x and y.
Polygon	Encapsulates a polygon.
PopupMenu	Encapsulates a pop-up menu.
Printjob	An abstract class that represents a print job.
Rectangle	Encapsulates a rectangle.
Robot	Support automated testing of AWT-based applications Added by java 2, V1.3.
Scrollbar	Creates a scroll bar control.
ScrollPane	A container that provides horizontal and/or vertical scroll bars for another component.
SystemColour	Contains the colours of GUI widgets such as windows, scroll bars, text, and others.
TextArea	Creates a multiline edit control.
TextComponent	A superclass for TextArea and TextField.
TextField	Creates a single-line edit control.
Toolkit	Abstract class implemented by the AWT.
Window	Creates a window with no frame, no menu bar, and no title.

Although the basic structure of the AWT has been the same since Java 1.0, some of the original methods were deprecated and replaced by new ones when Java 1.1 was released. For backward-compatibility, Java 2 still supports all the original 1.0 methods.

3.4. WINDOW FUNDAMENTALS

The AWT defines windows according to a class hierarchy that adds functionality and specificity with each level. The two most common windows are those derived from Panel, which is used by applets and those derived from Frame, which creates a standard window. Much of the functionality of these windows is derived from their parent classes. Thus, a description of the class hierarchies relating to these two classes is fundamental to their understanding. Figure 3.1 shows the class hierarchy for Panel and Frame.

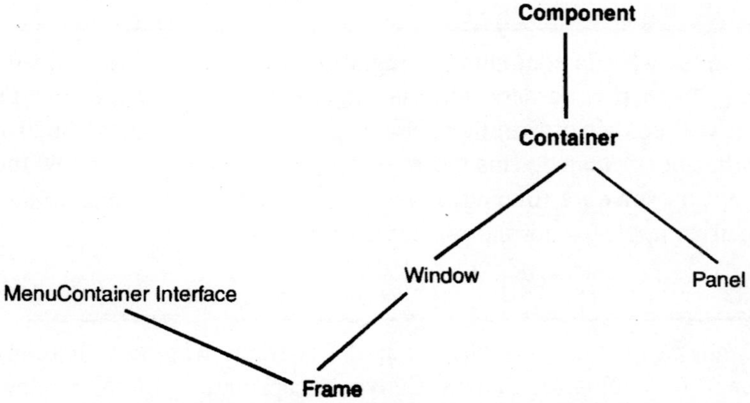

Fig. 3.1. The Class Hierarchy for Panel and Frame

3.5. COMPONENT

At the top of the AWT hierarchy is the Component class. Component is an abstract class that encapsulates all of the attributes of a visual component. All user interface elements that are displayed on the screen and that interact with the user are subclass of Component. It defines over a hundred public methods that are responsible for managing events, such as mouse and keyboard input, positioning and sizing the window, and repainting. A component object is responsible for remembering the current foreground and background colours and the currently selected text font.

3.6. CONTAINER

The Container class is a subclass of Component. It has additional methods that allow other component object to be nested within it. Other Container objects can be stored inside of a Container (Since they are themselves instances of Component). This makes for a multileveled containment system. A container is responsible for laying out any components that it contains. It does this through the use of various layout managers.

3.7. PANEL

The Panel class is a concrete subclass of Container. It doesn't add any new methods; it simply implements container. A Panel may be thought of as a recursively nestable, concrete screen component. Panel is the superclass for Applet. When screen output is directed to an applet, it is drawn on the surface of a Panel object. In essence, a Panel is a window that does not contain a title bar, menu bar, or border. This is why we don't see these items when an applet is run inside a browser. When you run an applet using an applet viewer, the applet viewer provides the title and border.

Other components can be added to a Panel object by its add() method (inherited from container). Once these components have been added, you can position and resize them manually using the setLocation( ), setSize( ), or setBounds( ) methods defined by component.

3.8. WINDOW

The Window class creates a top-level window. A top-level window is not contained within any other object; it sits directly on the desktop. Generally, you won't create Window objects directly. Instead, you will use a subclass of Window called Frame.

3.9. FRAME

Frame encapsulates what is commonly thought of as a "window". It is a subclass of Window and has a title bar, menu bar, borders, and resizing corners. If you create a Frame object from within an applet, it will contain a warning message, such as "Java Applet Window", to the user that an applet window has been created. This message warns users that the window they see was started by an applet and not by software running on their computer. When Frame window is created by a program rather than an applet, a normal window is created.

3.10. CANVAS

Although it is not part of the hierarchy for applet or frame windows, there is one other type of window that you will find valuable: Canvas. Canvas encapsulates a blank window upon which you can draw.

3.11. AWT CONTROLS

Controls are components that allow a user to interact with your application in various ways, for example, a commonly used control is the push button. A layout manager automatically positions components within a container. Thus, the appearance of a window is determined by a combination of the controls that it contains and the layout manager used to position them.

The AWT supports the following type of controls:

1. Labels
2. Push buttons
3. Check boxes
4. Choice lists
5. Lists
6. Scroll bars
7. Text editing

These controls are subclasses of **Component**.

3.12. LABEL

The Label component is present in the java.awt package and is a subclass of the Object. Component class. Label are used to write text on the GUI, like the headings or subheadings etc. Label class has the following constructors :

```
public Label( );

public Label(String text);

public Label(String text, int alignment);
```

The first constructor is used to create an empty label, which can be filled during runtime. The next constructor creates a label with some text, and the last one has an alignment parameter, which decides whether the label string is left, centre or right aligned.

The following program creates two labels, main heading and subheading label. Then it changes their font and colour. After creating the controls, they must be added to the container object which by default is the applet itself. The add (component) function adds label to the applet.

//Program to create two labels

```
import java.applet.*;
import java.awt.*;

public class AddLabel extends Applet
{
   public void init()
   {
```

```
        Label header = new Label("Enrollment Form");
        header.setFont(new Font("Courier",Font.BOLD,16));

        Label subheader = new Label("Enrollment Form");
        subheader.setFont(new Font("TimesRoman",Font.BOLD,14));

        header.setForeground(Color.black);
        header.setBackground(Color.white);

        subheader.setForeground(Color.black);
        subheader.setBackground(Color.white);

        add(header);
        add(subheader);
    }
}
```

3.13. BUTTON

Push buttons are present in the java.awt package and it is a subclass of the Component class. They can be created with the help of the following Constructors:

```
public Button( );
public  Button(String label);
```

The first constructor creates a button without a label and the second constructor creates a button with a label.

For example : Consider the following example in which a button object is made.

```
import java.applet.*;
import java.awt.*;
public class AButton extends Applet
{
    public void init()
    {
        Button beepButton = new Label("Beep");
        add(BeepButton);
    }
}
```

3.14. CHECKBOX

Checkbox component belongs to the java.awt. Checkbox class and it is created with the help of the following constructors:

```
public Checkbox( )

public Checkbox(String text)

public Checkbox(String text, Boolean state)
```

The Checkbox( ) constructor without any parameters create a checkbox component without a prompt. The constructor with the String parameter creates a checkbox with a label. If you provide a Boolean value true or false along with a string as parameter, it display a label as well as sets the checkbox state to either checked or unchecked.

For example : The following example demonstrates how to create a set of check boxes:

```
import java.applet.*;
import java.awt.*;

public class Select extends Applet
{
   public void init()
   {
      Label header = new Label("Select Toolbar");

      Checkbox c1= new Checkbox("Drawing",true);
      Checkbox c2= new Checkbox("Picture");

      c1.setBackground(Color.cyan);
      c2.setBackground(Color.cyan);

      add(header);
      add(c1);
      add(c2);

   }
}
```

3.15. LAYOUT MANAGERS

AWT works on the container-component relationship. It has a number of components available in the form of classes, but all these are not useful if they are not placed inside a container. Containers in turn place the components inside it in a specific style, *i.e.*, if you want to add an object in a panel, it starts placing it from center or left or around the edges of the panel etc. The style or the layout of the object placements in the container is decided through the layout manager.

When a component is to be placed inside a container, the container consults its layout manager which determines the place of the component. There are different kinds of layout managers, like

1. Flow Layout
2. Border Layout
3. Grid Layout
4. Card Layout
5. Gridbag Layout etc.

It is sometimes difficult to adapt to these layout as they have their own order of placement. If you want to decide the position of the components rather than leaving it to the layout manager then there is a null layout. This layout nullifies all the settings and allows you to use coordinates using the function setBounds(int x, int y, int width, int height). The null layout can be specified using the function setLayout(null).

Despite having different features, the components can be acted upon by certain common functions. These functions are given below:

The add( ) method adds the components as the next item of the container.

```
public synchronized Component add(Component obj)
```

The remove( ) method removes the specified component from the container.

```
public synchronized void remove(Component obj)
```

If you want to remove all the components using only one command, you can use the removeAll( ) method.

```
public synchronized void removeAll(Component obj)
```

The getComponents( ) method returns the reference of all the components present in the container in the form of an array. You can act upon these controls collectively using this array.

```
public synchronized Component[] getComponents( )
```

3.16. FLOW LAYOUT

Flow Layout is the default layout. It consists of continuous rows, the height of which is determined by the height of the items placed in them. It can align the items center, left or right. The default alignment is the center alignment, *i.e.*, when the component is placed it is placed in the center. It keeps on placing the items in a row until it encounters an item exceeding the applet size. It then wrap that item to the next row and continues from there on. Flow layout is created using the constructors:

```
public FlowLayout( )

public FlowLayout(int alignment)

public FlowLayout(int alignment, horizontalgap, int verticalgap)
```

The first constructor creates a flow layout with the default center alignment and a five pixel gap between the components. In the second constructor the alignment parameter see the alignment through the constants:

```
FlowLayout.CENTER
FlowLayout.LEFT
FlowLayout.RIGHT
```

Through the last constructor we can also decide upon the horizontal and vertical gaps between the components.

3.17. BORDER LAYOUT

The border layout divides a container into five regions, east, west, north, south, and center region. You can place one component in each of these regions. The components are added using a special form of add( ) function which takes the first parameters as the region and the second parameter as the component to be added to that region. The constructors for creating border layout are:

```
public BorderLayout( )

public BorderLayout(int horizontalgap, int verticalgap)
```

Both the constructor create border layout with five sections, but in the second one you can also specify the horizontal ad vertical gaps between the regions.

```
import java.awt.*;
import java.applet.*;

public class BLayout extends Applet
{
    BorderLayout b= new BorderLayout( );
    Button est,wst,nrth,sth;
    TextArea cen;

    public void init( )
    {
        est = new Button("East");
        wst= new Button("West");
        nrth = new Button("North");
        sth= new Button("South");
        cen = new TextArea( );

        setLayout(b);
```

```
        add("East",est);
        add("West",wst);
        add("North",nrth);
        add("South",sth);
        add("Center",ce,)
        }
    }
```

3.18. GRID LAYOUT

Grid Layout lays out components in a two dimensional grid. When you instantiates a GridLayout, you define the number of rows and columns. The constructors supported by GridLayout are show here:

```
GridLayout( )
GridLayout(int numRows, int numColumns)
GridLayout(int numRows, int numColumns, int horz, int vert)
```

The first form creates a single column grid layout. The second form creates a gridlayout with the specified number of rows and columns. The third form allows you to specify the horizontal and vertical space left between components in horz and vert respectively.

3.19. CARD LAYOUT

The card layout arranges the components in the form of a queue of cards. In order to create a card layout you can use the following constructor:

```
public CardLayout( )
```

It creates a simple card layout which can be set using the function setLayout.

3.20. INSETS

Insets are the instructions to the layout manager about how much of space to be left around the edges of the container. Insets can be created using the following constructor:

```
public Insets(int top, int left, int bottom, int right)
```

It creates an inset specifying the space to be left from the top, left, bottom and right borders of the container. To implement the insets you have to override the get Insets( ) method which should return the object of the Insets class.

SUMMARY

1. AWT stands for Abstract window toolkit, which is a collection of number of common graphical widgets.
2. Three steps we use to create GUI application contains :
   - Compose the GUI,

- Setup Event Handlers and
- Display the GUI

3. There are numerous of AWT classes which are contained in java.awt package.
4. Component is an abstract class that encapsulates all the attributes of visual component.
5. Container class has additional methods that allow other component objects to be nested with it.
6. Panel class doesn't add any new methods, it simply implements container.
7. The tools that AWT package contains are Labels, Buttons, Check box, Drop down box, list etc.
8. There are three layout managers namely Flow layout, Border layout, Card layout and Grid layout.
9. Insets are the instructions to the layout manager about how much of space to be left around the edges of the container.

REVIEW QUESTIONS

1. What is AWT? Elaborate AWT classes.
2. Explain in brief container and component in AWT package.
3. How many layout are available in AWT package in Java? Explain each layout in brief.

❑❑❑

CHAPTER 4

Event Handling in AWT

INSIDE THIS CHAPTER

Well friends, this chapter examine an important aspect of Java that relates us to the world of graphical user interface: events. We had learned earlier in chapter1 that applets are event driven programs. Thus, event handling is the core of java programming. Let us learn what these events are and how to handle these events.

4.1. WHAT IS EVENT HANDLING

With the help of AWT we can create components like Buttons, Labels, Checkboxes, Radio buttons, etc. But it is equally important to handle the user response to these components. For example, if the checkbox is checked, the program should be able to record this information. In this case clicking of the checkbox is event.

An event is generated in response to anything that a user does, when a program is running.

Hence we can define event as :

Definition : An event is an object that describes a state change in a source. It can be generated as a consequence of a person interacting with the elements in a graphical user interface.

In other words, we can says that, when the user interacts with a GUI application, an event is generated. Examples of user events are clicking a button, selecting an item or closing a window. Events are represented as Objects in Java technology. The super class of all event classes is java.util.EventObject. Some of the important classes and their hierarchy is shown in Fig. 4.1.

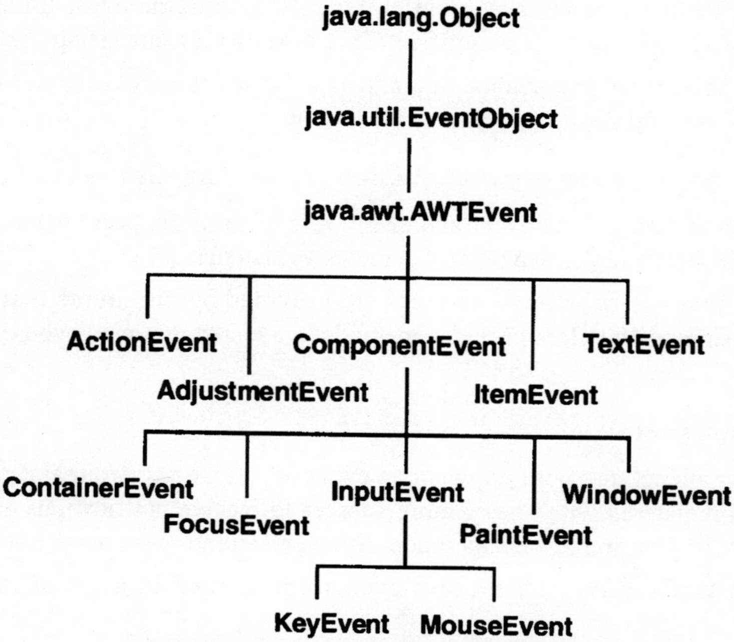

Fig. 4.1. Elaborating java.util.EventObject

Some of the activities that cause events to be generated are pressing a button, entering a character via keyboard, selecting an item in a list, and clicking the mouse.

Events may also be generated when a timer expires, a counter exceeds a value, a software or hardware failure occurs, or an operation is completed.

4.1.1. Event Sources

A Source is an object that generates an event. This occurs when the internal state of that object changes in some way. Sources may generate more than one type of event.

A source must register listeners in order for the listeners to receive notifications about a specific type of event. Each type of event has its own registration method.

Here is the general form :

```
public void addTypeListener(TypeListener el)
```

Here, Type is the name of the event and el is the reference to the event listener. For example, the method that registers a keyboard event listener is called addKeyListener( ).

The method that registers a mouse motion listener is called addMouseMotionListener( ).

When an event occur, all registered listeners are notified and receive a copy of the event object. This is known as multicasting the event. In all cases, notifications are sent only to listeners that register to receive them.

Some sources may allow only one listener to register. The general form of such a method is this:

```
public void addTypeListener(TypeListener el)

throws java.util.TooManyListenersException
```

Here, Type is the name of the event and el is a reference to the event listener. When such an event occurs, the registered listener is notified. This is known as unicasting the event.

A source must also provide a method that allows a listener to unregister an interest in a specific type of event. The general form of such method is this:

```
public void removeTypeListener(TypeListener el)
```

Here, Type is the name of the event and el is a reference to the event listener. For example, to remove a keyboard listener, you would call removekeyListener( ).

The methods that add or remove listeners are provided by the source that generates events. For example, the Component class provides methods to add and remove keyboard and mouse event listeners.

4.1.2. Event Listeners

A listener is an object that notified when an event occurs. It has two major requirements. First, it must have been registered with one or more sources to receive notifications about specific types of events. Second, it must implement methods to receive and process these notifications.

The methods that receive and process events are defined in a set of interfaces found in java.awt.event.

4.2. EVENT DELEGATION MODEL

The modern approach to handling events is based on the delegation event model, which defines standard and consistent mechanisms to generate and process events. Its concept is quite simple which is as follows:

" a source generates an event and sends it to one or more listeners. In this scheme, the listener simply waits until it receives an event. Once received, the listener process the event and then returns."

The advantage of this design is that the application logic that processes the events is cleanly separated from the user interface logic that generates those events. A user interface element is able to "delegate" the processing of an event to a separate piece of code.

In the delegation event model, listeners must register with a source in order to receive an event notification. This provides an important benefit:

Notifications are sent only to listeners that want to receive them. This is more efficient way to handle events than the design used by the old java 1.0 approach. Previously, an event was propagated up the containment hierarchy until it was handled by a component. This required the components to receive events that they did not process, and it wasted valuable time. The delegation event model eliminates this overhead.

4.3. EVENT METHODS

Some methods related to events are :

1. Object getSource()

This method is defined in the Event Object class. It returns the object that originated the event. So if the user has clicked a Push button, the method getSource returns the object corresponding to Push button is generated.

2. int getID()

This method returns the integer value corresponding to the type of event. For example, if the user has clicked on the mouse, the method getID returns the integer defined as MouseEvent.MOUSE_CLICKED.

4.4. EVENT CLASSES

The classes that represent events are at the core of Java's event handling mechanism.

At the root of java event class hierarchy is EventObject, which is in java.util. It is the superclass for all events.

The other class is AWTEvent which is superclass of all AWT events that are handled by the delegation event model. Another class GUIEvent which is the superclass of all the components like buttons, labels etc.

4.4.1. AWT Event Classes

The subclasses of AWT Event can be categorized into two groups :

1. Semantic events
2. Low-level events.

1. Semantic Event : Semantic events directly correspond to high level user interactions with a GUI component. Clicking of a button is an example of a semantic event. Following event classes are semantic classes.

- ActionEvent
- AdjustmentEvent
- ItemEvent
- TextEvent

2. Low-level Events : Multiple low-level events may get generated for each high level user event. Following event classes are low level event classes.

- ComponentEvent
- ContainerEvent
- FocusEvent
- KeyEvent
- MouseEvent
- PaintEvent
- WindowEvent

4.4.2. GUI Controls Event Classes

For each Java GUI component a set of events of above type are generated. It is important to understand which events are generated for each component. This is explained below.

The GUI component that generate **ActionEvent** are :

1. **Button :** When the user clicks on a PushButton.
2. **List :** When an item in list box is double clicked.
3. **MenuItem :** When a MenuItem is selected.

4. **TextField :** When the user clicks the Enter key in a text box.

AdjustmentEvent is generated when the user adjusts the position of a scrollbar. Scrollbar is the only GUI control that receives the AdjustmentEvent.

ItemEvent is generated when an item is selected or deselected. Following components generate ItemEvents.

1. **CheckBox :** When the state of the CheckBox is changed.
2. **CheckBoxMenuItem :** When the state of a MenuItem is changed.
3. **Choice :** When the state of a ChoiceBox is changed.
4. **List :** When an item in list is selected or deselected.

TextEvent is generated when the contents of text component are changed. The components that generate TextEvent are TextArea and TextField.

The GUI components corresponding to low level event classes are :

FocusEvent : This event is generated when a component gains or looses focus. Focus may be gained by bringing the mouse over a component (or by using the tab key). The component that has the focus receives all user keyboard events. Focus events are generated by objects of Component class and all its subclasses.

KeyEvent and **MouseEvent** are subclasses of abstract InputEvent class. Both these events are generated by objects of type Component class and its subclasses. The KeyEvent is generated when the user presses or releases a key on the keyboard. The MouseEvent is generated when the user presses the mouse or moves the mouse.

WindowEvent are generated for the Window class and its subclasses. These events are generated if an operation is performed on a window. The operation could be closing of window, opening of window, activating a window etc.

PaintEvent is generated when a component needs to be repainted (for example, when an application which is in front is closed and the component needs to be redrawn.) PaintEvents are internally handled by AWT, and cannot (and should not) be handled by you in the application.

ComponentEvent are also generated by objects of type Component class and its subclasses. This event is generated when a component is hidden, shown, moved or resized.

ContainerEvents are generated when a component is added or removed from a container. ComponentEvent and ContainerEvent are handled by AWT and are not normally handled by the user.

Event types and corresponding EventSource and EventListener are given below:

Event Type	Event Source	Event Listener interface
ActionEvent AdjustmentEvent	Button, List, MenuItem, TextField Scrollbar	ActionListener AdjustmentListener
Itemevent	Choice, Checkbox, CheckboxMenuItem, List	ItemListener
TextEvent	TextArea, TextField	TextListener
ComponentEvent	Component	ComponentListener
ContainerEvent	Container	ContainerListener
FocusEvent	Component	FocusListener
KeyEvent	Component	KeyListener
MouseEvent	Component	MouseListener, MouseMotionListener
WindowEvent	Window	WindowListener

Event Listener Interfaces and corresponding methods which it defines are given below:

Event Listener Interface	Event Listener Methods
ActionListener	actionPerformed(ActionEvent evt)
AdjustmentListener	adjustmentValueChanged(AjustmentEvent evt)
ItemListener	itemStateChanged(ItemEvent evt)
TextListener	textValueChanged(TextEvent evt)
ComponentListener	componentHidden(ComponentEvent evt), componentMoved(ComponentEvent evt), componentResized(ComponentEvent evt), componentShown(ComponentEvent evt)
ContainerListener	componentAdded(ContainerEvent evt), componentRemoved(ContainerEvent evt)
FocusListener	focusGained(FocusEvent evt), focusLost(FocusEvent evt)
KeyListener	keyPressed(KeyEvent evt), keyReleased(KeyEvent evt), keyTyped(KeyEvent evt)
MouseListener	mouseClicked(MouseEvent evt), mouseEntered(MouseEvent evt), mouseExited(MouseEvent evt), mousePressed(MouseEvent evt), mouseReleased(MouseEvent evt)
MouseMotionListener	mouseDragged(MouseEvent evt), mouseMoved(MouseEvent evt)
WindowListener	windowActivated(WindowEvent evt), windowClosed(WindowEvent evt), windowClosing(WindowEvent evt), windowDeactivated(WindowEvent evt), windowDeiconified(WindowEvent evt), windowIconified(WindowEvent evt), windowOpened(WindowEvent evt)

4.5. ADAPTER CLASSES

Event adapters facilitate implementing listener interfaces. Many event listener interfaces have more than one event listener methods. For such interfaces, Java technology defines adapter classes. These have empty implementation (stubs) of all the event listener methods defined in the interface they implement. A listener can subclass the adapter and override only stub methods for handling events of interest. These classes are useful when you want to receive and process only some of the events that are handled by a particular event listener interface.

The table below lists the low level event listener interfaces and their adapters.

Event Listener interface	Event Listener Adapter
ComponentListener	ComponentAdapter
ContainerListener	ContainerAdapter
FocusListener	FocusAdapter
KeyListener	KeyAdapter
MouseListener	MouseAdapter
MouseMotionListener	MouseMotionAdapter
WindowListener	WindowAdapter

SUMMARY

1. An event is an object that describes a stage change in a source. When the user Interacts with a GUI application, an event is generated.
2. An event source is an object that generates events.
3. A listener is an object that notified when an event occurs.
4. Event delegation model—" a source generates an event and sends it to one or more listeners. In this scheme, the listener simply waits until it receives an event. Once received, the listener process the event and then returns."
5. There are various methods related to event like getSource( ), int getId( ) etc.
6. An AWT event classes can be categorized into two groups :
   (*i*) Semantic Events (Action Events, Adjustment Event, Item Event, Text Event etc.)
   (*ii*) Low Level Events (Component Event, Container Event, Focus Event, Key Event, Mouse Event, Paint Event, Windows Event etc.)
7. An adapter class provides an empty implementation of all methods in an event listener interface.

REVIEW QUESTIONS

1. Define the following terms :
   (*i*) Events
   (*ii*) Events sources
   (*iii*) Event listeners
2. Describe the event class hierarchy in brief.
3. Explain Event Delegation model in brief.
4. Write short notes on Adapter Classes.

❑❑❑

CHAPTER 5

Applets

INSIDE THIS CHAPTER

Well friends, this chapter introduce another important graphical user interface concept contained in package named as java.applet. The concept of applets have created the improvements in the scope of Java program. So friends, let us understand the core of this concept and have fun with java programming.

5.1. OVERVIEW OF APPLETS

As discussed earlier, Java Programs can be of two types :

1. Applications
2. Applets

Applications are the programs that we run on the system while applets are the programs that we run on the internet. The browser on which the applets run must support the features of java, this means that they must have Java-enabled inside it. Internet Explorer 3.0 and above, Google Chrome, Netscape navigator and Sun's Hot Java are some of the most popular Java enabled browsers.

The applets can be transported over the internet from one computer to another and run using the Applet Viewer or any web browser that uses java. The applet is similar to an application program in the sense that we can perform arithmetic operations, display graphics, play sounds, accept user input, create animation and play interactive games.

An applet can be made locally and can be stored in a local system is known as **Local Applet**.

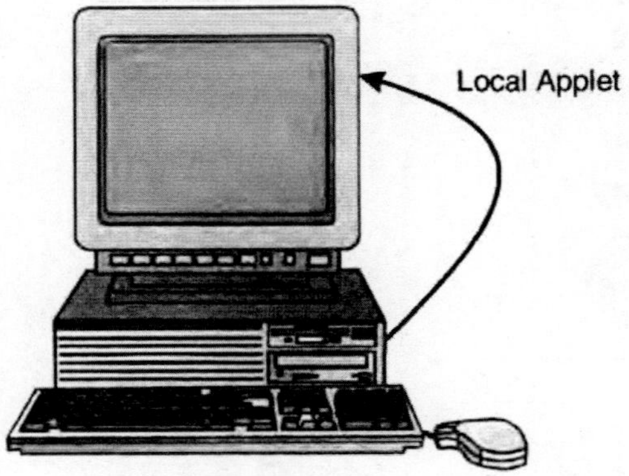

Fig. 5.1. Loading Local Applets

An Applet which is developed on one computer and stored on the remote computer connected to the internet is known as **Remote Applet**.

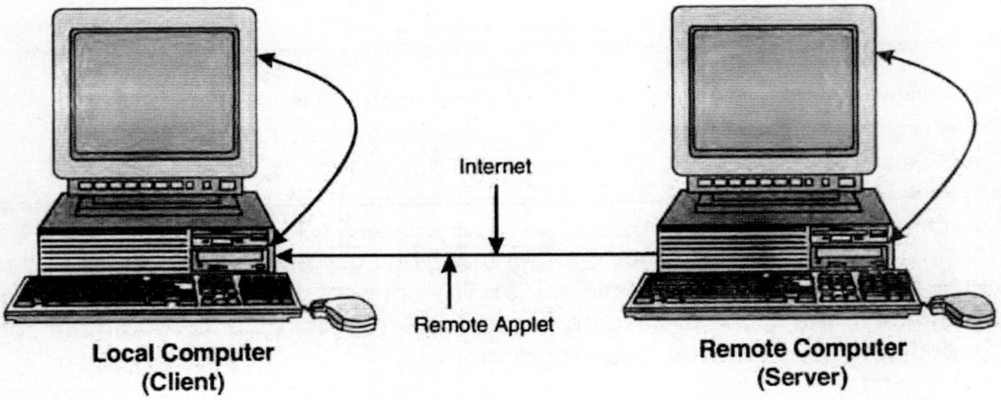

Fig. 5.2. Remote Applet

5.2. RESTRICTION TO APPLET DESIGN

1. The applet doesn't use the main method for initiating the execution of the code. It automatically calls certain inbuilt methods of applet class to start and execute the applet code.
2. Applets cannot read from or write to the files in the local computer.
3. Applets cannot be run independently as application run. They are run with the help of web page using a special feature known as **HTML Tag**.
4. The communication of applets is restricted to other servers on the internet
5. Applets cannot run any program from the local computer.
6. Applets are also restricted to access libraries of any other languages such as C or C++.

5.3. APPLICATION VS. APPLETS

The following table below shows the difference between application and the applet.

S.No.	Application	Applets
1.	Applications are the programs that run on the System.	Applets are the programs that run on the browser.
2.	Application can read, write or execute files in the local computer.	Applets cannot read, write or execute files in the local computer.
3.	Application doesn't require any browser to run.	Applets require a browser to run.
4.	It takes less time to execute an application.	It takes longer to execute an applet.
5.	Application uses system memory to execute.	The amount of memory that can be used by an applet is decided by the browser.

5.4. THE APPLET CLASS

The applet class defines the methods shown below :

S.No.	Applet Classes	Description
1.	void destroy( )	Called by the browser just below an applet is terminated. Your applet will override this method if it needs to perform any cleanup prior to its destruction.
2.	AccessibleContext getAccessibleContext( )	Returns the accessibility context for the invoking object.
3.	AppletContext getAppletContect( )	Returns the context associated with the applet
4.	String getAppletInfo( )	Returns a string that describes the applet
5.	AudioClip getAudioClip (URL url)	Returns an AudioClip object that encapsulates the audio clip found at the location specified by url
6.	AudioClip getAudioClip(URL url, String clipName)	Returns an AudioClip object that encapsulates the audio clip found at the location specified by url and having the name specified by clipName.
7.	URL getCodeBase( )	Returns the URL associated with the invoking applet.
8.	URL getDocumentBase( )	Returns the URL of the HTML document that invokes the applet
9.	Image getImage(URL url)	Returns an Image object that encapsulates the image found at the location specified by url.
10.	Image getImage(URL url, String ImageName)	Returns an Image object that encapsulates the image found at the location specified by url and having the name specified by imageName
11.	Local getLocale( )	Returns a Locale object that is used by various locale-sensitive classes and methods
12.	String getParameter(String paramName)	Returns the parameter associated with paramName. Null is returned if the specified parameter is not found.
13.	void init( )	Called when an applet begins execution. It is the first method called for any applet.
14.	Boolean isActive( )	Returns true if the applet has been started. It returns false if the applet has been stoped

S.No.	Applet Classes	Description
15.	void play(URL url)	If an audio clip is found at the location specified by url, the clip is played.
16.	void resize(Dimension dim)	Resizes the applet according to the dimension specified by dim
17.	void resize(int width, int height)	Resizes the applet according to the dimension specified by width and height
18.	void start( )	Called by the browser when an applet should start execution.
19.	void stop( )	Called by the browser to suspend execution of the applet.
20.	void showStatus(String str)	Display str in the status window of the browser or applet viewer.

5.5. LIFE CYCLE OF AN APPLET

We have already seen that how an applet is created and executed in chapter 1. An Applet requires an HTML envelop around it to be able to get executed. Applications contain a main() program that is the starting point of execution of an application. An applet, however, doesn't contain a main() function, so how an applets can be run? An answer to this is that there are several methods in an applet that get executed at different times. These methods are known as **Life Cycle of Applet** which are shown in Fig. 5.3.

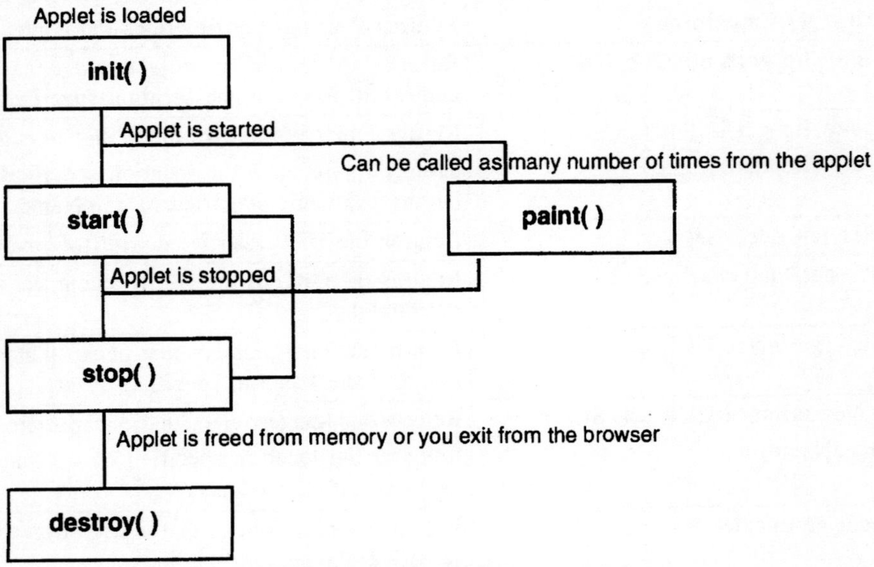

Fig. 5.3. Life Cycle of an applet

The five most important methods of an applet are :

1. init( )
2. start( )
3. stop( )

4. destroy( )
5. paint( )

Initialization : When an applet is loaded in the memory, init( ) function is called. This Function sets the initial behavior of the applet. We can set fonts, load images, initialize variables or set parameters here. To give an applet the type of functionality you want, you must override the init( ) method.

```
Public void init( )
{
// Write necessary code }
```

Starting: This phase happens after an applet has been initialized or when the user comes back to the page that contained the applet in the browser. The main difference between initialization and starting is that initialization happens only once whereas starting can happen any number of times in an applet.

```
Public void start(){
//write necessary code
}
```

Stopping : The stop( ) method is called when an explicit call to the method is made or when the user leaves the current page in which the applet is running. Again we have to override the function stop() to provide your own functionality to the applet.

```
Public void stop()
{
//write necessary code
}
```

Destroying : The destroy() method is called when the memory used for the applet has to be freed or when the user exits the browser. Again we need to override the function destroy() to provide our own functionality to the applet.

```
Public void destroy()
{
//Write necessary code
}
```

Painting : The paint() method can be called any number of time in an applet. This method is responsible for displaying text, graphics, image etc. on the screen, paint() function must be overridden if we want to provide our own functionality to the applet.

```
Public void(Graphics g)
{
    // Write necessary code
}
```

5.6. HTML TAGS FOR APPLET

As explained in chapter 1, an applet has to be enveloped inside an HTML file to be able to run in a browser.

```
<html>
<head>
<title>"The Applet is Running"</title>
</head>
<body>
<applet code="ClassName" height=200 width=200>
</applet>
</html>
```

The description of the above will be :

<html></html> tag specifies the beginning and the end of the HTML document

<head></head> tag specifies the header in which title section has been specified through**<title></title>**

<body></body> tag specifies the document region where text can be written and in which we want our applet to appear.

Finally, the applet is called through the **<applet></applet>** tag. The code specifies the .class filename, height and width determine the size of the applet. Now we can call the HTML document in the browser. As soon as the file is opened, the applet enveloped inside the HTML file also starts running.

For example : Let us now look at how an applet runs:

```
import java.applet.*;
import java.awt.*;
public class Apple extends Applet
{
public void paint(Graphics g)
{
g.drawString("An Applet a day keeps a doctor away",50,50);
}
}
```

The first two statements are for importing or including the packages in the applet. A package is a set of classes categorized under a specific name and kept in the library. This program has included the java.awt package as it is using the method paint() and program also include the java.applet package as the main class must be inherited from the applet class. The 'extends' keyword is used for inheritance.

The paint(Graphics g) is a method used to draw a picture or text on the applet. It gets the applets graphics context automatically as the parameter. The graphics context is nothing but an area to write or draw something. So, the 'Graphics g' in the paint( ) function gets the applets graphics context, area where drawing etc. would happen. We are using the function drawString(String text,int position X, int position Y) in order to write some text on the applet.

The above applet must be saved as the same class name, *i.e.,* Apple.java and compiled as:

```
javac Apple.java.
```

This makes the .class file which contains the byte code. Since this is an applet, the .class file now have to be embedded inside an HTML document and run through a browser.

A very basic HTML document may be written as:

```
<html>
<head>
<title>"The Applet is Running"</title>
</head>
<body>
<applet code="Apple" height=200 width=200>
</applet>
</html>
```

Save as : The above program can be saved as:

```
Apple.html
```

Compiled as : javac Apple.java

Run as : appletviewer Apple.html

SUMMARY

1. Applets are the programs that we run on the internet.
2. An applet doesn't have main method. It can be run through applet viewer.
3. An applet can be made locally and can be stored in a local system. This type of applet is known as Local Applet.
4. An applet which is developed on one computer and stored on remote computer connected to the internet is known as Remote Applet.
5. The applet class contains numerous of methods that supports graphics.
6. The life cycle of applet contains the following steps :
    1. Initialization(init( )).
    2. Starting (start( )).
    3. Stopping (stop( )).
    4. Destroying(destroying( )).
    5. Painting(paint( )).
7. An applet need to be enveloped into html file to be able to run on a browser.

REVIEW QUESTIONS

1. What are applets ? Explain the life cycle of applet.
2. Elaborate applet class in details.
3. Difference between application and applet.
4. Create applet in which one string moves from left to right.

❑❑❑

CHAPTER 6

Introduction to Swing

INSIDE THIS CHAPTER

Well friends, lets take a tour to a superchanged alternative of AWT, called Swing. Swing provides more powerful and flexible components than AWT.

So friends lets go to the concept and have fun with Swing.

6.1. INTRODUCTION TO SWING

In chapter 3, we have seen how to build user interfaces with AWT classes. Here we will take a tour to an alternative approach known as **Swing**.

Swing is a set of classes that provides more powerful and flexible components than the concept of AWT. In addition to the familiar components, such as buttons, check boxes and labels, Swing supplies several additions including tabbed panes, scroll panes, trees and tables. Even familiar components such as buttons have more capabilities in Swing.

For example, a button may have both an image and a text string associated with it. Also, the image can be changed as the state of the button changes.

6.2. SWING LIBRARY

Swing library will contains swing packages and swing components. All elements of swing are part of java.swing package. To use a swing class one can either use an import statement for a specific class to be imported or import all classes from the swing packages. Swing packages and swing components are given below in table below.

S.No.	Swing Packages	Description
1.	javax.swing	This high level swing package primarily contains components, adapters, default components models and interfaces for all delegates and models.
2.	javax.swing.border	The border package declares the Border interface and classes, which define specific border rendering styles.
3.	javax.swing.event	The event package is for the Swing-specific event types and listener. Swing components can generate their own event types, in addition to the java.awt.event package.
4.	javax.swing.table	The table package contains the interfaces and classes that supports the Swing JTable components.
5.	javax.swing.text	The text package contains the support classes for the swing documents framework.
6.	javax.swing.text.html	The text.html package contains the support classes for basic HTML rendering
7.	javax.swing.undo	The undo package provides the support classes for implementing the undo/redo capabilities in a GUI.

S.No.	Swing Packages	Description
1.	JApplet	An extended version of java.applet.Applet that adds support for root panes and other panes.
2.	JButton	A push or command button
3.	JCheckBox	A check box that can be selected or deselected, displaying its state visually.
4.	JCheckMenuItem	A menu item that can be selected or deselected and that display its state visually
5.	JComboBox	A combo box, which is a combination of a text field and dropdown list
6.	JDialog	The base class for creating dialog window
7.	JFrame	An extended version of java.awt.Frame that adds support root panes and other panes.
8.	JLabel	A display area for a shot text string or an image
9.	JList	A Component that allows the user to select one or more objects from a list.
10.	JMenu	A pop-up menu containing JMenuItem that's displayed when the user selects it in the JMenuBar componet.
11.	JMenuBar	An implementation of a menu bar
12.	JMenuItem	An implementation of a menu item
13.	JOptionPane	Make it easy to pop up a standard dialog box.
14.	JPanel	A generic lightweight container
15.	JPasswordField	Allows editing of a single line of text where the view does not show the original
16.	JPopupMenu	A pop-up menu

S.No.	Swing Packages	Description
17.	JPopupMenuSeparator	A Pop-up menu-specific separator
18.	JprogressBar	A Component that displays an integer value within an interval
19.	JRadioButton	A radio button that can be selected or deselected, displaying its state visually
20.	JRadioButtonMenuItem	A radio button menu item.
21.	JRootPane	The fundamental component in the container hierarchy
22.	JScrollPane	A container that manages a viewport, optional vertical and horizontal scrollbars, and optional row and column heading viewports
23.	JSlider	A Component that lets the user select a value by sliding a knob within an interval.
24.	JTabbedPane	Lets the user switch between a group of components by clicking tabs.
25.	JTable	Presents data in a two dimensional table format
26.	JTextArea	A multiline area that displays plain text
27.	JTextField	Allows the editing of a single line of text
28.	JTextPane	A text component that can marked up with attributes that are represented graphically
29.	JToolBar	A toolbar, useful for displaying commonly used controls
30.	JTree	Displays a set of hierarchical data as an outline.

6.3. BUILDING APPLICATION USING SWING

6.3.1. Program to understand the concept of swing that display six buttons with shortcut key and tooltips on a panel using frame.

```
import javax.swing.*;
import java.awt.event.*;

public class MasterForm extends JFrame
{
   public MasterForm()
   {
      super("Master Form");

   JButton btnInsert= new JButton("Insert");
   JButton btnUpdate= new JButton("Update");
   JButton btnDelete= new JButton("Delete");
   JButton btnView= new JButton("View");
   JButton btnPrevious= new JButton("Previous");
```

```
JButton btnNext= new JButton("Next");

JPanel pnlMenu=new JPanel();
pnlMenu.add(btnInsert);
pnlMenu.add(btnUpdate);
pnlMenu.add(btnDelete);
pnlMenu.add(btnView);
pnlMenu.add(btnPrevious);
pnlMenu.add(btnNext);

btnInsert.setMnemonic('i');
btnUpdate.setMnemonic('u');
btnDelete.setMnemonic('d');
btnView.setMnemonic('v');
btnPrevious.setMnemonic('p');
btnNext.setMnemonic('n');

btnInsert.setToolTipText("To Insert New Records");
btnUpdate.setToolTipText("To Update New Records");
btnDelete.setToolTipText("To Delete New Records");
btnView.setToolTipText("To View Existing Records");
btnPrevious.setToolTipText("Go to Previous Record");
btnNext.setToolTipText("Go to Next Record");
setContentPane(pnlMenu);
}

public static void main(String args[])
{
   MasterForm frmMaster=new MasterForm();
   frmMaster.setSize(500,300);
   frmMaster.setVisible(true);

   WindowListener listener= new WindowAdapter()
   {
      public void windowClosing(WindowEvent winEvt)
      {
            System.exit(0);
      }
   };
```

```
            frmMaster.addWindowListener(listener);
        }
    }
```

Save as: The above program can be saved as:

MasterForm.java

Compile as: javac MasterForm.java

Run as: java MasterForm

Output: The output of the program will be:

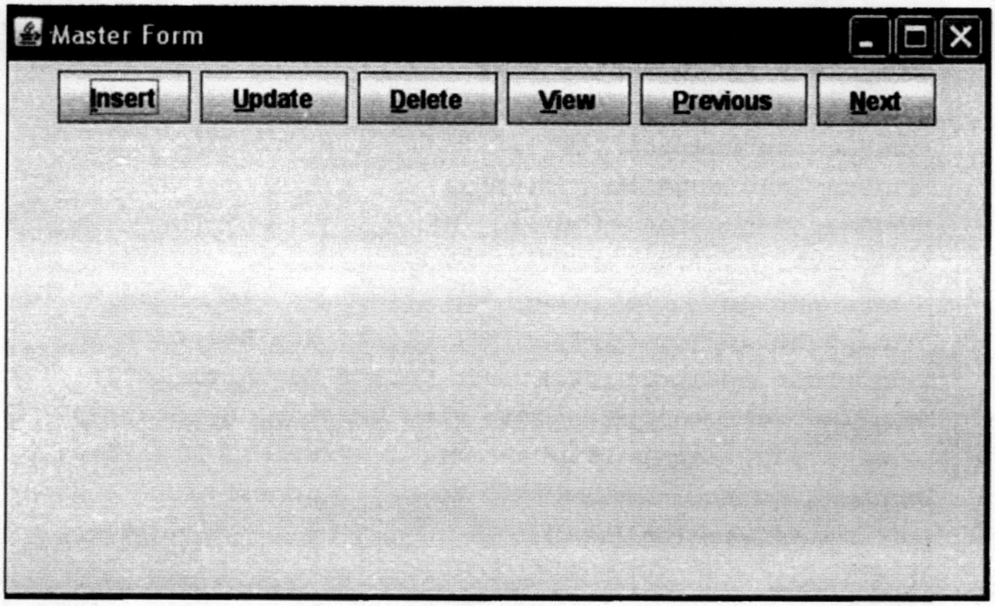

Fig. 6.1.

6.3.2. Program to print your name and address in text box with the button submit. On clicking submit the entered information should be shown.

```
import javax.swing.*;
import java.awt.event.*;
public class TextAreaDemo extends JPanel implements ActionListener
{
    JLabel lblName, lblAdd;
    JTextField txtName,txtAdd;
    JTextArea taRemarks;
    JButton btnIcon;

    public TextAreaDemo()
    {
```

```
setLayout(null);

lblName  = new JLabel("Enter Your Name");
lblAdd   = new JLabel("Enter Your Address");
txtName  = new JTextField(15);
txtAdd   = new JTextField(25);
taRemarks= new JTextArea(10,10);
btnIcon  = new JButton("Submit");

btnIcon.addActionListener(this);

lblName.setBounds(10,20,120,25);
txtName.setBounds(150,20,150,25);
lblAdd.setBounds(10,60,120,25);
txtAdd.setBounds(150,60,200,25);
btnIcon.setBounds(120,100,150,30);
taRemarks.setBounds(30,140,330,100);

add(lblName);
add(txtName);
add(lblAdd);
add(txtAdd);
add(btnIcon);
add(taRemarks);
}

public void actionPerformed(ActionEvent actEvt)
{
   if(actEvt.getSource()==btnIcon)
   {
      taRemarks.append("Name:" +txtName.getText()+"\n");
      taRemarks.append("Address:"+txtAdd.getText()+"\n");
   }

}

public static void main(String args[])
{
   TextAreaDemo tademo= new TextAreaDemo();
```

```
        JFrame frm=new JFrame("Text Area Demo");

        frm.setContentPane(tademo);

        frm.setSize(400,300);

        frm.setVisible(true);

        WindowListener listener=new WindowAdapter()
        {
           public void windowClosing(WindowEvent winEvt)
           {
                System.exit(0);
           }
        };
        frm.addWindowListener(listener);
    }
}
```

Save as: The above program can be saved as:

TextAreaDemo.java

Compile as: javac TextAreaDemo.java

Run as: java TextArea

Output: The output of the program will be:

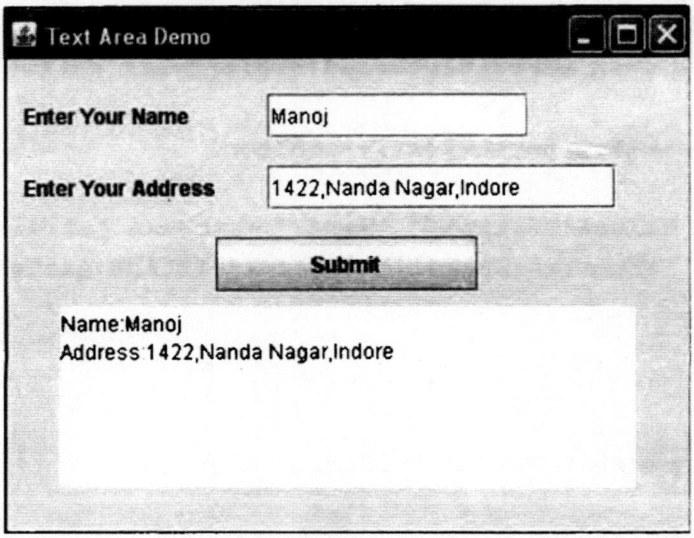

Fig. 6.2.

SUMMARY

1. Swing is a set of classes that provides more powerful and flexible components than the concept of AWT.
2. Swing library contains various packages which makes the programming approach easy to understand and build.

REVIEW QUESTIONS

1. Wrtie short note on Swing.
2. Explore swing library in brief.
3. What are the steps used to build a swing application ?

❑❑❑

UNIT-III

- ➤ **Multithreading in Java**
- ➤ **Exception Handling**

SYLLABUS

Multithreading and Exception Handling : Overview of simple threads, Basic idea of multithreaded programming,Thread synchronization: Locks, synchronized methods, synchronized block, Thread scheduling Producer-consumer relationship, Daemon thread, Basic idea of exception handling, stack based execution and exception propagation, Exceptiontypes. Exception Handling : Try, Catch, Finally, Throw statement, Assertions.

CHAPTER 7

Multithreading in Java

INSIDE THIS CHAPTER

Well friends, in the first chapter we had seen that Java provides built in support for multithreaded programming. A multithreaded program contains two or more parts that can run simultaneously. This chapter deals with the basic concept of multithreaded programming. So let's have fun with the concept of multithreaded programming.

7.1. WHAT IS MULTITHREADING?

Java provides built-in support for multithreaded programming. A multithreaded program contains two or more parts that can run concurrently. Each part of such a program is called a thread, and each thread defines a separate path of execution.

A multithreading is a specialized form of multitasking. Multitasking threads require less overhead than multitasking processes.

Let us define another definition of Threads, but before that lets take an overview on the definition of **process:** Program in Execution is known as **Process.**

Definition : A small process is known as **Thread.**

Hence, we can says that, process is a collection of multiple threads.

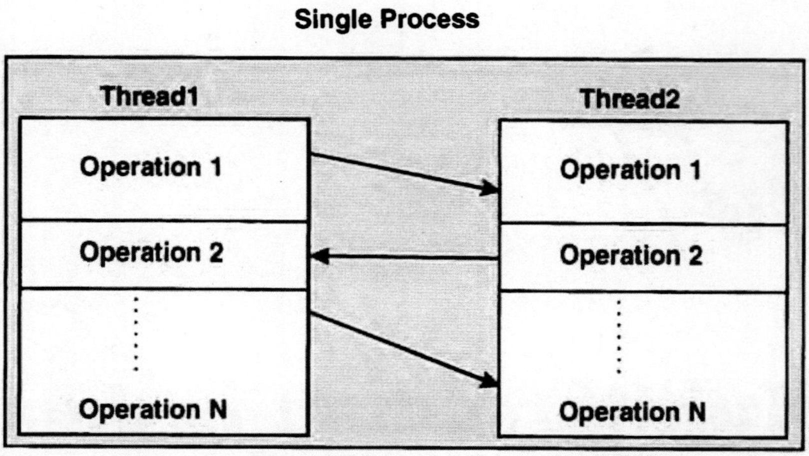

Fig. 7.1. Single Process Consist of Multiple Threads

From the example above, we can says that single process consist of multiple threads. Multithreading enables us to write very efficient programs that make maximum use of the CPU, because idle time can be kept to a minimum.

7.2. LIFE CYCLE OF A THREAD

A thread goes through various stages in its life cycle. For example, a thread is born, started, runs, and then dies. The diagram below shows complete life cycle of a thread.

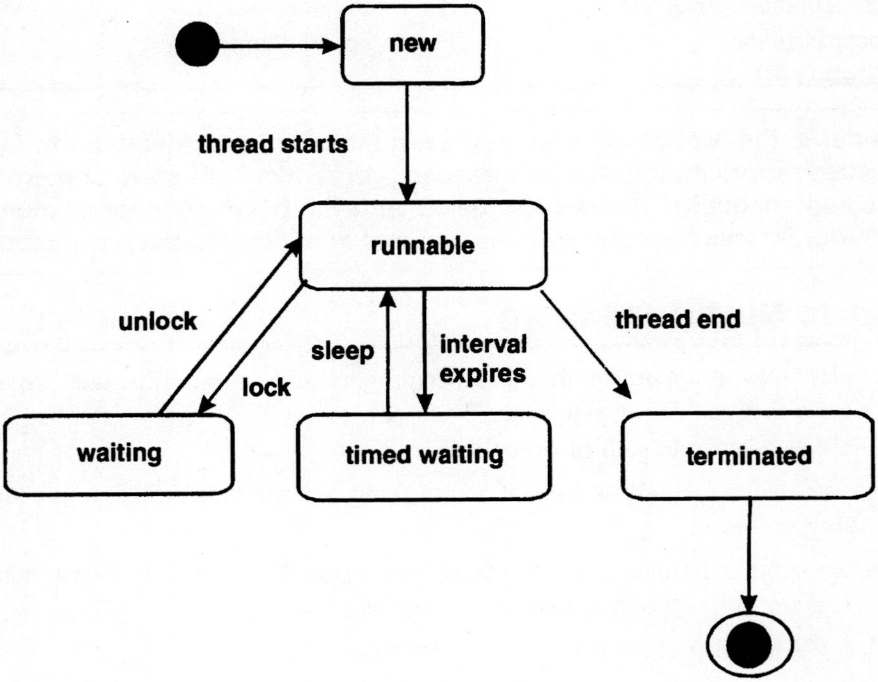

Fig. 7.2. Life Cycle of Thread

The description of above mentioned stages are explained below:

1. **New :** A new thread begins its life cycle in the new state. It remains in this state until the program starts the thread. It is also referred to as a born thread.
2. **Runnable :** After a newly born thread is started, the thread becomes runnable. A thread in this state is considered to be executing its task.
3. **Waiting :** Sometimes a thread transitions to the waiting state while the thread waits for another thread to perform a task. A thread transitions back to the runnable state only when another thread signals the waiting thread to continue executing.
4. **Timed Waiting :** A runnable thread can enter the timed waiting state for a specified interval of time. A thread in this state transitions back to the runnable state when that time interval expires or when the event it is waiting for occurs.
5. **Terminated :** A runnable thread enters the terminated state when it completes its task or otherwise terminates.

7.3. THREAD PRIORITIES

Every Java thread has a priority that helps the operating system determine the order in which threads are scheduled.

Java priorities are in the range between MIN_PRIORITY (a constant of 1) and MAX_PRIORITY (a constant of 10). By default, every thread is given priority NORM_PRIORITY (a constant of 5).

Threads with higher priority are more important to a program and should be allocated processor time before lower-priority threads. However, thread priorities cannot guarantee the order in which threads execute and very much platform dependentant.

7.4. CREATING A THREAD

Java defines two ways in which this can be accomplished:

1. Implement the Runnable interface.
2. Extend the Thread class, itself.

7.4.1. Create Thread by Implementing Runnable

The easiest way to create a thread is to create a class that implements the **Runnable** interface. To implement Runnable, a class need only implement a single method called **run( )**, which is declared like this:

```
public void run( )
```

You will define the code that constitutes the new thread inside run() method. It is important to understand that run() can call other methods, use other classes, and declare variables, just like the main thread can.

After you create a class that implements Runnable, you will instantiate an object of type Thread from within that class. Thread defines several constructors. The one that we will use is shown here:

```
Thread(Runnable threadObject, String threadName);
```

Here threadObject is an instance of a class that implements the Runnable interface and the name of the new thread is specified by threadName.

After the new thread is created, it will not start running until you call its **start( )** method, which is declared within Thread. The start( ) method is shown here:

```
void start( );
```

Example : Let us take an example that creates a new thread and starts it running:

```
// Create a new thread.
class NewThread implements Runnable {
   Thread t;
   NewThread() {
      // Create a new, second thread
      t = new Thread(this, "Demo Thread");
      System.out.println("Child thread: " + t);
      t.start(); // Start the thread
   }

   // This is the entry point for the second thread.
   public void run() {
      try {
         for(int i = 5; i > 0; i–) {
            System.out.println("Child Thread: " + i);
            // Let the thread sleep for a while.
            Thread.sleep(500);
         }
      } catch (InterruptedException e) {
         System.out.println("Child interrupted.");
      }
      System.out.println("Exiting child thread.");
   }
}

class ThreadDemo {
   public static void main(String args[]) {
      new NewThread(); // create a new thread
      try {
         for(int i = 5; i > 0; i–) {
            System.out.println("Main Thread: " + i);
            Thread.sleep(1000);
         }
      } catch (InterruptedException e) {
```

```
            System.out.println("Main thread interrupted.");
        }
        System.out.println("Main thread exiting.");
    }
}
```

Output :

```
The output of the program will be:
Child thread: Thread[Demo Thread,5,main]
Main Thread: 5
Child Thread: 5
Child Thread: 4
Main Thread: 4
Child Thread: 3
Child Thread: 2
Main Thread: 3
Child Thread: 1
Exiting child thread.
Main Thread: 2
Main Thread: 1
Main thread exiting
```

7.4.2. Create Thread by Extending Thread

The second way to create a thread is to create a new class that extends **Thread**, and then to create an instance of that class.

The extending class must override the **run( )** method, which is the entry point for the new thread. It must also call **start( )** to begin execution of the new thread.

Example : Let us again take the same example by Extending Thread:

```
// Create a second thread by extending Thread
class NewThread extends Thread {
    NewThread() {
        // Create a new, second thread
        super("Demo Thread");
        System.out.println("Child thread: " + this);
        start(); // Start the thread
    }

    // This is the entry point for the second thread.
    public void run() {
        try {
```

```
            for(int i = 5; i > 0; i–) {
               System.out.println("Child Thread: " + i);
            // Let the thread sleep for a while.
               Thread.sleep(500);
            }
        } catch (InterruptedException e) {
          System.out.println("Child interrupted.");
        }
       System.out.println("Exiting child thread.");
    }
}

class ExtendThread {
   public static void main(String args[]) {
       new NewThread(); // create a new thread
        try {
            for(int i = 5; i > 0; i–) {
               System.out.println("Main Thread: " + i);
               Thread.sleep(1000);
            }
        } catch (InterruptedException e) {
          System.out.println("Main thread interrupted.");
        }
       System.out.println("Main thread exiting.");
    }
}
```

Output :

This would produce following result:

```
Child thread: Thread[Demo Thread,5,main]
Main Thread: 5
Child Thread: 5
Child Thread: 4
Main Thread: 4
Child Thread: 3
Child Thread: 2
Main Thread: 3
Child Thread: 1
Exiting child thread.
Main Thread: 2
Main Thread: 1
Main thread exiting
```

7.5. THREAD METHODS

Following is the list of important methods available in the Thread class.

S.No.	Methods with Descriptions
1	**public void start()** Starts the thread in a separate path of execution, then invokes the run() method on this Thread object.
2	**public void run()** If this Thread object was instantiated using a separate Runnable target, the run() method is invoked on that Runnable object.
3	**public final void setName(String name)** Changes the name of the Thread object. There is also a getName() method for retrieving the name.
4	**public final void setPriority(int priority)** Sets the priority of this Thread object. The possible values are between 1 and 10.
5	**public final void setDaemon(boolean on)** A parameter of true denotes this Thread as a daemon thread.
6	**public final void join(long millisec)** The current thread invokes this method on a second thread, causing the current thread to block until the second thread terminates or the specified number of milliseconds passes.
7	**public void interrupt()** Interrupts this thread, causing it to continue execution if it was blocked for any reason.
8	**public final boolean isAlive()** Returns true if the thread is alive, which is any time after the thread has been started but before it runs to completion.

The previous methods are invoked on a particular Thread object. The following methods in the Thread class are static. Invoking one of the static methods performs the operation on the currently running thread.

S.No.	Methods with Descriptions
1	**public static void yield()** Causes the currently running thread to yield to any other threads of the same priority that are waiting to be scheduled
2	**public static void sleep(long millisec)** Causes the currently running thread to block for at least the specified number of milliseconds
3	**public static boolean holdsLock(Object x)** Returns true if the current thread holds the lock on the given Object.
4	**public static Thread currentThread()** Returns a reference to the currently running thread, which is the thread that invokes this method.
5	**public static void dumpStack()** Prints the stack trace for the currently running thread, which is useful when debugging a multithreaded application.

Example : The following ThreadClassDemo program demonstrates some of these methods of the Thread class :

```
// File Name : DisplayMessage.java
// Create a thread to implement Runnable
public class DisplayMessage implements Runnable
{
   private String message;
   public DisplayMessage(String message)
   {
      this.message = message;
   }
   public void run()
   {
      while(true)
      {
        System.out.println(message);
      }
   }
}

// File Name : GuessANumber.java
// Create a thread to extentd Thread
public class GuessANumber extends Thread
{
   private int number;
   public GuessANumber(int number)
   {
      this.number = number;
   }
   public void run()
   {
      int counter = 0;
      int guess = 0;
      do
      {
         guess = (int) (Math.random() * 100 + 1);
         System.out.println(this.getName()
                          + " guesses " + guess);
         counter++;
      }while(guess != number);
```

```
      System.out.println("** Correct! " + this.getName()
                              + " in " + counter + " guesses.**");
    }
  }

// File Name : ThreadClassDemo.java
public class ThreadClassDemo
{
   public static void main(String [] args)
   {
      Runnable hello = new DisplayMessage("Hello");
      Thread thread1 = new Thread(hello);
      thread1.setDaemon(true);
      thread1.setName("hello");
      System.out.println("Starting hello thread...");
      thread1.start();

      Runnable bye = new DisplayMessage("Goodbye");
      Thread thread2 = new Thread(hello);
      thread2.setPriority(Thread.MIN_PRIORITY);
      thread2.setDaemon(true);
      System.out.println("Starting goodbye thread...");
      thread2.start();

      System.out.println("Starting thread3...");
      Thread thread3 = new GuessANumber(27);
      thread3.start();
      try
      {
         thread3.join();
      }catch(InterruptedException e)
      {
         System.out.println("Thread interrupted.");
      }
      System.out.println("Starting thread4...");
      Thread thread4 = new GuessANumber(75);

      thread4.start();
      System.out.println("main() is ending...");
   }
}
```

This would produce following result. You can try this example again-and-again and you would get different result every time.

```
Starting hello thread...
Starting goodbye thread...
Hello
Hello
Hello
Hello
Hello
Hello
Hello
Hello
Hello
Thread-2 guesses 27
Hello
** Correct! Thread-2 in 102 guesses.**
Hello
Starting thread4...
Hello
Hello
and more...
```

7.6. MAJOR THREAD CONCEPTS

While doing Multithreading programming, you would need to have following concepts very handy:

1. Thread Synchronization
2. Interthread Communication
3. Thread Deadlock
4. Thread Control: Suspend, Stop and Resume

7.7. SYNCHRONIZATION

When two or more threads need access to a shared resource, they need some way to ensure that the resource will be used by only one thread at a time. The process by which this is achieved is called **Synchronization**.

Key to Synchronization is the concept of **monitor**. A **monitor** is an object that is used as mutually exclusive lock or mutex. Only one thread can own a monitor at a given time. When a thread acquires a lock, it is said to entered the monitor. All other threads attempting to enter the locked monitor will be waiting for the monitor.

7.8. THREAD SYNCHRONIZATION

When multiple threads share an object and one or more of them modify that object, indeterminate results may occur unless access to the shared object is managed properly. When the object finishes manipulating it, one of the threads that was waiting is allowed to proceed. This process is called as Thread Synchronization which coordinates access to shared data by multiple concurrent threads.

By synchronizing threads, one can ensure that each thread accessing a shared object excludes all other threads from doing so simultaneously- this is called mutual exclusion.

A common way to perform synchronization is to use Java's built in monitors. Every object has a monitor and monitor lock. The monitor ensures that its object's monitor lock is held by a maximum of only one thread at any time, and thus can be used to enforce mutual exclusion.

If an operation requires the executing thread to hold a lock while the operation is performed, a thread must acquire the lock before it can proceed with the operation. Any other threads attempting to perform an operation that requires the same lock will be blocked until the first thread releases the lock, at which point the blocked thread may attempt to acquire the lock.

7.9. SYNCHRONIZED STATEMENTS

To specify that a thread must hold a monitor lock in order to execute a block of code, the code should be placed in a synchronized statement. Such code is said to be guarded by a monitor lock, a thread must acquire the lock to execute the synchronized statements.

The synchronized statements are declared by using the "synchronized" keyword-

```
synchronized(object)
{
statements
}
```

Here, object refers to the object whose monitor lock will be acquired.

7.10. SYNCHRONIZED METHOD AND SYNCHRONIZED BLOCK

First of all to achieve Multithreading mechanism in java we should go for synchronization. And this can be done in two ways depending on the requirement.

1. Synchronized block and
2. Synchronized method.

If we go for synchronized block it will lock a specific object.

If we go for synchronized method it will lock all the objects.

In other words, both the synchronized method and block are used to acquires the lock for an object. But the context may vary. Suppose if we want to invoke a critical method which is in a class whose access is not available then synchronized block is used. Otherwise synchronized method can be used.

Synchronized methods are used when we are sure all instance will work on the same set of data through the same function Synchronized block is used when we use code which we cannot modify ourselves like third party jars etc.

For example :

```
    //Synchronized block

class A
{ public void method1() {...} }
class B
{
public static void main(String s[])
{ A objecta=new A();
A objectb=new A();
synchronized(objecta){objecta.method1();}
objectb.method1(); //not synchronized
}
}


//synchronized method
class A
{ public synchronized void method1() { ...}
}
class B
{
public static void main(String s[])
{
A objecta=new A();
A objectb =new A();
objecta.method1(); objectb.method2();

}
}
```

7.11. THREAD SCHEDULING

Every java thread priority that helps the operating system determines the order in which threads are scheduled. Java priorities range between MIN_PRIORITY and MAX_PRIORITY, by default every thread is given priority NORM_PRIORITY.

An operating system's thread scheduler determines which thread runs next. One simple thread scheduler implementation keeps the highest-priority thread running at all times and if there more than one highest priority thread, ensures that all such threads executes in a round robin fashion.

Figure 7.3 shows the multilevel priority queue for threads. In figure, assuming a single processor computer, threads A and B each executes for a quantum in round robin fashion until both threads complete execution. This means that A gets a quantum of time to run. Then B gets a quantum. Then A gets another quantum. Then B gets another quantum. This continues until one thread completes. The processor then devotes all its power to the thread that remains. Next, thread C runs to completion. Threads D, E and F each execute for a quantum in round robin fashion until they complete execution. This process continues until all threads run to completion.

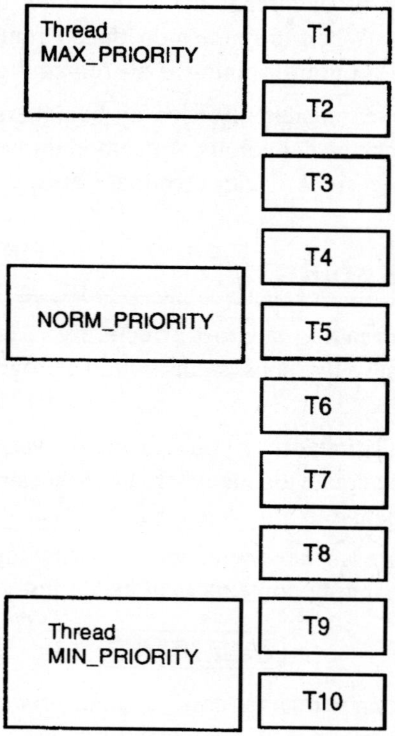

Fig. 7.3. Example

7.12. PRODUCER/CONSUMER RELATIONSHIP

In a producer/consumer relationship, the producer portion of an application generates data and stores it in a shared object, and the consumer portion of an application reads data from shared object. The producer/consumer relationship separates the task of identifying work to be done from the tasks involved in actually carrying out the work. One example of the producer/consumer relationship is an application that copies data onto CDs by placing data in a fixed size buffer, which is emptied as the CD-RW drive "burns" the data onto the CD.

In a producer consumer relationship, a producer thread generates data and places it in a shared object called a buffer. A consumer thread reads data from the buffer. This relationship requires synchronization to ensures that values are produced and consumed properly. Operations on the buffer data shared by a producer and consumer thread are also state dependent, the operations should proceed only if the buffer is in the correct state. If the buffer is in a not empty state, the consumer may consume. All operations that access the buffer or read from the buffer only if the buffer is in the proper state. If the producer is attempeting to put data into the buffer determines that it is full, the producer thread should wait until there is space to write a new value.

7.13. DAEMON THREAD

A Daemon is simply a thread that has no other role in life than to serve others. We can turn a thread into daemon thread by calling

```
t.setDaemon(true);
```

For example : Examples are timer threads that send "timer ticks" to other threads or threads that clean up state cache entries. When only daemon thread remains, the virtual machine exists. There is no point in keeping the program running if all remaining threads are daemons.

Daemon threads are sometimes mistakenly used by beginners who don't want to think about shut down action. However, this can be dangerous. A daemon thread should never access a persistent resource such as file or database since it can terminate at any time, even in the middle of an operation.

7.14. USING MULTITHREADING

The key to utilizing multithreading support effectively is to think concurrently rather than serially. For example, when you have two subsystems within a program that can execute concurrently, make them individual threads.

With the careful use of multithreading, you can create very efficient programs. A word of caution is in order, however: If you create too many threads, you can actually degrade the performance of your program rather than enhance it.

Remember, some overhead is associated with context switching. If you create too many threads, more CPU time will be spent changing contexts than executing your program.

SUMMARY

1. Program in execution is known as process. A small process is known as Thread.
2. A multithreaded program contains two or more parts that can run simultaneously.
3. A thread goes through various stages in its life cycle like—New, Runnable, Waiting, Time Waiting and Terminated.
4. Every Java thread has a priority that helps the operating system determine the order in which threads are scheduled.
5. Java supports various methods to implement the concept of multithreaded programming like start(), run() etc.
6. The process to ensure that the resource will be used by only one thread at a time is known as Synchronization.
7. A Daemon Thread is simply a thread that has no other role in life than to serve others.

REVIEW QUESTIONS

1. What are the basic idea of multithreaded programming and its synchronization?
2. What are Threads ? Explain Life Cycle of Thread.
3. Explain the following term briefly.
   (*i*) Multithreading (*ii*) Daemon thread
   (*iii*) Thread Synchronization
4. Write a program which contains three thread.
5. Write short note on Producer consumer relationship.
6. What is stack based execution and exception propogation ?

❑❑❑

CHAPTER 8

Exception Handling

INSIDE THIS CHAPTER

Well friends, while dealing with the real world we find various abnormal conditions which are difficult to handle. Similarly in Java programming, while executing the program we find such abnormal conditions, we call it exceptions. There is difference between error and the exception. So friends have fun with the concept of exception and how to handle such exception.

8.1. EXCEPTION IN JAVA

Any abnormal condition that occurs in our program is known as **Exception**. When such a condition occurs in the program, an appropriate code is written so that it can be handled.

Whatever value the function returns can be checked, and depending upon the value user can make out whether it is executed successfully or were there any errors. If there was an error then user need to match the error code with the errorlist and find out what error occurred.

Java runtime environment has adopted this feature extensively using object oriented methodology in the form of exception handling.

By using exception handling, user can prevent program from abruptly ending, flashing surprising and annoying error messages.

All exceptions are subclasses of the built-in class called **Throwable**. There are two main subclasses under Throwable:

- Exception
- Error

Exception : Exception class caters to all the problems that should be caught by the user program.

Error : Exceptions that are not expected to be caught by user program and more or less fatal in nature come under the **Error Subclass**.

For example : Stack Overflow, Linkage Error.

Note : A part from the system generated exception the user also can explicitly define the exceptions.

The hierarchy of the exception class is shown below:

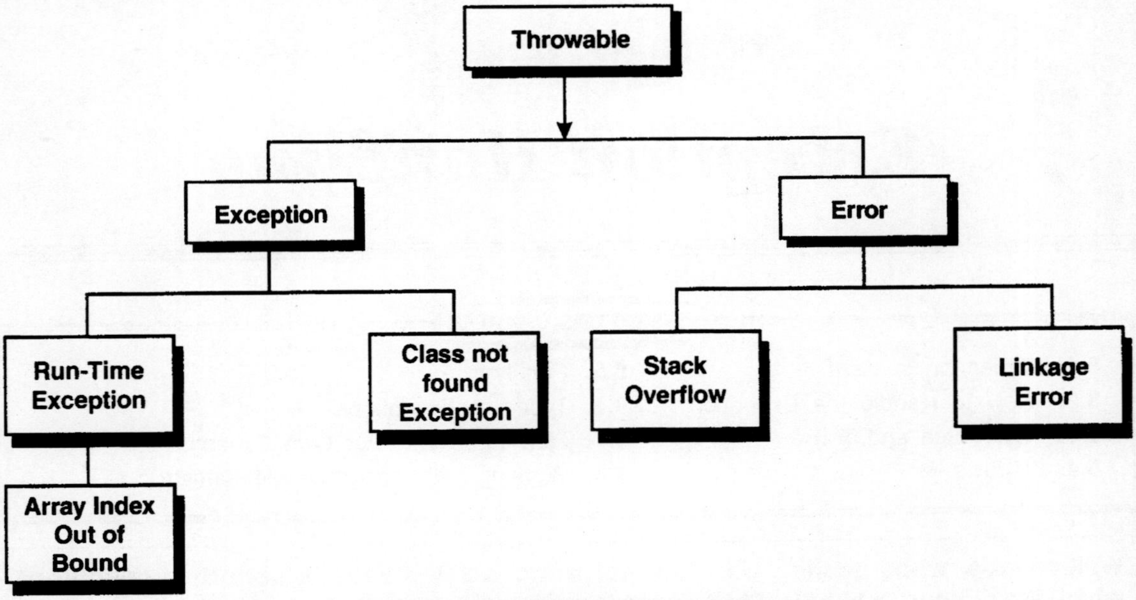

Fig. 8.1. Exception Handling in Java

8.2. HOW TO HANDLE THE EXCEPTION?

Java manages the exceptions through five clauses :

1. try
2. catch
3. throw
4. throws
5. finally

As soon as exception condition is encountered in the program, an object of the related type of exception is thrown in the same method that causes the exception. Now, the method is supposed to catch the object thrown and handle the exception in its own way. If it chooses not to do so and lets, the exception go, then the caller function should handle it, else the run-time environment catches it and terminate the program.

8.3. TRY, CATCH AND THROW

The code which is expected to generate the exception must be enclosed in the try and catch block.

The very basic form of the exception handling is the following:

```
try
{
//Statements

}catch(<ExceptionTypeClass> Object 1)
{
   //Statement
}
```

Inside the try and catch block, as soon as the exception condition arises, an object of that specific type of exception is automatically created and thrown. The thrown object is then matched with the appropriate catch block *i.e.,* the catch block having the same parameter type as the object thrown. If the block matches, then the statements for handling the exception are written within the catch block are executed.

/*Code without exception Handling*/

```
class  NumFormExcp
{
   public static void main(String args[])
   {
      String str1= new String("text12");
      int num1 = Integer.parseInt(str1); //converts string to number
      System.out.println(num1);
}}
```

Save as : NumFormExcp.java

Compile as : javac NumFormExcp.java

Run as : java NumFormExcp

Output : The output is

```
Exception in thread "main" java.lang.NumberFormatException: text12

at java.lang.Integer.parseInt(Compiled Code)
at java.lang.Integer.parseInt(Integer.java.458)
at numformexcp.main(numformexcp.java:6)
```

In the above program the string str1 doesnot store the number in an appropriate format, *i.e.,* it contain a mix of text as well as numbers. When str1 is tried to be converted into a number, the object of the type NumberFormatException is thrown. Since, we are not catching this object, it is handeled by default exception handler that is the runtime environment.

It prints the stack trace showing what exception has been thrown, which statement has caused it and the method and the line number from where it is generated.

/*Code with Exception Handling*/

```
class NumFormExcp
{
    public static void main(String args[])
    {
        try
        {
            String str1= new String("text12");
            int num1= Integer.parseInt(str1);
            System.out.println(num1);

        }catch(NumberFormatException e)
        {
            System.out.println("##Wrong Number##");
        }
    }
}
```

Output : The output of the program is:

```
##Wrong Number##
```

Here, the NumberFormatException is not left unhandled and there is a catch block ready to catch it. Once the exception is caught the statements inside the catch block execute, giving the appropriate message.

In the previous example, the exception which occurred is implicit, *i.e.*, thrown automatically. If a user want to throw an exception explicitly then he need to use the throw clause. The throw clause is used when we create our own exceptions and we want to throw them.

Note : All the system-defined exceptions are thrown automatically, but the user-defined exception must be thrown explicitly using the throw clause.

The syntax for throw clause is as:

```
try
{
    //Statement
throw new Udef_Exception( );
}catch(Udef_Exception obj1)
{
    System.out.println("User Defined Exception Caught");
}
```

```
/*Program to throw the exception*/

class Throw_clause
{
Public static void main(String args[])
{
try
{
   throw new NullPointerException();
}catch(NullPointerException e)
{
System.out.println("Invalid Reference Use ");
}}}
```

Save : Throw_Clause.java

Compile : javac Throw_Clause.java

Run : java Throw_Clause

Output : In the above example, output will be

```
Invlaid reference use
```

Here, the throw clause throws an object of a system defined exception NullPointerException, which is actually thrown when an object storing a null-pointer is referenced.

Thus, as soon as the exception is raised it is caught with the catch claused, the statement inside the catch clause are executed and we get the output.

8.4. THROWS

Till now we have seen that an exception is thrown either implicitly or explicitly in the try block and there is a catch block ready to handle it. But there are methods, which throw the exception, but do not catch it within the method body. In this case the method which is throwing the exception must use **throws** clause with its definition.

The throws clause acts as a warning message which makes the calling module aware that the module is throwing an exception which it is not handling and it has to handle the thrown exception. Incase of runtime exception, the method that leaves them unhandled need not use throw clause, the runtime environment will handle them.

Consider the following class structure that has a method, namely, method_one(). This method is using the throws clause which is throwing an exception object. Note that in the same method there is no subsequent catch clause. This method is being called from the main() method which in turn is made to catch the exception thrown by method_one(), although main is not responsible for throwing it directly. Now, if the main() method is not handling this exception it can specify a throws clause and let the exception be handled by runtime environment.

```
class<ClassName>
{
```

```
    Static void method_one() throws<exception>
  {
    throw new <exception>
          //method is throwing the exception but not catching it

  }

  public static void main(String args[])
  {
    Try
  {
    method_one();
  //main() is not throwing the exception, but it has to catch it
  }catch(<exception> object)
  {
    //Statement for exception handling
  }}
  }
```

/* Program without throws clause*/

```
  class Throws_Clause
  {
  static void throwExcp()
  {
  try{
  throw new IllegalAccessException();                //exception thrown
  }catch(IllegalAccessException e)                   //exception caught
  System.out.println("Catch Block");
  Throw new IllegalAccessException( );               //exception thrown
  again
  }

  public static void main(String arg[])
  {
  throwExcp();
  System.out.println("does not reach here");
  }
  }
```

Output : The result of the program is:

```
Throws_clause.java:12: Exception java.lang.IllegalAccessException
must be caught, ot it must be declared in the throws clause of
this method.

Throw new IllegalAccessException;
```

/*Program with Throws Clause*/

```
Class Throws_clause
{
   static void throwExcp() throws IllegalAccessException
{
Throw new IllegalAccessException();

}

public static void main(String arg[])
{
   Try
{
   throwExcp();
}catch(IllegalAccessException e)
{
   System.out.println("Exception Caught");
}}}
```

Save as : Throws_clause.java

Compile as : javac Throws_clause.java

Run as : java Throws_clause

Output : The output of the above program is

```
Exception Caught
```

8.5. FINALLY

The finally clause is written with the try statement, rather the try statement must have either the catch or finally block, or having both of them.

The benefit of the finally block is that it is definitely executed after a catch block or before the method quits.

Syntax :

```
try
   {
      // Statements
```

```
} finally
{
    //Statements
}
```

OR

```
try
{
    //Statement
}catch(exception object)
{
    //Statement
}
finally
{
    //Statement
}
```

Program: Program to understand the usage of finally block

```
Class Finally_Block
{
    static void division()
    {
        try
        {
            int numerator=34,denominator=0;
            int div = numerator/denominator;
        }catch(ArithmeticException e)
        {
            System.out.println("Divide by zero");
        }finally
        {
            System.out.println("In the finally block");
        }
    }
    public static void main(String args[])
    {
        division();
    }
}
```

Save as : Finally_Block.java

Compile as : javac Finally_Block.java

Run as : java Finally_Block

Output : The output of the program will be:

```
Divide by zero
In the finally block
```

8.6. TYPES OF EXCEPTIONS

There are several types of exceptions :

(*i*) **Arithmetic Exception :** Very common exception which occurs when there is any error in the arithmetic operation.

(*ii*) **Null Pointer Exception :** Null pointer exception occurs if wrong and unavailable destination is referenced.

(*iii*) **Array Index Out of Bounds Exception :** It occurs if we points to the unavailable index of the array.

(*iv*) **Negative Array Size Exception :** It occurs when we specify negative size for array.

(*v*) **Number Format Exception :** Number format exception arises when we try to convert a string to number format, and the string is either empty or does not contain the number in a proper format.

(*vi*) **Illegal Access Exception :** This exception occurs when we try to access a class for which we don't have permission.

Note : Java defines several built in classes for exception handling. All these classes are a part of the java.lang package which is automatically imported. That is why, while throwing the exceptions we did not specifically include any package for exception class.

8.7. HOW TO CREATE OUR OWN EXCEPTION

A part from the built in exception classes we can define our own exception classes. This is very useful when we want to define exception types which are having a behaviour different from the standard exception types.

Program : Program to create user defined exception

```
class Validate_Range extends Exception
{
    String mesg;

    validate_Range()
    {
        mesg=new String("Enter digit between 20 and 100");
    }
```

```
    public String toString()
    {
        return(mesg);
    }
}

public class My_Exception
{
    public static void main(String args[])
    {
        try{
            int x=10;
        if(x<20||x>100)
        throw new validate_Range();
    }catch(Validate_Range e)
    {
        System.out.println("***"+e);
    }
   }
```

The exception class here is the Validate_Range class. We have seen that this class is derived from the exception class. For any class to behave as an exception type it must become the subclass of the exception class. A variable message of String type is defined and in the constructor it is initialized with appropriate message. We are also overriding the function toString so that the caught exception object can convey some message when used in a print statement.

8.8. WORKING WITH ASSERTION MECHANISM

The Assertion mechanism can be explained as :

1. Assertion gives us way to test our assumptions during development and debugging
2. Assertions are typically enabled during testing but disabled during deployment.
3. We can use assert as a keyword or an identifier, but do not use both together.
4. Assertions are disabled at runtime by default. To enable them, we use a command line flag –ea or –enableassertions.
5. Selectively disable assertions by using –da or disableaassertions flag.
6. If we enable or disable assertions using the flag without any arguments, we are enabling or disabling assertions in general. We can combine enabling and disabling switches to have assertions enabled for some classes and/or packages, but not other.
7. We can enable and disable assertions on a class-by-class basis, using the following syntax:

   ```
   java -ea  -da:MyClass   TestClass
   ```

8. We can enable and disable assertions on package-by-package basis and any package we specify also includes any subpackages.

9. Do not use assertions to validate arguments to public methods.
10. Do not uses assert expressions that cause side effects. Assertions aren't guaranteed to always run.
11. Use assertions even in public methods to validate that a particular code block will never reached.

SUMMARY

1. Exception is an abnormal condition that arise when executing a program.
2. All exceptions are subclass of the buill-in class called Throwable.
3. Try keyword is applied on that statement from which chances of exception takes place.
4. Catch keyword is used to provide solution of particular exception.
5. Throw keyword is used to generate manual exception.
6. Throws keyword is used to forward exception towards JRE.
7. Finally block is a block which executes always.
8. Assertion gives us way to test our assumptions during development and debugging

REVIEW QUESTIONS

1. Explain the term try, catch and throw with respect to exception handling in Java.
2. List ten different exception defined in Java.
3. Write a program to demonstrate "IndexOutOfBounds-Exception".
4. What are assertions ? Explain in brief.

❑❑❑

UNIT-IV

- **Exploring Java Input/Output**
- **Java Database Connectivity**

SYLLABUS

Input/Output : Exploring Java I/O, Directories, Stream Classes.

The Byte stream : Input stream, output stream, file input stream, file output stream, print stream. Random access file, the character streams, Buffered reader, buffered writer, print writer, serialization.

JDBC : JDBC-ODBC bridge; The connectivity model; The driver manager; Navigating the result set object contents; java.sql Package; The JDBC exception classes; Connecting to Remote database.

CHAPTER 9

Exploring Java Input/Output

INSIDE THIS CHAPTER

Well friends, this chapter introduces Java's most important packages: io. The io package supports Java's basic I/O (Input/Output) system, which is a collection of classes required for input/output manipulation. So friends, lets have fun with the concept of I/O.

9.1. EXPLORING JAVA INPUT OUTPUT

As we know that, Java standard library (or API) includes hundreds of classes and methods grouped into several functional packages, one of the package that it support is **Input/Output Package** abbreviated as I/O package in java, which is a collection of classes required for input/output manipulation.

The syntax, used to explore the I/O package is:

```
import java.io.*;
```

This package provides support for input output operations. The data is retrieved from the input source and the result of a program is sent to the output destination through output source.

9.2. INTRODUCTION TO STREAM

Most of the program cannot accomplish their goal without reading and writing data from some external source. The java.io package caters to such requirements of input output. In java the input output is based upon the concept of streams, which is the sequence of bytes or characters travelling over a communication path. The communication path may be a memory to memory transfer of bytes, may be a file system or even networks.

1. A stream is a logical entity or abstraction that either produces or consumes information.
2. A stream is linked to a physical device by the java I/O System.
3. All streams behave in the same manner, even if the actual physical devices they are linked to differ.

The I/O classes defined by java.io are listed below :

BufferedInputStream	FileDescriptor	LineNumberReader
BufferedOutputStream	FileInputStream	ObjectInputStream
BufferedReader	FileOutputStream	ObjectInputStream.GetField
BufferWriter	FilePermission	ObjectOutputStream
ByteArrayInputStream	FileReader	ObjectOutputStream.PutField
ByteArrayOutputStream	FileWriter	ObjectStreamClass
CharArrayReader	FilterInputStream	ObjectStreamField
CharArrayWriter	FilterOutputStream	OutputStream
DataInputStream	FilterReader	OutputStreamWriter
DataOuputStream	FilterWriter	PipedInputStream
File	InputStream	PipedOutputStream
PipedReader	PipedWriter	PrintStream
PrintWriter	PushbackInputStream	PushbackReader
RandomAccessFile	Reader	SequenceInputStream
SerializablePermission	StreamTokenizer	StringReader
StringWriter	Writer	

9.3. TYPES OF STREAM

Java defines two major classes of Streams

- Byte Stream
- Character Stream

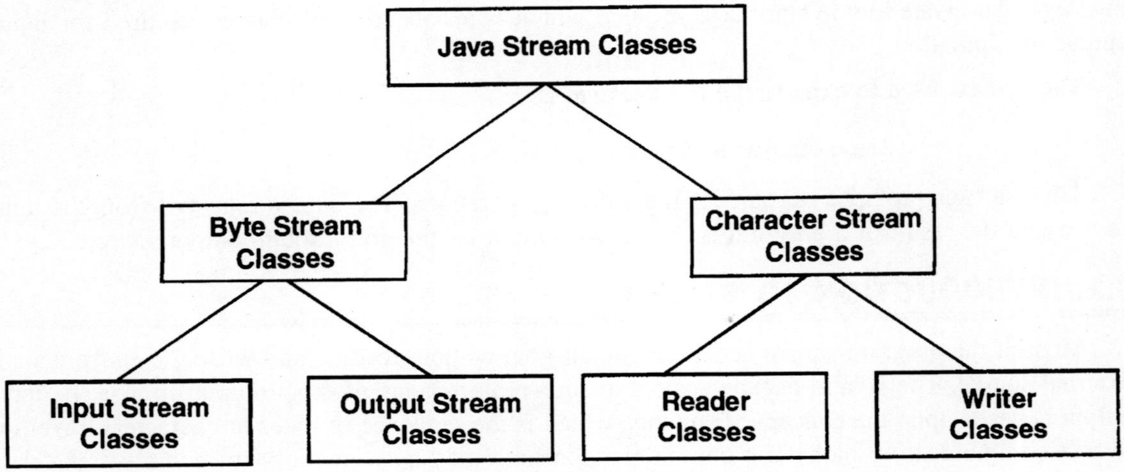

Fig. 9.1. Types of Stream Classes

Byte Stream is convenient for handling input output of bytes. Byte Stream are used when we are reading or writing binary data.

Character Stream is convenient for handling input and output of characters. They use Unicode.

9.4. BYTE STREAM CLASSES

As discussed earlier, byte stream is the sequence of bytes travelling over a communication path. Byte streams are defined by using two class hierarchies. At the top of the hierarchy there are two abstract classes :

- Input Stream
- Output Stream

These abstract classes has several concrete subclasses, that handle the differences between various devices.

The abstract classes InputStream and OutputStream defines several keymethods that the other stream classes implement.

For example : Two (abstract) methods are read() and write(), which respectively, read and write bytes of data. They are overridden by stream classes.

Several Byte stream classes with their meanings are given below in table as :

S. No.	Stream Classes	Meaning
1.	InputStream	Abstract class that describe stream input
2.	OutputStream	Abstract class that describe stream output
3.	BufferedInputStream	Buffered Input Stream
4.	BufferedOutputStream	Buffered Output Stream
5.	ByteArrayInputStream	Input Stream that reads from byte array
6.	DataInputStream	An input Stream that contains methods for reading the java standard data types
7.	DataOutputStream	An output Stream that contains methods for writing the java standards data type
8.	FileInputStream	Input Stream that reads from a file
9.	FileOutputStream	Output Stream that writes to a file
10.	FilterInputStream	Implements Input Stream
11.	FilterOutputStream	Implements Output Stream
12.	PipedInputStream	Input pipe
13.	PipedOutputStream	Output pipe
14.	PrintStream	Output Stream that contains print() and println()
15.	PushbackInputStream	An input Stream that supports one byte "unget" which returns a byte to the input stream
16.	RandomAccessFile	Supports RandomAccessFile I/O
17.	SequenceInputStream	Input Stream that is a combination of two or more input streams that will be read sequentially, one after another.

9.5. CHARACTER STREAM CLASSES

As discussed earlier, character stream is the sequence of characters travelling over a communication path. Character streams are defined by using two class hierarchies. At the top are two abstract classes :

- Reader
- Writer.

These abstract classes handle Unicode character streams.

Several character stream classes with their meanings are given below in table as :

S. No.	Stream Classes	Meaning
1.	BufferedReader	Buffered Input Character Stream
2.	BufferedWriter	Buffered Output Character Stream
3.	CharArrayReader	Input Stream that reads from character array
4.	CharArrayWriter	Output Stream that writes to Character array
5.	FileReader	Input stream that reads from a file
6.	FileWriter	Output Stream that Writes to file
7.	FilterReader	Filtered Reader
8.	FilterWriter	Filtered Writer
9.	InputStreamReader	Input Stream that translates bytes to character
10.	OutputStreamReader	Output Stream that translates character to byte
11.	OutputStreamWriter	Output Stream that translate characters to bytes
12.	LineNumberReader	Input Stream that counts line
13.	PipedReader	Input pipe
14.	PipedWriter	Output pipe
15.	PrintWriter	Output Stream that contains print() and println()
16.	PushbackReader	Input stream that allows characters to be returned to the input stream
17.	Reader	Abstract class that describes character stream input
18.	StringReader	Input Stream that reads from a String
19.	StringWriter	Output Stream that writes to stream
20.	Writer	Abstract Class that describes character stream output

9.6. SERIALIZATION

Serialization is the process of writing the state of an object to a byte stream. This is useful when you want to save the state of your program to a persistent storage area, such as a file.

Serialization is also needed to implement Remote Method Invocation (RMI). RMI allows a java object on one machine to invoke a method of a java object on a different machine. An object may be supplied as an argument to that remote method. The sending machine serializes the object and transmits it. The receiving machine deserialize it.

For example: Let us assume that, an object is to be serialized has references to other objects, which, have references of another object, *i.e.,* object obj1 contain a reference to object obj2, and object obj2 have the reference back to obj1.

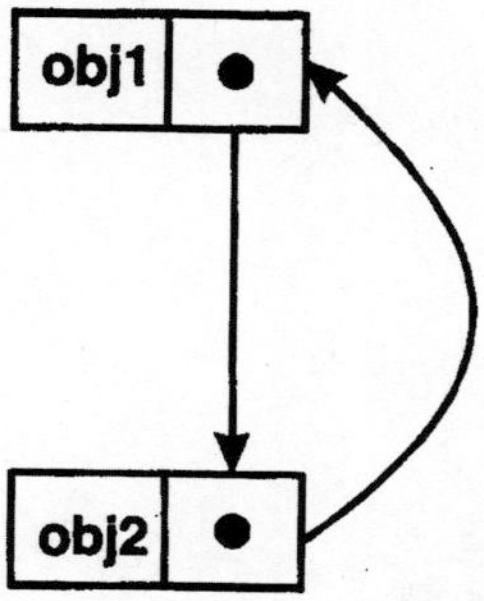

Fig. 9.2. Reference Object

This example tells us that, object may contain references to themselves which means that if we attempt to serialize an object, all the other referenced objects are recursively located and serialized.

SUMMARY

1. Input/Output package is a collection of classes requires for input/output manipulation.
2. A stream is a logical entity or abstraction that either produces or consumes information.
3. Byte stream is convenient for handling input/output of bytes.
4. Character stream is convenient for handling input/output of characters.
5. Serialization is the process of writing the state of an object to a byte of stream.

REVIEW QUESTIONS

1. Explain java input and output stream.
2. Write a program to illustrate reading data with the help of StringTokenizer.
3. Why do we need stream objects?
4. What is serialization? Explain in brief.

❑❑❑

CHAPTER 10

Java Database Connectivity

INSIDE THIS CHAPTER

Well friends, connecting to database is tough task to achieve. Java provides bundle of drivers to support the concept of connectivity. This chapter deals with the JDBC overview. So friends, have a fun with the concept of JDBC.

10.1. JAVA DATABASE CONNECTIVITY

Database is a collection of interrelated data and set of program to access those data. The collection of data is known as **Database**. Java provides bundle of drivers to support the concept of connectivity.

10.2. CLASSIFICATION OF JDBC DRIVERS

Java has classified JDBC drivers into four categories, which are shown in Fig. 10.1.

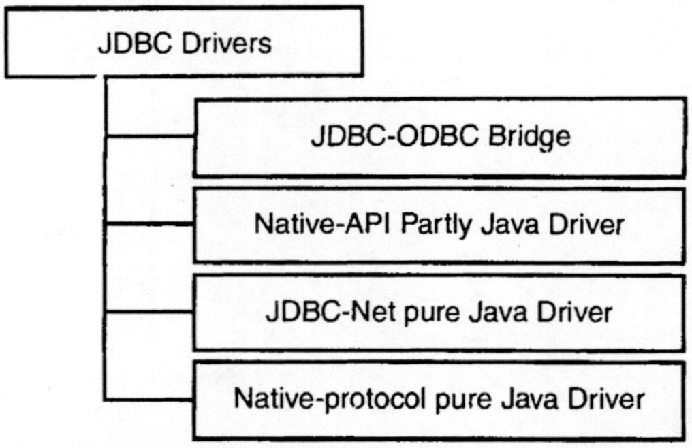

Fig. 10.1. Classification of JDBC Drivers

10.3. JDBC-ODBC BRIDGE

It is a bridge developed between Java Database connectivity with Microsoft's Open Database Connectivity driver's to communicate with database servers. This driver has to be pre-installed on the client's machine before their utilization. The ODBC drivers for that database should also be present on the client machine.

Syntax: The syntax used for JDBC-ODBC connectivity is given below:

```
Class.forName("com.mysql.jdbc.Driver");

Connectioncon=DriverManager.getConnection("jdbc:mysql://
localhost:3306/Name of Application","UserName,"Password");
```

The JDBC-ODBC bridge is shown below in Fig. 10.2.

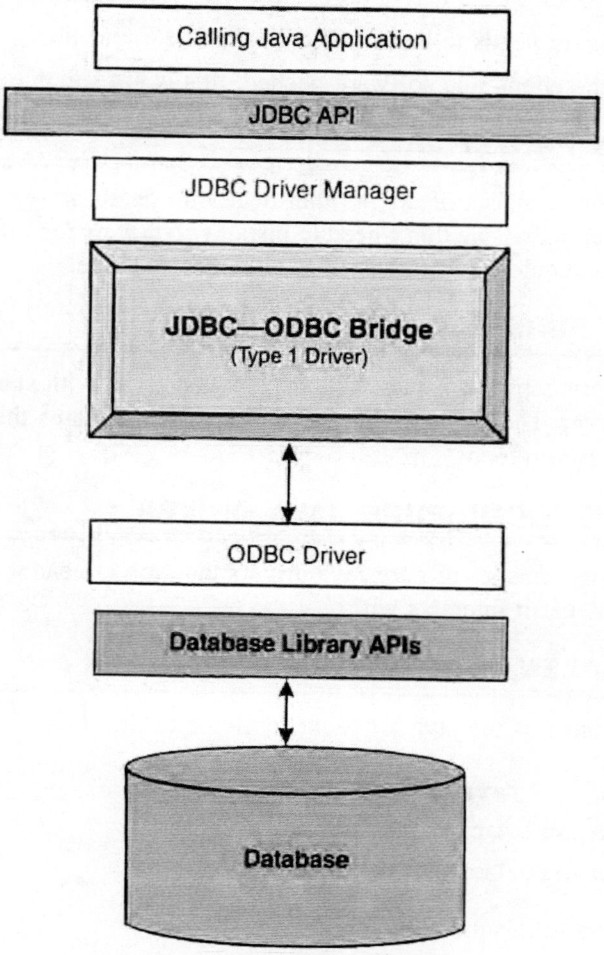

Fig. 10.2. JDBC-ODBC Bridge

10.4. FUNCTION OF JDBC

1. Translates query obtained by JDBC into corresponding ODBC query, which is then handled by the ODBC driver.

2. Sun provides a JDBC-ODBC Bridge driver. sun.jdbc.odbc.JdbcOdbcDriver. This driver is native code and not Java, and is closed source.
3. Client -> JDBC Driver -> ODBC Driver -> Database
4. There is some overhead associated with the translation work to go from JDBC to ODBC.

10.5. ADVANTAGES OF JDBC

1. Almost any database for which ODBC driver is installed, can be accessed.
2. A type 1 driver is easy to install.

10.6. DISADVANTAGES OF JDBC

1. Performance overhead since the calls have to go through the JDBC overhead bridge to the ODBC driver, then to the native db connectivity interface.
2. The ODBC driver needs to be installed on the client machine.
3. Considering the client-side software needed, this is not suitable for applets.

10.7. NATIVE-API PARTLY JAVA DRIVER

This driver category consists of drivers that deal with database server's native protocol. The advantage of this driver is that, we don't need to install two drivers for a database. The disadvantage of this driver is that it should be atleast present on client machine.

10.8. JDBC-NET PURE JAVA DRIVER

This driver category consists of pure java drivers that deals with standard network protocol to a database access server. The database access server then translates the network protocol into a vendor specific database protocol.

10.9. NATIVE-PROTOCOL PURE JAVA DRIVER

This driver category consists of pure Java drivers that talk to vendor specific database protocol of the database server that it interacts with.

10.10. JDBC IMPLEMENTATION

JDBC is implemented as the java.sql package. Some of the classes of this package are:

```
Drivers    java.sql.Driver
     java.sql.DriverManager
     java.sql.DriverPropertyInfo
```

Connection : java.sql.Connection

Statements : java.sql.Statement

```
     java.sql.PreparedStatement
     java.sql.CallableStatement
```

ResultSet :

```
java.sql.ResultSet
```

Exceptions :

```
java.sql.SQLException
```

Date :

```
java.sql.Date
```

10.11. JAVA.SQL PACKAGE

Provides the API for accessing and processing data stored in a data source (usually a relational database) using the Java programming language. This API includes a framework whereby different drivers can be installed dynamically to access different data sources. Although the JDBCTM API is mainly geared to passing SQL statements to a database, it provides for reading and writing data from any data source with a tabular format. The reader/writer facility, available through the javax.sql.RowSet group of interfaces, can be customized to use and update data from a spread sheet, flat file, or any other tabular data source.

The java.sql package contains API for the following:

1. Making a connection with a database via the Driver Manager facility

- DriverManager class — makes a connection with a driver.
- SQLPermission class — provides permission when code running within a Security Manager, such as an applet, attempts to set up a logging stream through the DriverManager.
- Driver interface — provides the API for registering and connecting drivers based on JDBC technology ("JDBC drivers"); generally used only by the DriverManager class.
- DriverPropertyInfo class — provides properties for a JDBC driver; not used by the general user.

2. Sending SQL statements to a database

- Statement — used to send basic SQL statements
- PreparedStatement — used to send prepared statements or basic SQL statements (derived from Statement)
- CallableStatement — used to call database stored procedures (derived from PreparedStatement)
- Connection interface — provides methods for creating statements and managing connections and their properties
- Savepoint — provides savepoints in a transaction

3. Retrieving and updating the results of a query

- ResultSet interface

4. Standard mappings for SQL types to classes and interfaces in the Java programming language

- Array interface — mapping for SQL ARRAY
- Blob interface — mapping for SQL BLOB
- Clob interface — mapping for SQL CLOB
- Date class — mapping for SQL DATE
- Ref interface — mapping for SQL REF
- Struct interface — mapping for SQL STRUCT
- Time class — mapping for SQL TIME
- Timestamp class — mapping for SQL TIMESTAMP
- Types class — provides constants for SQL types

5. Custom mapping an SQL user-defined type (UDT) to a class in the Java programming language

- SQLData interface — specifies the mapping of a UDT to an instance of this class.
- SQLInput interface — provides methods for reading UDT attributes from a stream.
- SQLOutput interface — provides methods for writing UDT attributes back to a stream.

6. Metadata

- DatabaseMetaData interface — provides information about the database.
- ResultSetMetaData interface — provides information about the columns of a ResultSet object.
- ParameterMetaData interface — provides information about the parameters to PreparedStatement commands.

7. Exceptions

- SQLException — thrown by most methods when there is a problem accessing data and by some methods for other reasons.
- SQLWarning — thrown to indicate a warning.
- DataTruncation — thrown to indicate that data may have been truncated.
- BatchUpdateException — thrown to indicate that not all commands in a batch update executed successfully.

10.12. SQL INTERFACE

Array : The mapping in the Java programming language for the SQL type ARRAY.

Blob : The representation (mapping) in the JavaTM programming language of an SQL BLOB value.

CallableStatement : The interface used to execute SQL stored procedures.

Clob : The mapping in the JavaTM programming language for the SQL CLOB type.

Connection : A connection (session) with a specific database.

DatabaseMetaData : Comprehensive information about the database as a whole.

Driver : The interface that every driver class must implement.

ParameterMetaData : An object that can be used to get information about the types and properties of the parameters in a PreparedStatement object.

PreparedStatement : An object that represents a precompiled SQL statement.

Ref : The mapping in the Java programming language of an SQL REF value, which is a reference to an SQL structured type value in the database.

ResultSet : A table of data representing a database result set, which is usually generated by executing a statement that queries the database.

ResultSetMetaData : An object that can be used to get information about the types and properties of the columns in a ResultSet object.

Savepoint : The representation of a savepoint, which is a point within the current transaction that can be referenced from the Connection.rollback method.

SQLData : The interface used for the custom mapping of an SQL user-defined type (UDT) to a class in the Java programming language.

SQLInput : An input stream that contains a stream of values representing an instance of an SQL structured type or an SQL distinct type.

SQLOutput : The output stream for writing the attributes of a user-defined type back to the database.

Statement : The object used for executing a static SQL statement and returning the results it produces.

Struct : The standard mapping in the Java programming language for an SQL structured type.

SUMMARY

1. Java provides bundle of driver to support the concept of connectivity.
2. JDBC-ODBC bridge is developed to connection with database server.
3. Java sql package contains API for metadata, exceptions, creating connection etc.

REVIEW QUESTIONS

1. Explain JDBC and ODBC bridge and role of driver manager.
2. Explain the architecture of JDBC.
3. How to establish connection with database in Java? Write a code for connection.
4. Write short note on JDBC exception classes.

❑❑❑

UNIT-V

- **Java Networking**
- **Remote Method Invocation**

SYLLABUS

Java Networking : Exploring java.net package, Networking Basics : Socket, Client server, reserved sockets, proxy servers, Internet addressing, TCP sockets, UDP sockets.

RMI : Client/Server architecture, RMI registry services; Steps of creating RMI Application and an example.

CHAPTER 11

Java Networking

INSIDE THIS CHAPTER

Well friends, the creators of Java called it as "Programming for the Internet", this chapter help us to explore the java.net package. This package provides support for networking. So friends, read this chapter and have fun with the concept of networking.

11.1. NETWORKING IN JAVA

The networking in Java explores the java.net package, which provides support for networking. Its creators have called Java "**Programming for the Internet**". Java is so called good language for networking because there are classes defined in **java.net package**.

These Network classes encapsulate the "Socket" paradigm pioneered in the Berkeley Software Distribution (BSD) from the University of California at Berkeley.

11.2. NETWORKING BASIC

Ken Thompson and Dennis Ritchie developed UNIX in concert with the C language at Bell Laboratories, Murray Hill, New Jersey, in 1969. For many years, the development of UNIX remained in Bell Labs and in a few universities where it was designed to run on. In 1978, Bill Joy was leading a project at Cal Berkeley to add many new features to UNIX, such as virtual memory and full-screen display capabilities. By early 1984, just as Bill was leaving to found Sun Microsystems, he shipped 4.2 BSD, commonly known as Berkeley Unix.

4.2 BSD came with fast file system, reliable signals, interprocess communication, and most important networking. The networking support first found in 4.2 eventually become the defacto standard for the internet. Berkeley's implementation of TCP/IP remains the primary standard for communications within the internet. The socket paradigm for the interprocess and network communication has also been widely adopted outside of Berkely. Even windows and the Macintosh started talking "Berkeley Sockets" in late 1980's.

11.3. SOCKET OVERVIEW

A network socket is a lot like an electrical socket. Various plugs around the network have a standard way of delivering their payload. Anything that understand the standard protocol can "plug-in" the socket and communicate. With electrical sockets, it doesn't matter if you plug in a lamp or a toaster, as they are expecting 60 Hz, 115-volt electricity, the devices will work. Think how your electricity bill is created. There is a meter somewhere between your house and the rest of the network. For each kilowatt of power that goes through the meter, you are billed. The bill comes to your "address". So even though the electricity flows freely around the power grid, all of the sockets in your house have particular address.

The same idea applies to network sockets, except we talk about TCP/IP packets and IP addresses rather than electrons and streets addresses. Internet Protocol(IP) is a low-level routing protocol that breaks data into small packets and sends them to an address across a network, which doesnot guarantee to deliver said packets to the destination. Transmission Control Protocol (TCP) is a higher-level protocol that manages to robustly string together these packets, sorting and retransmitting them as necessary to reliably transmit your data. A third protocol, User Datagram Protocol (UDP), sits next to TCP and can be used directly to support fast, connectionless, unreliable, transport of packets.

11.4. CLIENT/SERVER

There is common term referred to as "Client/Server" always mentioned in the context of networking. It seems complicated when we read about it in corporate marketing statements, but it is actually quite simple. A server is anything that has some resource that can be shared. There are

1. Computer servers, which provide computing power;
2. Print Servers, which manages a collection of printers
3. Disk Servers, which provides network disk space
4. Web Server, which stores web pages

The interaction between a client server is just like an interaction between a lamp and an electrical socket. The power grid of the house is the server and the lamp is a power client.

The server is a permanently available resource, while the client is free to "unplug" after it has been served.

In Berkeley sockets, the notion of socket allows a single computer to serve many different clients at once, as well as serving many different types of information. This feat is managed by the introduction of a port, which is numbered socket on a particular machine. A server process is said to "listen" to a port until a client connects to it. A server is allowed to accept multiple clients connected to the same port number, although each session is unique. To manage multiple client connections, a server process must be multithreaded or have some other means of multiplexing the simultaneous I/O.

11.5. RESERVED SOCKETS

Once connected to a higher level protocol, *i.e.,* TCP decides which port you are using for which. TCP/IP reserves the lower 1,024 ports for specific protocols. Many of these will seem familiar to you if you have spent any time surfing the internet. Port number 21 is for FTP, 23 is for Telnet, 25 is for e-mail, 79 is for finger, 80 is for HTTP, 119 is of netnews and the list goes on. It is up to each protocol to determine how a client should interact with the port.

For example : HTTP is the protocol that web browser and servers use to transfer hypertext pages and images. It is quite a simple protocol for a basic page-browsing web server, Here's how it works. When a client requests a file from HTTP server, an action known as hit, it simply prints the name of file in a special format to a predefined port and read back the contents of the file. The server also responds with a status code number to tell the client whether the request can be fulfilled or not.

11.6. PROXY SERVER

In computer networks, a **proxy server** is a server (a computer system or an application program) that acts as an intermediary for requests from clients seeking resources from other servers. A client connects to the proxy server, requesting some service, such as a file, connection, web page, or other resource, available from a different server. The proxy server evaluates the request according to its filtering rules. For example, it may filter traffic by IP address or protocol. If the request is validated by the filter, the proxy provides the resource by connecting to the relevant server and requesting the service on behalf of the client. A proxy server may optionally alter the client's request or the server's response, and sometimes it may serve the request without contacting the specified server. In this case, it 'caches' responses from the remote server, and returns subsequent requests for the same content directly.

A proxy server has a large variety of potential purposes, including:

1. To keep machines behind it anonymous (mainly for security).
2. To speed up access to resources (using caching). Web proxies are commonly used to cache web pages from a web server.
3. To apply access policy to network services or content, *e.g.*, to block undesired sites.
4. To log/audit usage, *i.e.*, to provide company employee Internet usage reporting.
5. To bypass security/parental controls.
6. To scan transmitted content for malware before delivery.
7. To scan outbound content, *e.g.*, for data leak protection.
8. To circumvent regional restrictions.

A proxy server that passes requests and replies unmodified is usually called a gateway or sometimes **Tunneling proxy**.

A proxy server can be placed in the user's local computer or at various points between the user and the destination servers on the Internet.

A reverse proxy is (usually) an Internet-facing proxy used as a front-end to control and protect access to a server on a private network, commonly also performing tasks such as load-balancing, authentication, decryption or caching.

11.7. INTERNET ADDRESSING

Every computer on the Internet has an address. An Internet address is a number that uniquely identifies each computer on the Net. Originally, all internet addresses consisted of 32-bit values.

This address type was specified by IPv4 (Internet Protocol, version 4). However, a new addressing scheme, called IPv6 (Internet Protocol, version 6) has come into play. IPv6 uses a 128-bit value to represent an address. Although there are several advantages to IPv6, the main one is that it supports a much larger address space than does IPv4. Fortunately, IPv6 is downwardly compatible with IPv4 is by far the most widely used scheme, but this situation is likely to change over time.

Because of the emerging importance of IPv6, JAVA 2, version 1.4 has begun to add support for it. However, at the time of this writing, IPv6 is not supported by all environments. Furthermore, for the next few years, IPv4 will continue to be dominant form of addressing.

There are 32 bits in an IPv4 IP address, and we often reffer to them as sequence of four numbers between 0 and 255 separated by dots(.). This makes them easier to remember, because they are not randomly assigned—they are hierarchically assigned. The first few bits define which class of network A, B, C, D, E the address represents. Most internet users are on class C network, since there are over two millions network in the class. The first byte of a class C network is between 192 and 224, with the last byte actually identifying the individual computer among the 256 allowed on single class C network. This scheme allows for half a billion devices to live on class C network.

11.8. DIFFERENCE BETWEEN IP VERSION6 AND IP VERSION4

IPv4 stands for **Internet Protocol version 4** and the IPv6 stands for **Internet Protocol version 6**.

The Internet Protocol version 4 (IPv4) is, as indicated by the number, the fourth edition/ revision in the Internet Protocol (IP). The Internet Protocol version 4 (IPv4) is the most widely adopted and implemented version of the Internet Protocol (IP) where as the Internet Protocol version 6 (IPv6) is still in its nascent stages of adoption and implementation.

The Internet Protocol version 4 (IPv4) is a simple protocol that is used on Ethernet and other packet switching networks and simply looks to deliver the message by the best delivery mode. This means that the message may or may not be received or delivered. There may be also redundancy and duplication of the message bring propagated.

The Internet Protocol Version 6 (IPv6) on the other hand is designed as the successor of the Internet Protocol version 4 (IPv4). The IPv6 is also an Internet Layer protocol that works on on Ethernet and other packet switching networks. However, it was designed primarily to address the issues of the exhaustion of the number of unique IP addresses that the Internet Protocol version 4 (IPv4) could offer.

The Internet Protocol Version 6 (IPv6) inherently sports a much wider scope and space for addresses than IPv4. This is due the change in the basic bits used for address storage. The **Internet Protocol Version 6 (IPv6) uses a 128-bit address**, whereas **IPv4 uses only 32-bits**. Thus, it can be easily computed that the Internet Protocol Version 6 (IPv6) supports 2128 (about 3.4 × 1038) addresses. This expansion will provide a great deal of leeway in providing unique IP addresses to the rapidly booming number of internet devices.

Another upgrade provided by the Internet Protocol Version 6 (IPv6) over the Internet Protocol Version 4 (IPv4) is the **ability to eliminate the need for network address translation (NAT).**

Also, a particularly noteworthy difference between IPv6 and IPv4 is that there is a simplification of the aspects of address assignment (stateless address auto-configuration) and network renumbering (prefix and router announcements). This makes it much easier to switch between various internet service providers. Also, there has been a standardization of the Internet Protocol version 6 (IPv6) subnet size. This has enabled automatic formatting of the host identifier from media addressing information (MAC address).

11.9. TCP SOCKET

A **TCP socket is defined as an endpoint for communication**. A socket consists of the pair **<IP Address, Port>**. For our purposes, a port will be defined as an integer number between 1024 and 65535. This is because all port numbers smaller than 1024 are considered well-known — for example, telnet uses port 23, http uses 80, ftp uses 21, and so on. On UNIX machines, the file/etc./services contains a list of services provided by that machine, along with their well-known ports.

A TCP connection consists of a pair of sockets. Sockets are distinguished by client and server sockets. A server listens on a port, waiting for incoming requests from clients.

For example, a web server listens at port 80 for incoming request from clients (web browsers). When a client wishes to make a connection with a server socket, the client is assigned a port from the local host. Suppose that client X (at IP address 146.86.3.15) wishes to browse a web page on the server 146.86.5.20. If the port the local host assigned client X is port 12345, the connection between the client and the server is uniquely identified by the socket pair.

```
<146.86.3.15 : 12345, 146.86.5.20 : 80>
```

11.10. UDP SOCKET

UDP is short for User Datagram Protocol that (just as TCP) runs on top of IP. It is typically used in conjunction with IP (Internet Protocol): UDP/IP. The difference with TCP is that UDP doesn't guarantee delivery of packets. On the other hand, it doesn't have the TCP overhead of setting up a connection and acknowledging packets. UDP is mostly used in streaming video and audio data to one or more destinations (multicast). Also, check out the parent category if you don't find what you are looking for.

SUMMARY

1. To support concept of networking in Java, there are bundles of classes defined in java.net package.
2. A server is anything that has same resources to share.
3. There are various types of server.
4. Proxy server is a server that acts as an intermediary for request from accessing resources from other server.
5. A proxy server passes requests and replies unmodified is usually called gateway or tunnelling proxy.
6. A TCP socket is defined as an endpoint for communication.
7. The difference between TCP and UDP is that UDP doesn't guarantee delivery of service.

REVIEW QUESTIONS

1. Why do you need Java.net package to write Java networking program? Explain.
2. Explain the client server architecture.
3. What is the difference between TCP/IP programming and datagram programming?
4. Explain TCP/IP programming with example.

❑❑❑

CHAPTER 12

Remote Method Invocation

INSIDE THIS CHAPTER

Well friends, in the first chapter we have learned that java supports a package named as RMI. This package helps us to locate and execute methods of remote objects. So friends, lets have fun with RMI package and see how to create these packages.

12.1. WHAT IS RMI?

In procedural language we will rely on the notion of Remote Procedure Call. But in object oriented language, we will rely on the notion of RMI.

RMI is the acronym for Remote Method Invocation. As the name suggests, it helps us to locate and execute methods of remote objects. It is like placing a class on Machine A and calling methods of that class from Machine B as though they were from the same machine.

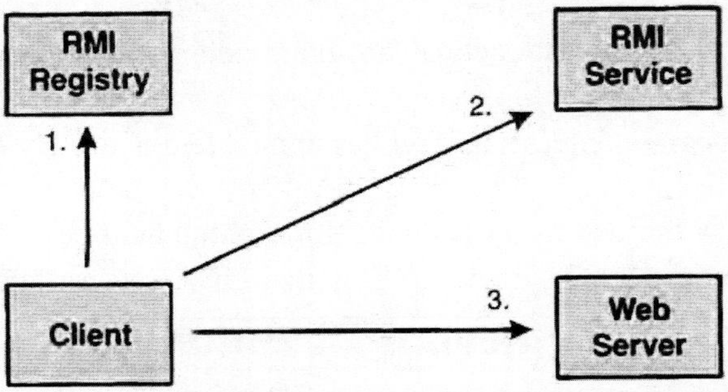

Fig. 12.1. Connection made when Client Uses RMI

In other word we can says that, RMI is a way that a programmer (using the Java programming language and development environment) can write object-oriented programming in which objects on different computers can interact in a distributed network.

As said earlier, RMI is the JAVA version of Remote Procedure Call, but with the ability to pass one or more objects along with the request.

The original implementation depends on Java Virtual Machine (JVM) class representation mechanisms and it thus only supports making calls from one JVM to another. The protocol underlying this Java-only implementation is known as Java Remote Method Protocol (JRMP).

12.2. FEATURES OF JAVA RMI

Some features of java RMI is given below as :

1. Provides a distributed object capability for Java applications
2. Allows a Java method to obtain a reference to a remote object and invoke methods of the remote object nearly as easily as if the remote object existed locally
3. The remote object can be in another JVM on the same host or on different hosts across the network.
4. Uses object serialization to marshal and unmarshal method arguments.
5. Supports the dynamic downloading of required class files across the network.

12.3. RMI-CLIENT SERVER ARCHITECTURE

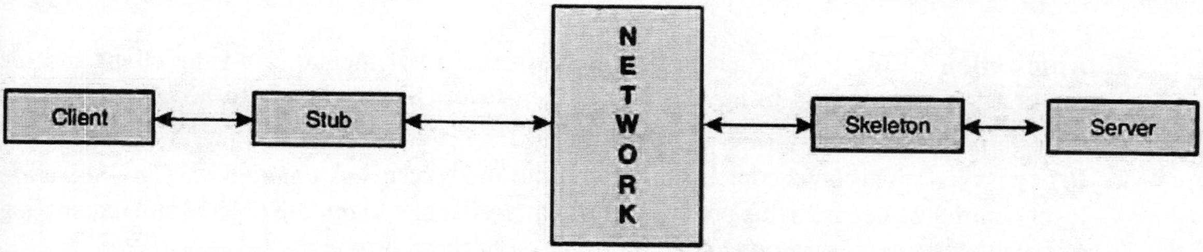

Fig. 12.2. A Typical Implementation of RMI Server Client Architecture

The Fig. 12.2 depicts the server-client architecture of RMI. The RMI architecture consist of four layers :

1. The application
2. Stubs/Skeleton
3. Remote Reference
4. Transport Layer

When a client application makes a remote method call, the call passes to the stub and then onto the remote reference layer, it then passes it via the network layer from the client to the server, where the remote reference layer, on the server side, unpacks the arguments and passes them to the skeleton and then to the server .class file. The return value of the method call then takes the reverse trip back to the client side.

A remote method invocation is made through a reference to a remote object. When a client makes a call to a remote method, that client receives a reference to the remote object, which implements the remote method. The remote object is not sent over the network to the client. In place of the remote object there is a stub that is client-side proxy for the remote object. All interactions by the client are performed with the stub class. The stub is responsible for data transfer between the local (client) system and remote (server) system.

Many clients may have references to a single remote object. Each of these clients will have their own stub object representing the remote object but the remote object will not be replicated. The stub on the client does not interact directly with the remote object on the server. There exists a server-side proxy object called Skeleton, which is responsible for transferring method calls and data between a stub and the actual object being referenced on the server. The RMI system implements a four layer model, which can be categorized as follows :

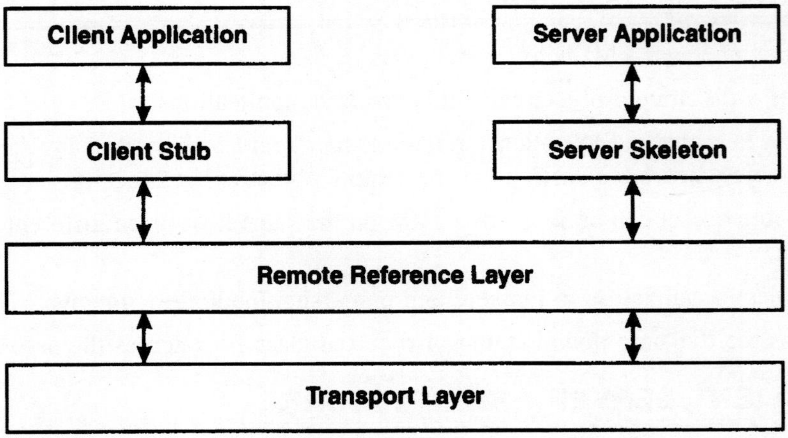

Fig. 12.3. RMI

1. **Application Layer :** This layer contains the actual implementation of the client and the server applications. It is in this layer that high-level calls are made to access and export remote object.
2. **Proxy Layer :** This layer contains the client stub and server skeleton objects. The application layer communicates with this proxy layer directly. All calls to remote objects and marshaling of parameters and return objects are done through these proxies.
3. **Remote Reference Layer (RRL) :** The RRL handles packaging of method call and its parameters and its return values for transport over the network. The RRK uses the server-side and the client-side component to communicate via the network layer.
4. **Transport Layer :** The transport layer sets up connections, manages existing connections and handles remote objects residing in its address space.

12.4. RMI REGISTRY SERVICES

In any distributed application, for the client side of the application to make a call to a remote object, that client application should first be able to locate the remote object. RMI provides a registry service or name service, which makes this possible.

A server registers any remote object that it is exporting with a name server called a registry. When a client wishes to obtain a reference to a remote objects, a lookup is performed with a known registry and a reference to the remote object is returned if the lookup is successful.

Registry services can be used in one of the two ways :

1. The first method is to maintain a registry server that is running on a well-known predefined port number. Any application that is exporting objects can register with this registry, as long as that application is running on the same physical machine as the registry.

2. The second method involves an application running its own registry services. This allows the application to have total control over the registry but at the same time makes it more difficult to define a well-known port number that clients applications can use to access remote objects.

RMI uses the first method to maintain a registry. The registry keeps track of the addresses of all the remote object that are being exported by their applications. All objects are assigned unique names that are used to identify them. Applications can add, remove and access remote objects in the registry's table of object by calling certain methods from the rmi.registry. Registry interface or from the rmi.Naming class.

12.5. STEPS OF CREATING RMI APPLICATIONS AND EXAMPLES

To create an application that uses RMI, one needs to use the classes and interfaces defined by the jave.rmi.package. To create an RMI application, the following steps needs to be followed :

1. Define an Interface for the Remote Classes

To implement the RMI based client/server application, an interface is created that contains all the methods that the remote object must support. All interfaces for remote object must extend the Remote interface defined in java.rmi package. All the methods in those interfaces must include a throws RemoteException with every remote method call and to specify the appropriate action to be taken when the call doen not succeed.

2. Implement the Interface in a Server-Side Application

The server application extends the UnicatRemoteObject class and implements the remote interface inside the class. All remote objects must extendUnicatRemoteObject, which provides functionality that is needed to make objects available from remote machines. The java class library includes a class called RMISecurityManager on a server to prevent random clients.

3. Binding Objects to a Registry Service

For an application to bind or register an object with the registry, both the registry service as well as the application must be running on the same machine. An application can bind any object to the registry, provided that object either extends the UnicastRemoteObject class, or extends a Remote interface.

For a server application to bind an object to a registry, the following is required :

(*a*) A reference to an instance of the object.

(*b*) The address of the registry server.

(*c*) A unique name that the object will be registered.

A client application invokes a remote object by using the name with which that object is registered with the registry service. As a result no two objects can be registered with the same name. The java.rmi.Naming class has provided two methods for binding objects to a registry service. These two methods are :

1. bind( ) *i.e.* java.rmi.Naming.bind (URL, Ref)
2. rebind( ) *i.e.* java.rmi.Naming.rebind (URL, Ref)

4. Creating Stubs and Skeletons Classes

The stubs and skeleton layers can be created using the rmic compiler, which comes along with the JDK.

5. Create and Compile the Client Program to Access Remote Object

The client is implemented to access the remoe objects created to use the remote interface and calls the method from that interface. A stub is a Java object that resides on the client machine. It's function is to present the same interface as the remote server. Remote method calls are actually directed to the stub. The stub works with the other parts of the RMI system to formulate a request that is sent to the remote machine. A remote machine may accept the arguments that simple types or objects. All of this information must be sent to the remote machine. A skeleton is a java object that resides on the server machine. It works with other parts of the RMI system to receive and invoke the appropriate code on the server. Obtaining a reference to a remote object is accomplished by making a call to the lookup( ) method of java.rmi.Naming Class.

6. Install Files on The Client and the Server Machines

Incase the server application and client application is run on separate machine then—

(*i*) Copy RMIClient.class, MethodImp.class, RMIServer_stub class to a directory on the client machine.

(*ii*) Copy RMIServer_stub.class, RMIServer_skel.class, MethodImpl.class to a directory on the server machine.

7. Starting the RMI Registry

Sun Microsystem has provided an RMI registry application as part of the JDK. The RMI registry application is normally started as a background application that will by default run on port 1099. On a windows machine, by issuing he following command at the DOS prompt—the RMI registry application can be started

```
rmiregisrty<port number>
```

The <port number> argument is optional. This command will load and execute RMI registry as a TSR application in windows. To run the RMI registry in a separate DOS shell, the registry can be started with the DOS "start" command.

SUMMARY

1. RMI is an acronym for Remote Method Invocation.
2. RMI is a way that a programmer can write object-oriented programming in which objects on different computers can interact in a distributed network.
3. RMI server-client architecture consist of four layers :
   (*i*) The Application
   (*ii*) Stubs/Skeleton
   (*iii*) Remote Reference
   (*iv*) Transport Layer.
4. There are 7 steps for creating RMI application.

REVIEW QUESTIONS

1. Explain Remote Method Invocation (RMI) and its client-server architecture.
2. Explain client/server architecture. What is RMI registry services ?
3. Write the steps of creating RMI application with example.
4. Write short note on RMI registry services.

❑❑❑

UNIT–VI

➤ **Programming Approach**

CHAPTER 13

Programming Approach

INSIDE THIS CHAPTER

13.1. PRACTICAL PROGRAMMING

"Theoretical approach alone is not sufficient for achieving goal."

Keeping this in mind, we are going to understand the practical implementation of all the theoretical terms that we had used in this book. But before implementing the terms just keep some points in mind.

1. First, assure that you had installed the jdk 1.6.0 (or any other version) on your computer.
2. Now, We can start writing our java program in any editor like Notepad, Newpad etc. but we need to save the program as:

   ```
   ClassName.java
   ```

   Keeping the firstletter of the class in uppercase.
3. Since, Java is Object Oriented Programming language, everything in java will be started from class.
4. Since, Java is Case Sensitive language, the class name will be start with the uppercase letters only.
5. For executing the program, lets open the command prompt. In command prompt we need to set the java path. We can set the java path as entering the location of java bin folder as:

   ```
   C:\set path=C:\Program Files\Java\jdk1.6.0_03\bin;
   ```
6. Execution of the program starts from main method.
7. Every program can be compiled as

   ```
   javac ClassName.java
   ```

8. Every program can be run as

```
java ClassName
```

Using the above eight points, now we are able to build java program applications. The sample programs are given below as:

13.1.0. Java 2 SDK 1.5 Installation Notes form Microsoft Windows

Installation Notes

```
Java 2 SDK, Standard Edition
Version 1.5
Microsoft Windows
```

System Requirements

Software : Java 2 SDK Standard Edition, 1.5 is supported on i586 Intel and 100% compatible platforms running Microsoft Windows.

Hardware : Intel and 100% compatible processors are supported. A Pentium 166 MHz or faster processor with at least 32 megabytes of physical RAM is required to run graphically based applications. At least 48 megabytes of RAM is recommended for applets running within a browser using the Java Plug-in. Running with less memory may cause disk swapping which has a severe effect on performance. Very large programs may require more RAM for adequate performance.

Installation Steps

In this procedure, you will find the easiest way to install Java 2 SDK software bundle. The procedure of complete installation is as follows:

Step 1: Check the download file size (Optional)

If you save the self-installing executable to disk without running it from the download page at the web site, notice that its byte size is provided on the download page. Once the download has completed, check that you have downloaded the full, uncorrupted software file. You can download JDK from the internet at site http://java.sun.com/products/jdk free of cost.

Step 2 : Run the Java 2 SDK installer

Note : You must have administrative permissions in order to install the Java 2 SDK on Microsoft Windows 2000 and XP.

The file j2sdk-1_5_0_08<version>-windows-i586-i.exe is the Java 2 SDK installer. If you downloaded it instead of running it directly from the web site, double-click on the installer's icon. Then follow the instructions the installer provides. The installer may ask you to reboot your computer. When done with the installation, you can delete the download file to recover disk space.

The directory structure for installing Java is shown in Fig. 13.1. The Java 2 SDK has the directory structure shown below.

```
                    j2sdk1.5.0.08_<version>
                              |
  ____________________________|________________________
 |    |    |    |    |    |      |          |    |
 |    |    |    |   bin  lib     |        demo   |
 |    |    | LICENSE |    |      |              jre
 |    | COPYRIGHT                |            ___|___
 | README.txt                 include        |       |
readme.html                                 bin     lib
```

Fig. 13.1.

Step 3: Update the PATH variable (Optional)

You can run the Java 2 SDK without setting the PATH variable, or you can optionally set it as a convenience.

Should I set the PATH variable?

Set the PATH variable if you want to be able to conveniently run the Java 2 SDK executables (javac.exe, java.exe, javadoc.exe, etc.) from any directory without having to type the full path of the command. If you don't set the PATH variable, you need to specify the full path to the executable every time you run it, such as:

```
C:\j2sdk1.5.0.08_<version>\bin\javac MyClass.java
```

It's useful to set the PATH permanently so it will persist after rebooting.

How do I set the PATH permanently?

To set the PATH permanently, add the full path of the **j2sdk1.5.0.08_<version>\bin** directory to the PATH variable.

```
C:\j2sdk1.5.0.08_<version>\bin;
```

Step 4: Start using the Java 2 SDK!

Your computer system should now be ready to use the Java 2 SDK. In this step, you'll run some simple commands to make sure it is working properly.

13.1.1. Program to print Welcome to the World of Java on Output Console

```
class JavaWorld
{
   public static void main(String args[])
   {
      System.out.println("Welcome to the World of Java");
   }
}
```

Save as : The above program can be saved as:

```
JavaWorld.java
```

Compile as : The above program can be compiled as:

```
javac JavaWorld.java
```

Run as : The above program can be run as:

```
java  JavaWorld
```

Output : The Output of the program will be:

```
Welcome to the World of Java
```

13.1.2. Program to write and use multiple System.out.println statement

```
public class Biodata
        {
public static void main(String args[])
{
 System.out.println("Name: Sagar Jha");
 System.out.println("Branch: IT");
 System.out.println("Subject: JAVA");
 }
 }
```

Save as : The above program can be saved as:

```
Biodata.java
```

Compile as : The above program can be compiled as:

```
javac Biodata.java
```

Run as : The above program can be run as:

```
java  Biodata
```

Output : The Output of the program will be:

```
Name: Sagar Jha
Branch: IT
Subject: JAVA
```

13.1.3. Program to Add two numbers

```
class Addition
{
```

```
        public static void main(String args[])
        {
            int a=10;
            int b=15;
            int c;
            c=a+b;
            System.out.println("The addition is"+c);
        }
    }
```

Save as : The above program can be saved as:

```
Addition.java
```

Compile as : The above program can be compiled as:

```
javac Addition.java
```

Run as : The above program can be run as:

```
java Addition
```

Output : The Output of the program will be:

```
The addition is30
```

13.1.4. Program to Subtract two number

```
class Subtract
        {
        public static void main(String arg[])
        {
         int x;
         int y;

         x=5;
         y=2;

       System.out.println("\n\tX="+x);
       System.out.println("\n\tY="+y);

        int z=x-y;

      System.out.println("The difference is=\t"+z);
        }
        }
```

Save as : The above program can be saved as:

```
Subtract.java
```

Compile as : The above program can be compiled as:

```
javac  Subtract.java
```

Run as : The above program can be run as:

```
java  Subtract
```

Output : The output of the program will be:

```
        X=5
        Y=2
The difference is= 3
```

13.1.5. Program to Divide two numbers

```
class Divide
 {
public static void main(String arg[])
{
   float x;
   float y;

   x=5;
   y=2;

 System.out.println("\n\tX="+x);
 System.out.println("\n\tY="+y);

  float z=x/y;

        System.out.println("Division is=\t"+z);
}
}
```

Save as : The above program can be saved as:

```
Divide.java
```

Compile as : The above program is compiled as:

```
javac Divide.java
```

Run as : The above program is run as:

```
java Divide
```

Output : The output of the above program will be:

```
X=5.0
Y=2.0
Division is=    2.5
```

13.1.6. Program to understand the concept of Type Casting in Java

```
class TypeCast
{
public static void main(String arg[])
{
char c='a';

System.out.println("Character="+c);

int x=(int)c;

System.out.println("Type Converted="+x);

}
}
```

Save as : The above program can saved as:

```
TypeCast.java
```

Compile as : The above program can be compiled as:

```
javac TypeCast,java
```

Run as : The above program can be run as:

```
java TypeCast
```

Output : The output of the program will be:

```
Character = a
Type Converted=97
```

13.1.7. Program to understand the concept of for loop in java

```
class Repeat
{
public static void main(String arg[])
{
```

```
            for(int i=0;i<=10;i++)
            {
         System.out.println("Repeat"+i);
            }
      }
      }
```

Save as : The above program is saved as:

```
Repeat.java
```

Compile as : The above program will be compile as

```
javac Repeat.java
```

Run as : The above program will be run as:

```
java Repeat
```

Output : The output of the program will be:

```
Repeat 0
Repeat 1
Repeat 2
Repeat 3
Repeat 4
Repeat 5
Repeat 6
Repeat 7
Repeat 8
Repeat 9
Repeat 10
```

13.1.8. Program to print Pyramid in JAVA

```
public class Pyramid
{
       public static void main(String arg[])
       {
for(int i=1;i<4;i++)
{
 System.out.println("");

for(int j=1;j<=i;j++)
{
```

```
System.out.print(j);
}
}
}
}
```

Save as : The above program can be saved as:

Pyramid.java

Compile as : The above program will be compile as:

javac Pyramid.java

Run as : The above program will be run as:

java Pyramid

Output: The output of the above program will be:

```
1
12
123
```

13.1.9. Program to print "\n" on Output Console

```
public class New
{
 public static void main(String arg[])
{
System.out.println("\"\\n\"");
}
}
```

Save as : The above program can be save as

New.java

Compile as : The above program run compiled as:

javac New.java

Run as : The above program can be run as:

java New

Output : The output of the program will be:

```
"\n"
```

13.1.10. Program to calculate the area of Circle

```
public class ComputeArea
{
   public static void main(String arg[])
{
   double pi=3.14;   //approximate value of pi
   double r=10.8;
   double a;

   System.out.println("pi="+pi);
   System.out.println("Radius of Circle="+r);

   a=pi*r*r;  //formula of area

   System.out.println("Area of Circle is:"+a);

}
}
```

Save as : ComputeArea.java

Compile : javac ComputeArea.java

Run : java ComputeArea

Output : The output of the program will be:

```
pi=3.14
Radius of Circle=10.8
Area of Circle is:366.2496000000001
```

13.1.11. Program to demonstrate character data

```
public class CharDemo
{
public static void main(String arg[])
{
 char ch1;

 ch1=88;   //Ascii Code for x

System.out.println(ch1+"");
}
}
```

Save as : The above program can be saved as:

```
CharDemo.java
```

Compile : The above program will be compile as:

```
javac CharDemo.java
```

Run as : The above program will be compile as:

```
java CharDemo
```

Output : The output of the program will be:

```
X
```

13.1.12. Program to understand the concept of Switch Case

```
public class Alphabet
{
public static void main(String arg[])
{
        char letter='A';

     switch(letter)
     {
     case'a':
     case'A':
        System.out.println("The letter is vowel");
        break;
     case'e':
     case'E':
        System.out.println("The letter is vowel");
        break;
     case'i':
     case'I':
        System.out.println("The letter is vowel");
        break;
     case'o':
     case'O':
        System.out.println("The letter is vowel");
        break;
     case'u':
     case'U':
        System.out.println("The letter is vowel");
        break;
```

```
        default:
            System.out.println("The letter is Consonant");
    }
    }
    }
```

Save as : The above program can be saved as:

```
Alphabet.java
```

Compile as : The above program will be compile as:

```
javac Alphabet.java
```

Run as : The above program will be run as:

```
java Alphabet
```

Output : The output of the program will be

13.1.13. Program to print Asterisk Pyramid

```
class Asterisk
{
    public static void main(String []k)
{
    int i,j;
    for(i=1;i<=5;i++)
    {
        System.out.println("");
        for(j=1;j<i;j++)
        {
        System.out.print(" * ");
        }
        System.out.println(" ");
       }
 }
 }
```

Save as : The above program can be saved as:

```
Asterisk.java
```

Compile as : The above program will be compile as:

```
javac Asterisk.java
```

Run as : The above program will be run as:

```
java Asterisk
```

Output : The output of the program will be:

```
*
*    *
*    *    *
*    *    *    *
```

13.1.14. Program to calculate which number is smaller

```
class Comparison
{
   public static void main(String args[])
{
 int number1=10;
 int number2=20;

 if(number1<number2)
 {
      System.out.println("Number1 is Smaller");
 }
 else
      System.out.println("Number2 is Smaller");
 }
 }
```

Save as : The above program can be saved as:

```
Comparison.java
```

Compile as : The above program will be compile as:

```
javac Comparison.java
```

Run as : The above program will be run as:

```
java Comparison
```

Output : The output of the program will be:

```
Number1 is Smaller
```

13.1.15. Program to print the Fibonacci Series

```
class FibonacciSeries
{
public static void main(String args[])
{
    int a,b,c,i;
    a=0;
    b=1;

    System.out.println(a);

    for(i=1;i<=15;i++)
    {
    c=a+b;
    System.out.println(""+c);
    a=b;
    b=c;
    }
}
}
```

Save as : The above program can be saved as:

```
FibonacciSeries.java
```

Compile as : The above program will be compile as:

```
java FibonaciSeries.java
```

Run as : The above program will be run as:

```
java FibonacciSeries
```

Output : The output of the program will be:

```
0
1
2
3
5
8
13
21
34
55
89
```

13.1.16. Program to find prime numbers between from 1 to 20

```
class PrimeNo
{
public static void main(String args[])
{
int i;
int num=20;

for(i=1;i<num;i++)
{
int j;
for(j=2;j<i;j++)
{
    int n=i%j;
    if(n==0)
    {
   break;
    }
}
if(i==j){
System.out.println(""+i);
}}}}
```

Save as : The above program can be save as

```
PrimeNo.java
```

Compile as : The above program will be compile as:

```
javac PrimeNo.java
```

Run as : The above program will be run as:

```
java PrimeNo
```

Output : The Output of the program will be:

```
2
3
5
7
11
13
17
19
```

13.1.17. Program to Swap two numbers

```
class Swap
{
public static void main(String args[])
{
  int i=10;
  int j=20;
  int k;

   System.out.println("The values are:\n\t i="+i+"\n\tj="+j);

   k=i;
   i=j;
   j=k;

   System.out.println("\nThe Swapped values are:\n\t
   i="+i+"\n\tj="+j);
   }
   }
```

Save as : The program can be save as:

```
Swap.java
```

Compile as : The above program will be compile as:

```
javac Swap.java
```

Run as : The above program will be run as:

```
java Swap
```

Output : The output of the program will be:

The values are:

```
i=10
j=20
```

The Swapped values are:

```
i=20
j=10
```

13.1.18. Program to Say Hello to Name

```
class SayHello
{
public static void main(String args[])
{
```

```
String name="Ram";
String msg= sayHello(name);
System.out.println(msg);
}
static String sayHello(String name)
    {
    return "Hello"+name;
    }
}
```

Save as : The above program can be saved as:

```
SayHello.java
```

Compile as : The above program will be compile as:

```
javac SayHello.java
```

Run as : The above program will be run as:

```
java SayHello
```

Output : The output of the program will be:

```
HelloRam
```

13.1.19. Program to check whether the given number is Even or Odd

```
class EvenOdd
{
static boolean isEven(int n)
{
    if(n%2==0)
    return true;
    else
    return false;
}
    public static void main(String []args)
{
    int x=3;
    if(isEven(x))
{
    System.out.println("Even No");
}
    else
    System.out.println("Odd No");
}
}
```

Save as : The above program can be saved as:

```
EvenOdd.java
```

Compile as : The above program will be compile as:

```
javac EvenOdd.java
```

Run as : The above program will be run as:

```
java EvenOdd
```

Output : The Output of the program will be:

```
Odd Number
```

13.1.20. Program to show the asterisk sign diagonally

```
class Diagonal
{
   public static void main(String []k)
{
   for(int i=1;i<5;i++)
{
   for(int j=1;j<=i;j++)
   {
      System.out.print("\t");

   }
     System.out.println("*");
   }
 }
 }
```

Save as : The above program can be saved as:

```
Diagonal.java
```

Compile as : The above program can be compiled as:

```
javac Diagonal.java
```

Run as : The above program will be run as:

```
java Diagonal
```

Output : The output of the program will be:

```
*
        *
                *
                        *
```

13.1.21. Program to understand the concept of Arithmetic Operator in java.

```
public class Arithmeticoperators
{
public static void main(String arg[])
{
    float a=20.5F,b=6.4F;

    System.out.println("a="+a);

    System.out.println("b="+b);

    System.out.println("a+b is="+(a+b));

    System.out.println("a-b is="+(a-b));

    System.out.println("a*b is="+(a*b));

    System.out.println("a/b is="+(a/b));

    System.out.println("a%b is="+(a%b));

}
}
```

Save as : The above program can be saved as:

```
Arithmeticoperators.java
```

Compile as : The above program can be compiled as:

```
javac Arithmeticoperators.java
```

Run as : The above program will be run as:

```
java Arithmeticoperators
```

Output : The output of program will be:

```
a=20.5
b=6.4
a+b is=26.9
a-b is=14.1
a*b is=131.2
a/b is=3.203125
a%bis=1.2999997
```

13.1.22. Program to understand the concept of Relational Operators in Java.

```
public class Relationaloperators
{
    public static void main(String arg[])
    {

        float a=15.0F,b=20.75F,c=15.0F;
        System.out.println("a="+a);
        System.out.println("b="+b);
        System.out.println("c="+c);
        System.out.println("a<b is="+(a<b));
        System.out.println("a>b is="+(a>b));
        System.out.println("a==c is="+(a==c));
        System.out.println("a<=c is="+(a<=c));
        System.out.println("a>=b is="+(a>=b));
        System.out.println("b!=c is="+(b!=c));
        System.out.println("b==a+c is="+(b==a+c));
}
}
```

Save as : The above program can be saved as:

```
Relationaloperators.java
```

Compile as : The above program can be compiled as:

```
javac Relationaloperators.java
```

Run as : The above program will be run as:

```
java Relationaloperators
```

Output : The output of program will be:

```
a=15.0
b=20.75
c=15.0
a<b is=true
a>b is=false
a==c is=true
a<=c is=true
a>=bis=false
b!=c is=true
b= =a+c is=false
```

13.1.23. Program to print the factorial of given number

```
class Factorial
{
public static void main(String[] args)
{
int num=4;
double result= factorial(num);
System.out.println(result);
}
public static double factorial(int x)
{
    if(x<0)
    return 0.0;
    double fact=1.0;
    while(x>1)
    {
    fact=fact*x;
    x=x-1;
}
return fact;
}
}
```

Save as : The above program can be saved as:

```
Factorial.java
```

Compile as : The above program can be compiled as:

```
javac Factorial.java
```

Run as : The above program will be run as:

```
java Factorial
```

Output : The output of the program will be:

```
24.0
```

13.1.24. Program to print average of given number

```
class Average
{
public static void main(String arg[])
{
```

```
int a=2,b=5,c=10,d=6;
double avg;
avg=(a+b+c)/3;
System.out.println("The average is"+avg);
}
}
```

Save as : The above program can be saved as:

```
Average.java
```

Compile as : The above program can be compiled as:

```
javac Average.java
```

Run as : The above program will be run as:

```
java Average
```

Output : The output of the program will be:

```
The average is 5.0
```

13.1.25. Program to calculate the area of rectangle

```
class RectArea
{
private int l;
private int w;
void setdata(int p,int q)
{
   l=p;
   w=q;
}
void show()
{
   System.out.println("Enter the length=" +l);
   System.out.println("width =" +w);
}
   int area()
{
   return l*w;
}
}
   class RectFun
{
```

```
    public static void main(string []k)
  {
    RectArea r1,r2;
    r1=new RectArea();
    r2=new RectArea();
    r1.setdata(2,5);
    r2.setdata(5,9);
    r1.show();
    int a1=r1.area();
    System.out.println("area=" +a1);
    r2.show();
    System.out.println("area=" +r.area());
    }
  }
```

Save as : The above program can be saved as:

```
RectFun.java
```

Compile as : The above program can be compiled as:

```
javac RectFun.java
```

Run as : The above program will be run as:

```
java RectFun
```

Output : The output of the program will be:

```
Enter the length= 2
width =5
area=10

Enter the length=5
Width=9
area=45
```

13.1.26. Program to take input in java

```
import java.util.Scanner;
class Input
{
   public static void main(String arg[])
   {
      int b;
      System.out.println("\n\t\tEnter Any Number");
      Scanner sc= new Scanner(System.in);
```

```
            b= sc.nextInt();
            System.out.println("\t\t"+b);
        }

    }
```

Save as : The above program can be saved as:

```
Input.java
```

Compile as : The above program can be compiled as:

```
javac Input.java
```

Run as : The above program will be run as:

```
java Input
```

Output : The output of program will be:

```
Enter Any Number
1
1
```

13.1.27. Program to understand the concept of one dimensional array.

```
public class Arraydec
{
    public static void main(String arg[])
    {
        int month_days[];               //declaration of array

        month_days=new int[12];         //creation of array

        month_days[0]=31;
        month_days[1]=28;
        month_days[2]=31;
        month_days[3]=30;
        month_days[4]=31;
        month_days[5]=30;         //Initializations of array
        month_days[6]=31;
        month_days[7]=31;
        month_days[8]=30;
        month_days[9]=31;
        month_days[0]=30;
        month_days[0]=31;
```

```
            System.out.println("April has"+month_days[3]+"days");
      }
      }
```

Save as : The above program can be saved as:

`Arraydec.java`

Compile as : The above program can be compiled as:

`javac Arraydec.java`

Run As :

`java Arraydec`

Output : The output of program will be:

`April has30days`

13.1.28. Program to understand the concept of 1-D Array

```
public class Arraydec1
      {
      public static void main(String args[])
      {
int month_days[]={31,28,31,30,31,30,31,31,30,31,30,31};
       //declaration,creation & initialization of array

System.out.println("April has"+month_days[3]+"days");
      }
      }
```

Save as : The above program can be saved as:

`Arraydec1.java`

Compile as : The above program can be compiled as:

`javac Arraydec1.java`

Run as : The above program will be run as:

`java Arraydec1`

Output : The output of the program will be

`April has 30 days`

13.1.29. Program to understand the concept of two dimensional array

```
class EmpBonus
{
public static void main(String arg[])
{
```

```
String ebonus[][]=new String[2][5];

ebonus[0][0]="P.K.Roy";
ebonus[0][1]="Anita Rana";
ebonus[0][2]="Rajesh Mandloi";
ebonus[0][3]="Sumit Sharma";
ebonus[0][4]="Shruti Yadav";
ebonus[1][0]="5000";
ebonus[1][1]="6000";
ebonus[1][2]="19000";
ebonus[1][3]="10000";
ebonus[1][4]="5500";

for(int i=0;i<5;i++)
{
System.out.println("\nEmployee name:\n"+ebonus[0][i]);
System.out.println("\t\tBonus Recorded is:"+ebonus[1][i]);
}
}
}
```

Save as : The above program can be saved as:

```
EmpBonus.java
```

Compile as : The above program can be compiled as:

```
javac EmpBonus.java
```

Run as : The above program will be run as:

```
java EmpBonus
```

Output : The output of program will be:

```
Employee name: P.K.Roy           Bonus Recorded is: 5000
Employee name: Anita Rana        Bonus Recorded is: 6000
Employee name: Rajesh Mandloi    Bonus Recorded is: 19000
Employee name: Sumit Sharma      Bonus Recorded is: 10000
Employee name: Shruti Yadav      Bonus Recorded is: 5500
```

13.1.30. Program to store some elements in an array

```
public class ArrayStorage
{
public static void main(String args[])
{
```

```
        int a[]={10,5,9,16,17};

        for(int i=0;i<a.length;i++)
        {
        System.out.println(a[i]);
        }
    }
    }
```

Save as : The above program can be saved as:

```
ArrayStorage.java
```

Compile as : The above program can be compiled as:

```
javac ArrayStorage.java
```

Run as : The above program will be run as:

```
java ArrayStorage
```

Output : The output of the program will be:

```
10
5
9
16
17
```

13.1.31. Program to reverse the elements of array

```
class ArrayReverse
{
    public static void main(String []k)
    {
        int a[]={10,28,43,24,15};
        int i;
        for(i=0;i<a.length;i++)
        {
        System.out.println(a[i]);
        }
        System.out.println("");
        for(i=4;i>=0;i--)
        {
        System.out.println(a[i]);
        }
        }
    }
```

Save as : The above program can be saved as:

```
ArrayReverse.java
```

Compile as : The above program can be compiled as:

```
javac ArrayReverse.java
```

Run as : The above program will be run as:

```
java ArrayReverse
```

Output : The output of the program will be:

```
The actual array is:
          10
          28
          43
          24
          25
The Reverse array is:
          25
          24
          43
          28
          10
```

13.1.32. Program to take average of all elements of array

```
class ArrayAverage
{
public static void main(String []k)
{
    int a[]={1,2,3,4,5};
    int i;
    double avg=0;
    for(i=0;i<a.length;i++)
    {
    avg=avg+a[i];
    }
    avg=avg/5;
    System.out.println("Avg=" +avg);
}
}
```

Save as : The above program can be saved as:

```
ArrayAverage.java
```

Compile as : The above program can be compiled as:

```
javac ArrayAverage.java
```

Run as : The above program will be run as:

```
java ArrayAverage
```

Output : The output of the program will be:

```
Avg=3.0
```

13.1.33. Program to sort maximum elements of Array

```
class ArrayMax
{
 public static void main(String []k)
 {
 int a[]={1,2,9,4,7};
 int i,max=0;

 for(i=0;i<a.length;i++)
 {
 System.out.println(a[i]);

 }
 System.out.println("");
 for(i=0;i<a.length;i++)
 {
    if(max<=a[i])
    max=a[i];
 }
 System.out.println(max);
         }
         }
```

Save as : The above program can be saved as:

```
ArrayMax.java
```

Compile as : The above program can be compiled as:

```
javac ArrayMax.java
```

Run as : The above program will be run as:

```
java ArrayMax
```

Output : The Output of the program will be:

```
1
2
9
```

```
4
7

9
```

13.1.34. Program to search out element in array

```
class ArraySearch
{
    public static void main(String []k)
            {
             int a[]={1,2,3,4,5};
             int i;
            double avg=0;
            for(i=0;i<a.length;i++)
             {
             if(a[i]==3)
            System.out.println("Element found at position:" +i);
            else
           System.out.println("Element not found");
         }
       }
}
```

Save as : The above program can be saved as:

```
ArraySearch.java
```

Compile as : The above program can be compiled as:

```
javac ArraySearch.java
```

Run as : The above program will be run as:

```
java ArraySearch
```

Output : The output of the program will be:

```
Element not found
Element not found
Element not found
Element found at position: 2
Element not found
Element not found
```

13.1.35. Program to sort list of Elements

```
class NumberSorting
{
   public static void main(String args[])
{
```

```
                int number[]={25,5,14,12,90};
                int n=number.length;

                System.out.println("Given list is:");

                for(int i=0;i<n;i++)
                {
                System.out.println(" "+number[i]);
                }
                System.out.println("\n");
                for(int i=0;i<n;i++)
                {
                for(int j=i+1;j<n;j++)
                {
                if(number[i]>number[j])
                    {
                    int temp=number[i];
                    number[i]=number[j];
                    number[j]=temp;
                    }
                }
            }
        }
    }
```

Save as : The above program can be saved as:

```
NumberSorting.java
```

Compile as : The above program can be compiled as:

```
javac NumberSorting.java
```

Run as : The above program will be run as:

```
java NumberSorting
```

Output : The output of the program will be:

```
Given list is:
        25
        5
        14
        12
        90
```

13.1.36. Program to find sum of array elements

```
class TwodArray
{
    public static void main(String []k)
    {
    int a[][];
    a=new int[3][2];
    a[0][0]=5;
    a[0][1]=9;
    a[1][0]=6;
    a[1][1]=2;
    a[2][0]=4;
    a[2][1]=5;
    for(int i=0;i<3;i++)
    {
        for(int j=0;j<2;j++)
        {
        System.out.print(a[i][j]+"   ");
        }
        System.out.println();
    }
    }
}
```

Save as : The above program can be saved as:

```
TwodArray.java
```

Compile as : The above program can be compiled as:

```
javac TwodArray.java
```

Run as : The above program will be run as:

```
java TwodArray
```

Output : The output of the program will be:

```
5    9
6    2
4    5
```

13.1.37. Program to show Upper array

```
import java.util.Scanner;
class TwodArrayUpper
    {
public static void main(String []k)
```

```
    {
        String a[][];
        String b;
        a=new String[3][3];
        System.out.println("Enter the Numbers :");
        for(int i=0;i<3;i++)
        {
            for(int j=0;j<3;j++)
            {
            Scanner sc=new Scanner(System.in);
            b=sc.next();
            }
            System.out.println();

        }

        for(int i=0;i<3;i++)
        {
            for(int j=0;j<3;j++)
            {
                  if(i<=j)

                  System.out.print("    *    ");
                  else
                  System.out.print("\t");

            }

            System.out.println();
        }
  }
  }
```

Save as : The above program can be saved as:

```
TwodArrayUpper.java
```

Compile as : The above program can be compiled as:

```
javac TwodArrayUpper.java
```

Run as : The above program will be run as:

```
java TwodArrayUpper
```

Output : The output of the program will be:

```
2
3
4

5
6
6

1
2
12

*    *    *
     *    *
          *
```

13.1.38. Program to implement 2D array without knowing no. of columns

```
import java.util.Scanner;
class TwodArrays
{
   public static void main(String []k)
   {
   int a[][];
   a=new int[3][];
   a[0]=new int[3];
   a[1]=new int[1];
   a[2]=new int[4];

   a[0][0]=5;
   a[0][1]=9;
   a[0][2]=10;
   a[1][0]=6;
   a[2][0]=2;
   a[2][1]=4;
   a[2][2]=5;
   a[2][3]=9;
   for(int i=0;i<a.length;i++)
   {
      for(int j=0;j<a[i].length;j++)
      {
```

```
            System.out.print(a[i][j]+"    ");
            }
            System.out.println();
        }
        }
        }
```

Save as : The above program can be saved as:

```
TwodArrays.java
```

Compile as : The above program can be compiled as:

```
javac TwodArrays.java
```

Run as : The above program will be run as:

```
java TwodArrays
```

Output : The output of the program will be:

```
5      9       10
6
2     4        5     9
```

13.1.39. Program to implement the concept of 2D array with the help of for each loop

```
import java.util.Scanner;
class TwodArraysUsingForEach
{
    public static void main(String []k)
{
    int a[][];
    a=new int[3][];
    a[0]=new int[3];
    a[1]=new int[1];
    a[2]=new int[4];

    a[0][0]=5;
    a[0][1]=9;
    a[0][2]=10;
    a[1][0]=6;
    a[2][0]=2;
    a[2][1]=4;
    a[2][2]=5;
    a[2][3]=9;
    for(int [] x:a)
    {
    for(int e:x)
```

```
        {
        System.out.print(e+"   ");
        }
        System.out.println();
        }
    }
}
```

Save as : The above program can be saved as:

```
TwodArraysUsingForEach.java
```

Compile as : The above program can be compiled as:

```
javac TwodArraysUsingForEach
```

Run as : The above programm will be run as :

```
java TwodArraysUsingForEach
```

Output : The output of the program will be:

```
5    9    10
6
2    4    5    9
```

13.1.40. Program to show lower Array

```
import java.util.Scanner;
class TwodArrayLower
{
    public static void main(String []k)
{
    String a[][];
    String b;
    a=new String[3][3];
    System.out.println("Enter the Numbers :");
    for(int i=0;i<3;i++)
    {
        for(int j=0;j<3;j++)
        {
        Scanner sc=new Scanner(System.in);
        b=sc.next();
        }
        System.out.println();

    }
```

```
        for(int i=0;i<3;i++)
        {
            for(int j=0;j<3;j++)
            {
                    if(i<=j)
                    System.out.print("*");
                    else

            System.out.print("\b");

            }
            System.out.println();
            }
        }
    }
```

Save as : The above program can be saved as:

```
TwodArrayLower.java
```

Compile as : The above program can be compiled as:

```
javac TwodArrayLower.java
```

Run as : The above program will be run as:

```
java TwodArrayLower
```

Output : The output of the above program will be:

```
Enter the Numbers :
            1
            2
            3

            4
            5
            6

            7
            8
            9

            *    *    *
            *    *
            *
```

13.1.41. Program to print Numbers in the form of Pyramid

```
class ForNumbers
{
    public static void main(String []m)
    {
    for(int i=5;i>=1;i–)
    {
    for(int k=5;k>i;k–)
    System.out.print(" ");
    for(int j=i;j>=1;j–)
    System.out.print(j);
    System.out.println("");
    }
}
}
```

Save as : The above program can be saved as:

```
ForNumbers.java
```

Compile as : The above program can be compiled as:

```
javac ForNumbers.java
```

Run as : The above program will be run as:

```
java ForNumbers
```

Output : The output of the program will be:

```
54321
 4321
  321
   21
    1
```

13.1.42. Program to understand the concept of recursion

```
class RecursionFact
{
static int fact(int n)
{
    return n*fact(n-1);
}
    public static void main(String []k)
{
    int x=fact(1);
```

```
        System.out.println(x);
        }
    }
```

Save as : The above program can be saved as:

```
RecursionFact.java
```

Compile as : The above program can be compiled as:

```
javac RecursionFact.java
```

Run as : The above program will be run as:

```
java RecursionFact
```

Output : The output of the program will be:

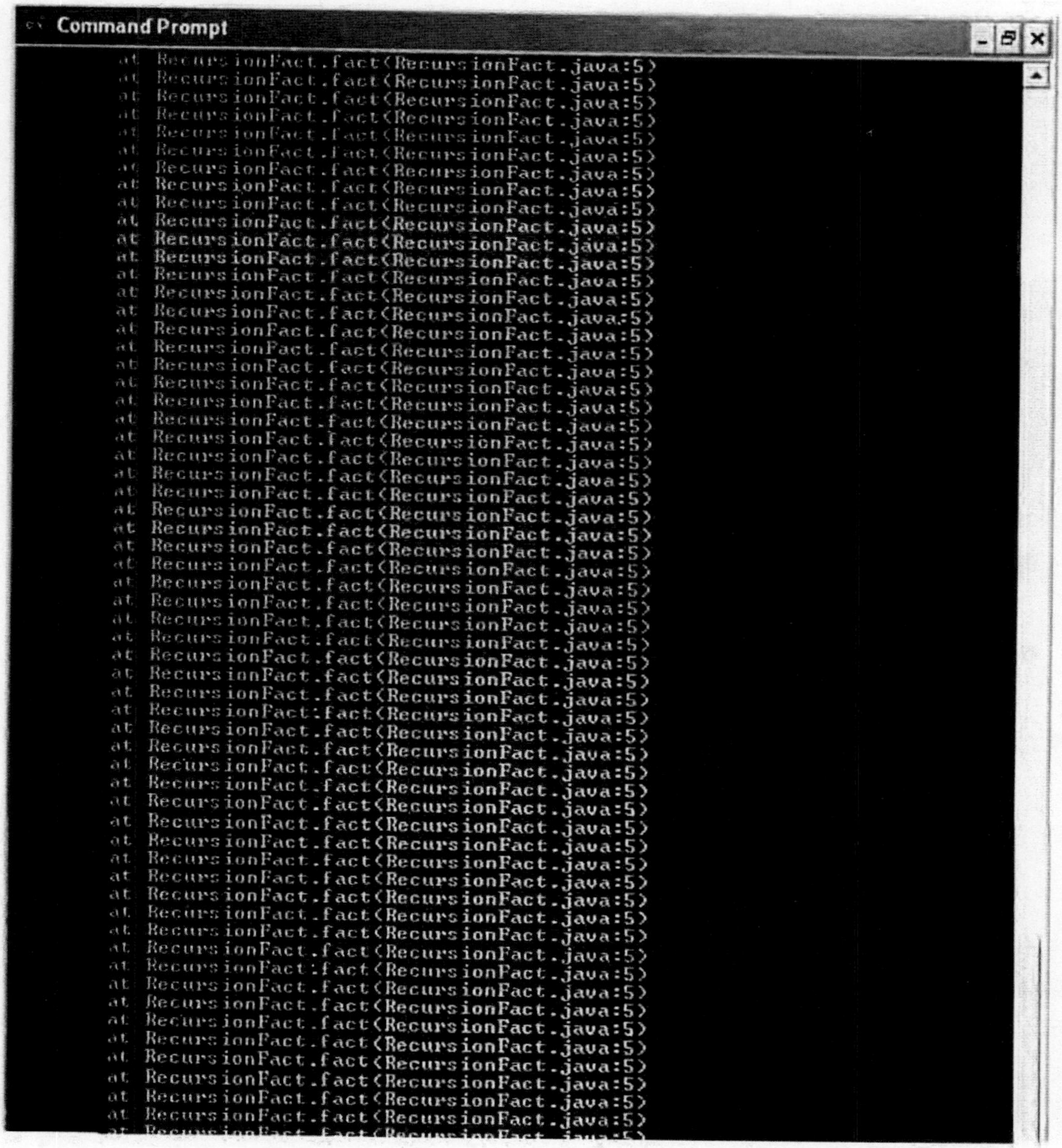

13.1.43. Program to understand the concept of Recursion in Java

```
class RecursionSum
{
    static int fact(int n,int m)
    {
    for(int i=0;m==0;i++)
    {
        n=n+1;
        m=m-1;
}

    return n;
    }
    public static void main(String []k)
    {
    int x=fact(5,6);
    System.out.println(x);
    }
}
```

Save as : The above program can be saved as:

```
RecursionSum.java
```

Compile as : The above program can be compiled as:

```
javac RecursionSum.java
```

Run as : The above program will be run as:

```
java RecursionSum.java
```

Output : The output of the program will be:

```
5
```

13.1.44. Program to convert Feet to Inch in Java.

```
class Distances
{
    private int ft;
    private double inch;
    void distances(int p,double q)
   {
    ft=p;
    inch=q;
    }
    void distances(int p)
```

```
{
    ft=p/12;
    inch=p%12;
}
    void distances(double p)
    {
        ft=(int)p;
        inch=(p-ft)*12;
    }
        void show()
    {
        System.out.println(ft + "'" + inch + "\"");
    }
        }
        class DistanceConverter
        {
        public static void main(String []k)
        {
      Distances d1;
      d1=new Distances();
      d1.distances(30);
      d1.show();
      d1.distances(3.75);
      d1.show();
      d1.distances(5,6);
      d1.show();
    }
  }
```

Save as : The above program can be saved as:

```
DistanceConverter.java
```

Compile as : The above program can be compiled as:

```
javac DistanceConverter.java
```

Run as : The above program will be run as:

```
java DistanceConverter
```

Output : The output of the program will be:

```
2'6.0"
3'9.0"
5'6.0"
```

13.1.45. Program to print address stored

```
import java.util.Scanner;
class Addresses
{
   private String name;
   private String ct;
   private String cu;
   private String st;
   private String zips;
   private String str;
   private int n;
   private int choise;
   private String uname;
   private String uct;
   private String ucu;
   private String ust;
   private String uzips;
   private String ustr;

   void setdata()
   {
   Scanner sc=new Scanner(System.in);
   System.out.println("Enter the City=");
   ct=sc.next();
   System.out.println("Enter the County=");
   cu=sc.next();
   System.out.println("Enter the State=");
   st=sc.next();
   System.out.println("Enter the Zip=");
   zips=sc.next();
   System.out.println("Enter the Name=");
   name=sc.next();
   System.out.println("Enter the Street=");
   str=sc.next();
   }
   void update()
   {
   Scanner sc=new Scanner(System.in);
   System.out.println("You have value of the n:");
   n=sc.nextInt();
   do
   {
        System.out.println("You have fallowing choice:");
```

```
System.out.println("1 update Name");
System.out.println("2 update Street");
System.out.println("3 update City");
System.out.println("4 update State");
System.out.println("5 update County");
System.out.println("6 update zip");
System.out.println("7 Exit=");
System.out.println("You have your choice:");
choice=sc.nextInt();

switch(choice)
{
case 1:
{
System.out.println(" update Name=");
uname=sc.next();
name=uname;
}
break;
case 2:
{
System.out.println(" update Street=");
ustr=sc.next();
str=ustr;
}
break;
case 3:
{
System.out.println(" update City=");
uct=sc.next();
ct=uct;
}
break;
case 4:
{
System.out.println(" update State=");
ust=sc.next();
st=ust;
}
break;
case 5:
{
System.out.println(" update Country=");
ucu=sc.next();
```

```
        cu=ucu;
        }
        break;
        case 6:
        {
        System.out.println(" update Zip=");
        uzips=sc.next();
        zips=uzips;
        }
        break;
        default:
        System.out.println(" Invalid choise=");

        }
        }while(n==7);
    }

    void show()
    {
    System.out.println(" the Name=" +name);
    System.out.println(" the Streate=" +str);
    System.out.println(" the City=" +ct);
    System.out.println(" the State=" +st);
    System.out.println(" the country=" +cu);
    System.out.println(" the Zip=" +zips);
    }
    }

    class AddressInformation
    {
    public static void main(String []k)
    {
    Addresses a1;
    a1=new Addresses();
    a1.setdata();
    a1.show();
    a1.update();
    a1.show();
    }
    }
```

Save as : The above program can be saved as:

```
AddressInformation.java
```

Compile as : The above program can be compiled as:

`javac AddressInformation.java`

Run as : The above program will be run as:

`java AddressInformation`

Output : The output of the program will be:

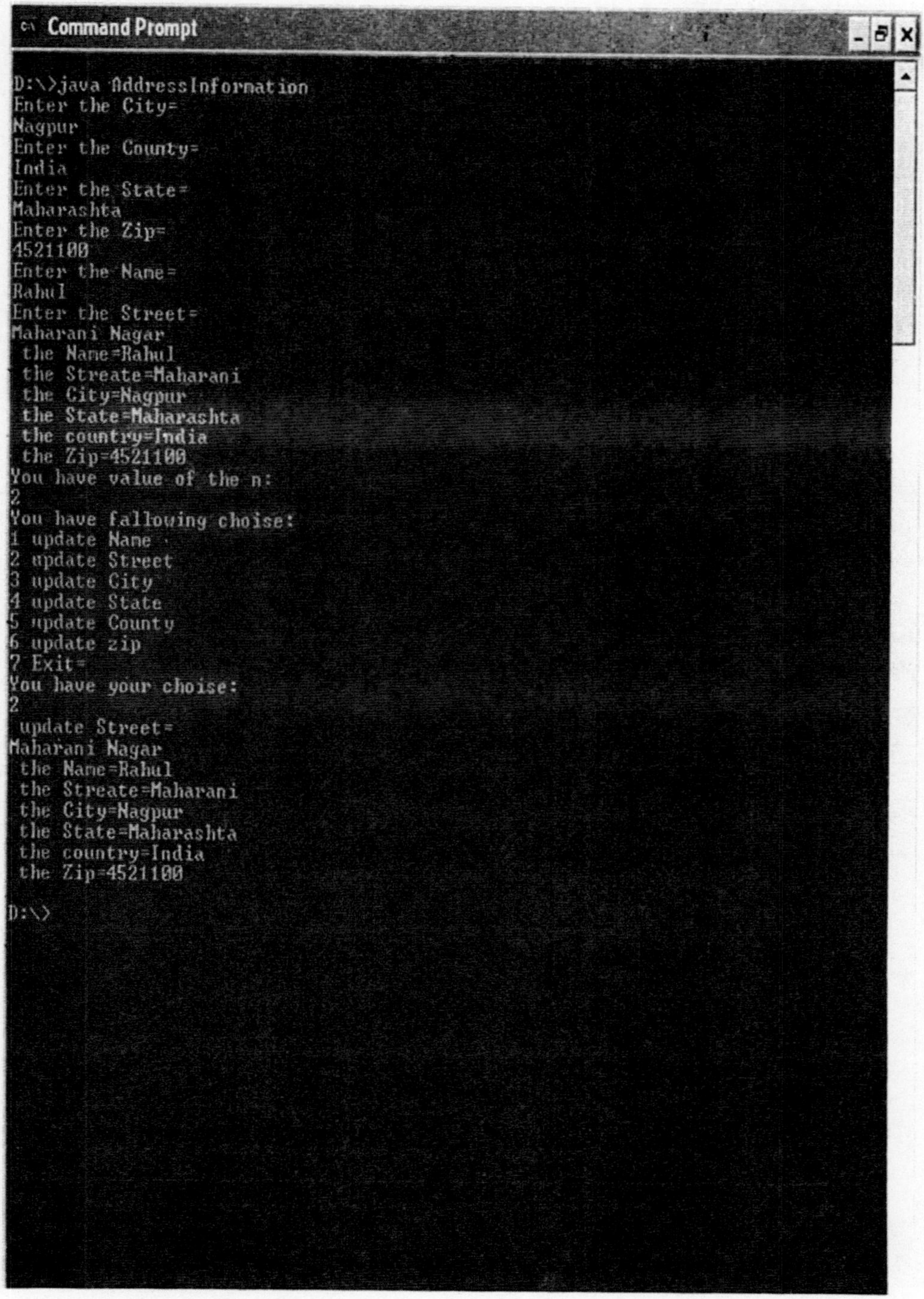

13.1.46. Program to Test Array

```
import java.util.*;
public class TestArray {
public static void main(String[] args) {
int a[]=new int[10];
int x,i,c=0;
int ch;
Scanner sc=new Scanner(System.in);

  do{
 System.out.println();
System.out.println("Enter Choice : ");
System.out.println("1. Add Element");
System.out.println("2. Delete Element");
System.out.println("3. Search Element");
System.out.println("4. Insert Element");
System.out.println("5. Show All");
System.out.println("6. Exit");
 ch=sc.nextInt();
 switch(ch)
 {
case 1:     System.out.println("Enter Data to Add : ");
      x=sc.nextInt();
      a[c++]=x;
      break;
case 2:     System.out.println("Enter Data to Delete : ");
      x=sc.nextInt();
      i=0;
      for(i=0;i<c;i++)
      {
            if(a[i]==x)
                  break;
      }
      if(i!=c)
      {
            c--;
            for(int k=i; k<c; k++ )
                  a[k]=a[k+1];
      }else
      {
```

```
                System.out.println("Data Not Found");
            }
            break;
    case 3:
            System.out.println("Enter Data to search : ");
            x=sc.nextInt();

            for(i=0;i<c;i++)
            {
                if(a[i]==x)
                    break;
            }
            if(i!=c)
            {
                System.out.println("Data fount at Location : "+i);
            }else
            {
                System.out.println("Data Not Found");
            }
            break;
    case 4:
            System.out.println("Enter Data to Insert : ");
            x=sc.nextInt();
            System.out.println("Enter Location : ");
            int l=sc.nextInt();
            for(i=c;i>l;i—)
            {
                a[i]=a[i-1];
            }
            a[i]=x;
            c++;
            break;
    case 5:
                for(int k=0;k<c; k++)
                {
                    System.out.print(a[k]+"\t");
                }
                break;
    case 6:     break;
    default: System.out.println("Invalid Entry . Try Again");
```

```
    }
  }while(ch!=6);
 }
}
```

Save as : The above program can be saved as:

`TestArray.java`

Compile as : The above program can be compiled as:

`javac TestArray.java`

Run as : The above program will be run as:

`java TestArray`

Output : The output of the program will be:

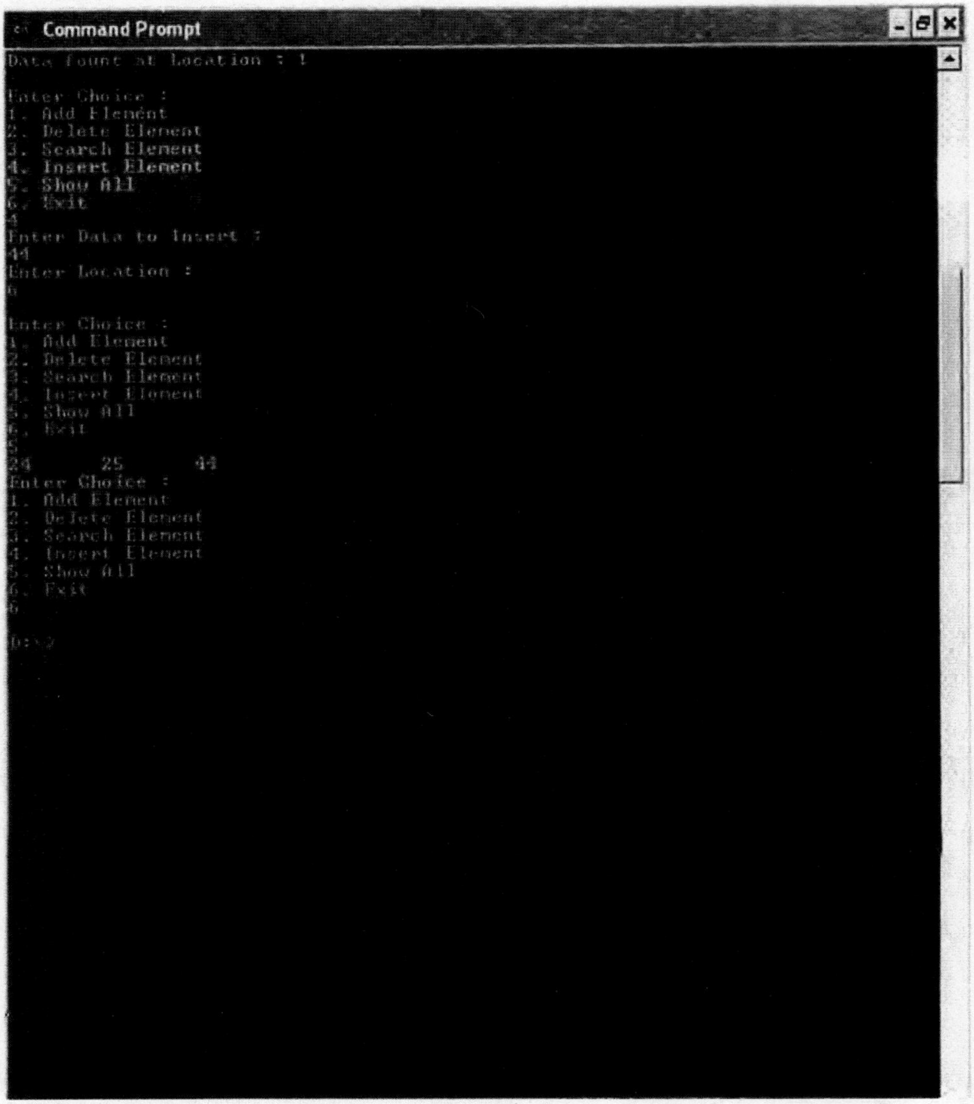

13.1.47. Program for Billing System

```
import java.util.Scanner;
class Bill
{  private int billno;
   private String cname;
   private String itemname;
   private int itemno;
   private double qty;
   private int n;
   private double price;
   private  double amount;
   void setdata()
   {
      Scanner sc=new Scanner(System.in);
      System.out.println("Enter the Bill Number:");
      billno=sc.nextInt();
      System.out.println("Enter the Custmor Name:");
      cname=sc.next();
      System.out.println("Enter the item Number:");
      itemno=sc.nextInt();
      System.out.println("Enter the item Name:");
      itemname=sc.next();
      System.out.println("Enter the item Qntity:");
      qty=sc.nextDouble();
      System.out.println("Enter the item  Price:");
      price=sc.nextDouble();
      amount=qty*price;
   }

   void show()
   {
      System.out.println(billno);
      System.out.println(cname);
      System.out.println( " itemno   itemname   qty price   amount");
      System.out.println(  itemno + "          " +itemname +"
" + qty + "    " +price+ "      "+ amount);
      }
   }
```

```
class BillsFuns
{
   public static void main(String []k)
   {
   Bill b1;
   b1=new Bill();
   b1.setdata();
   b1.show();
   }
}
```

Save as : The above program can be saved as:

BillsFuns.java

Compile as : The above program can be compiled as:

javac BillsFuns.java

Run as : The above program will be run as:

java BillsFuns

Output : The output of the program will be:

13.1.48. Program for Complex Number

```
class ComplexNumber
{
   private double real;
   private double imag;
   ComplexNumber(int p,int q)
   {
      real=p;
      imag=q;
   }

   void show()
   {
      if(real!=0 && imag>0)
      System.out.println(real +"+" +imag +"i" );
      if(real!=0 &&imag<0)
      System.out.println( real + ""  +imag +"i");
      if(real!=0 && imag==0)
      System.out.println( real  );
      if(real==0 && imag!=0)
      System.out.println( imag +"i" );
   }
}
class ComplexFun
{
   public static void main(String []k)
   {
   ComplexNumber c1;
   c1=new ComplexNumber(2,1);
   c1.show();
   c1=new ComplexNumber(-2,1);
   c1.show();
   c1=new ComplexNumber(2,-1);
   c1.show();
   c1=new ComplexNumber(-2,-1);
   c1.show();
   c1=new ComplexNumber(0,1);
   c1.show();
   c1=new ComplexNumber(2,0);
   c1.show();
   }
         }
```

Save as : The above program can be saved as:

ComplexFun.java

Compile as : The above program can be compiled as:

javac ComplexFun.java

Run as : The above program will be run as:

java ComplexFun

Output : The output of the program will be:

13.1.49. Program to implement the concept of Stack

```
class Stack
{
int stack[]=new int[10];
int tos;
Stack()
{
tos=-1;
}
void push(int item)
{
if(tos==9)
System.out.println("Stack is  full");
else
stack[++tos]=item;
}
int pop()
{
if(tos<0)
{
```

```
System.out.println("Stack is under flow");
return 0;
}
else
return stack[tos–];
}
}
class TestStack
{
public static void main(String []k)
{
Stack mystack1=new Stack();
Stack mystack2=new Stack();
for(int i=0;i<10;i++)
mystack1.push(i);
for(int i=10;i<20;i++)
mystack2.push(i);
System.out.println("Stack in My stack1");
for(int i=0;i<10;i++)
System.out.println(mystack1.pop());
System.out.println("Stack in My stack2");
for(int j=0;j<10;j++)
System.out.println(mystack2.pop());
}
}}
```

Save as : The above program can be saved as:

`TestStack.java`

Compile as : The above program can be compiled as:

`javac TestStack.java`

Run as : The above program will be run as:

`java TestStack`

Output: The output of the program will be:

13.1.50. Program to Understand the concept of Inheritance in Java

```
class A
{
    int x;
    int y;
    void setA(int p,int q)
    {
    x=p;
    y=q;
    }
    void showA()
    {
    System.out.println(x);
    System.out.println(y);
    }
}
class B extends A
{
int z;
void setB(int r)
{
z=r;
}
void showB()
{
System.out.println(z);
}
}

class InheriteTest
{
public static void main(String []k)
{
A a=new A();
a.setA(2,5);
B b1=new B();
b1.setB(8);
b1.showA();
b1.showB();
B b2=new B();
```

```
b2.setB(10);
b2.showA();
b2.showB();
b1.setA(100,200);
b1.showA();
}
}
```

Save as : The above program can be saved as:

```
InheriteTest.java
```

Compile as : The above program can be compiled as:

```
javac InheriteTest.java
```

Run as : The above program will be run as:

```
java InheriteTest
```

Output : The output of the program will be:

13.1.51. Program to show inheritance in java

```
class Person
{
   private String name;
   private String address;
   private String city;
   void setdataP(String p,String q,String r)
   {
      name=p;
      address=q;
      city=r;
   }
```

```
    void showp()
    {
    System.out.println("Name=" +name);
    System.out.println("Address=" +address );
    System.out.println("City=" +city);
    }
}
class Employe extends Person
{
    private int id;
    void setdata(int p)
    {
        id=p;
    }
    void showe()
    {
    System.out.println("Id=" +id);
    }
}

class InhertePerson
{
    public static void main(String []k)
    {
        Person p1=new Person();
        p1.setdataP("Devendra","Vijay Nagar","Indore");
        p1.showp();
        Employe e1=new Employe();
        e1.setdata(14);
        e1.showe();
    }
}
```

Save as : The above program can be saved as:

```
InhertePerson.java
```

Compile as : The above program can be compiled as:

```
javac InhertePerson.java
```

Run as : The above program will be run as:

```
java InhertePerson
```

Output : The output of the program will be:

13.1.52. Program to understand the concept of Inheritance in java

```
class Lion
{
    String voice;
    int speed;
    int height;
    void setdataL(String u,int v,int w)
    {
        voice=u;
        speed=v;
        height=w;
    }
    void showL()
    {
        System.out.println("Voice=" +voice);
        System.out.println("Speed in Km/h=" +speed );
        System.out.println("Height in ft=" +height);
    }
}
class Dog extends Lion
{
String sizeofhair;
void setdataD(String p)
{
sizeofhair=p;
}
void showD()
{
System.out.println("Size Of the Hair="+sizeofhair);
}
}
```

```
class InheriteLionByDog
{
public static void main(String []k)
{
Lion l1=new Lion();
Dog d1=new Dog();
l1.setdataL(“Loud”,18,3);
System.out.println(“content of the super class” );
l1.showL();
d1.setdataL(“Slow”,10,2);
d1.setdataD(“short”);
System.out.println(“content of the sub class” );
d1.showL();
d1.showD();

}
}
```

Save as : The above program can be saved as:

`InheriteLionByDog.java`

Compile as : The above program will be compile as:

`javac InheriteLionByDog.java`

Run as : The above program will be run as:

`java InheriteLion`

Output : The output of the program will be:

13.1.53. Program to understand the concept of Inheritance

```
class Student
{
    String name;
    String address;
```

```
     String city;
    void setdataS(String u,String v,String w)
     {
        name=u;
        address=v;
        city=w;
    }
    void showS()
    {
    System.out.println("Name=" +name);
    System.out.println("Address=" +address );
    System.out.println("City=" +city);
    }
}
class College extends Student
{
    String cname;
    String caddress;
    int stid;
    void setdataC(String p,String q,int r)
    {
    cname=p;
    caddress=q;
    stid=r;
    }
    void showC()
    {
    System.out.println("Colege Name=" +cname);
    System.out.println("College Address=" +address );
    System.out.println("Student Id=" +stid);
    }
}

class InheriteStudentByCollege
{
public static void main(String []k)
{

Student s1=new Student();
College c1=new College();
```

```
System.out.println("Content of the Super class");
s1.setdataS("Shahbaz Khan","MYH","Indore");
System.out.println("");
s1.showS();
System.out.println("Content of the Sub class");
c1.setdataC("PIES","Vijay Nagar",50);
c1.setdataS("Bhavya","Vijay Nagar","Indore");
c1.showS();
c1.showC();
}
}
```

Save as : The above program can be saved as:

`InheriteStudentByCollege.java`

Compile as : The above program can be compiled as:

`javac InheriteStudentByCollege.java`

Run as : The above program will be run as:

`java InheriteStudentByCollege`

Output : The output of the program will be:

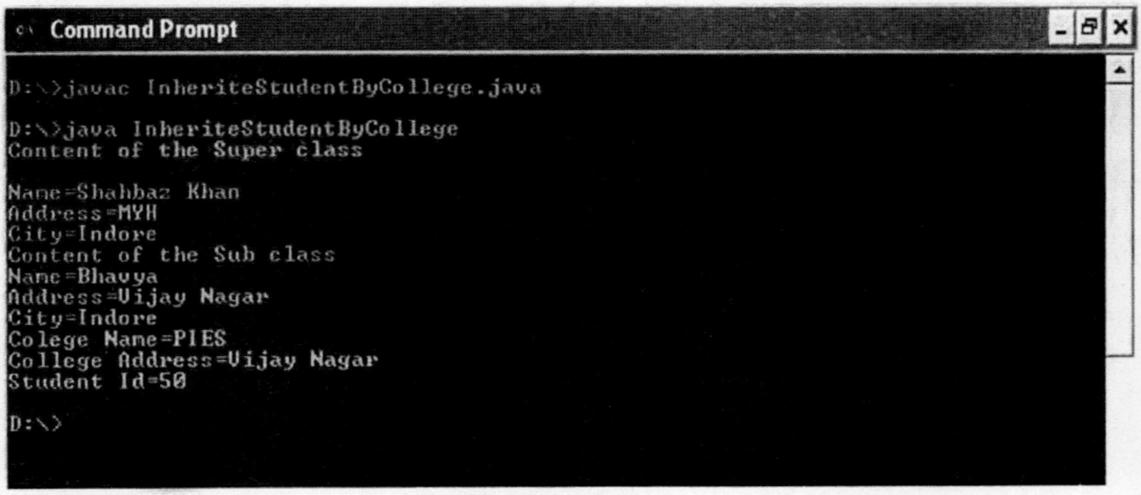

```
Command Prompt
D:\>javac InheriteStudentByCollege.java

D:\>java InheriteStudentByCollege
Content of the Super class

Name=Shahbaz Khan
Address=MYH
City=Indore
Content of the Sub class
Name=Bhavya
Address=Vijay Nagar
City=Indore
Colege Name=PIES
College Address=Vijay Nagar
Student Id=50

D:\>
```

13.1.54. Program to print series of log in java

```
class SeriesOfLog
{
public static void main(String []k)
{
int s=1;
int p=1;
```

```
for(int i=0;i<100;i++)
{
s=s+(s/s*i);

System.out.print(s+"+" );
}
}
}
```

Save as : The above program can be saved as:

`SeriesOfLog.java`

Compile as : The above program can be compiled as:

`javac SeriesOfLog.java`

Run as : The above program will be run as:

`java SeriesOfLog`

Output : The output of the program will be:

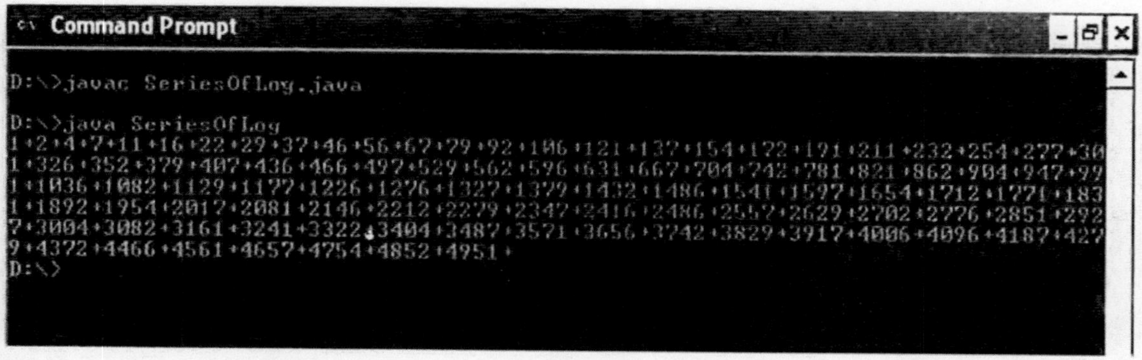

13.1.55. Program to show hierarchical inheritance in java

```
class Base
{
void show()
{
System.out.println("Show from Base");
}
void display()
{
System.out.println("display  from Base");
}
}
class Derived1 extends Base
{
```

```
void prints()
{
System.out.println("Print from Derived");
}
void show()
{
System.out.println("Show from Derived");
}
}
class Derived2 extends Base
{
void out()
{
System.out.println("Out from Drived");
}
void show()
{
System.out.println("Show from Derived2");
}
}
class TestHerarchical
{
static void info(Base b)
{
b.show();
b.display();
}
public static void main(String []k)
{
Base b=new Base();
Derived1 d1=new Derived1();
Derived2 d2=new Derived2();
info(b);
info(d1);
info(d2);
}
}
```

Save as : The above program can be saved as:

`TestHerarchical.java`

Compile as : The above program can be compiled as:

`javac TestHerarchical.java`

Run as : The above program will be run as:

`javac TestHerarchical`

Output : The output of the program will be:

13.1.56. Program to understand the concept of Run Time Polymorphism

```
class Figure
{
    double dim1;
    double dim2;
    Figure(double a,double b)
    {
    dim1=a;
    dim2=b;
    }
    double area()
    {
    System.out.println("Area of the Figure is undefined");
    return 0;
    }
}
class Rectangle extends Figure
{
    Rectangle(double a,double b)
    {
    super(a,b);
    }
//override area for the rectangle
    double area()
    {
```

```
    System.out.println("Inside area for the Rectangle:");
    return dim1*dim2;
    }
}
class Triangle extends Figure
{
    Triangle(double a,double b)
    {
    super(a,b);
    }
    double area()
    {
    System.out.println("Inside area for the tringle");
    return dim1*dim2/2;
    }
}
class FindAreas
{
    public static void main(String []k)
    {
    Figure f=new Figure(10,10);
    Rectangle r=new Rectangle(9,5);
    Triangle t=new Triangle(10,8);
    Figure figref;
    figref=r;
    System.out.println("Area is"+figref.area());//call the area
of the rectangle
    figref=f;
    System.out.println("Area is"+figref.area());//call the are a
of the Figure class
        figref=t;
    System.out.println("Area is"+figref.area());//call the are of
the tinangle class
    }
}
```

Save as : The above program can be saved as:

`FindAreas.java`

Compile as : The above program can be compiled as:

`javac FindAreas.java`

Run as : The above program will be run as:

`java FindAreas`

Output : The output of the program will be:

13.1.57. Program to understand the concept of Abstract class

```
abstract class A
{
void callmetoo()
{
System.out.println("this is the concreate method ");
}
}
class B extends A
{
void callme()
{
System.out.println("B is the implementation of the call me.");
}
}
class AbstractDemo
{
public static void main(String []k)
{
B b=new B();
b.callme();
b.callmetoo();
}
}
```

Save as : The above program can be saved as:

AbstractDemo.java

Compile as : The above program can be compiled as:

javac AbstractDemo.java

Run as : The above program will be run as:

```
java AbstractDemo
```

Output : The output of the program will be:

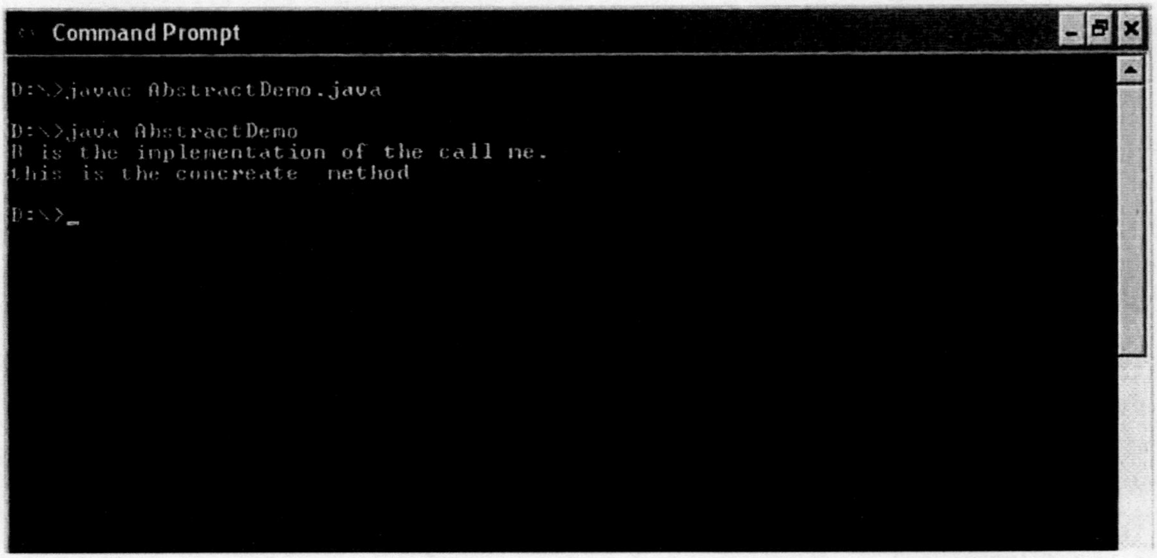

13.1.58. Program to understand the concept of Abstract class

```
abstract class Figure
{
double dim1;
double dim2;
Figure(double a,double b)
{
dim1=a;
dim2=b;
}
abstract double area();
}
class Rectangle extends Figure
{
Rectangle(double a,double b)
{
super(a,b);
}
double area()
{
System.out.println("inside area for rectangle");
return dim1*dim2;
```

```
}
}
class Triangle extends Figure
{
Triangle(double a,double b)
{
super(a,b);
}
double area()
{
System.out.println("Inside are for the triangle");
return dim1*dim2/2;
}
}
class AbstractArea
{
public static void main(String []k)
{
 //Figure  f=new  Figure(10,10);
Rectangle r=new Rectangle(9,5);
Triangle t=new Triangle(10,8);

Figure figref;
figref=r;
System.out.println("Area is "+figref.area());
System.out.println("Oject of the
class"+figref.getClass().getName());
System.out.println("");
figref=t;
System.out.println("Area is "+figref.area());
System.out.println("Oject of the
class"+figref.getClass().getName());
}
}
```

Save as : The above program can be saved as:

`AbstractArea.java`

Compile as : The above program can be compiled as:

`javac AbstractArea.java`

Run as : The above program will be run as:

`java AbstractArea`

Output : The output of the program will be:

13.1.59. Program to understand the concept of Command Line argument

```
class CommandLineSum
{
    public static void main(String []k)
    {
    for(int i=0;i<k.length;i++)
    {
    System.out.println(k[i]);
    }
    if(k.length!=2)
    System.out.println("Enter the two value");
    else
    {
    int x=Integer.parseInt(k[0]);
    int y=Integer.parseInt(k[1]);
    int z=x+y;
    System.out.println("sum="+z);
    }
    }
}
```

Save as : The above program can be saved as:

```
CommandLineSum.java
```

Compile as : The above program can be compiled as:

```
javac CommandLineSum.java
```

Run as : The above program will be run as:

```
java CommandLineSum
```

Output : The output of the program will be:

13.1.60. Program to perform division from command line

```
class CommandLineDiv
{
   public static void main(String []k)
   {
   for(int i=0;i<k.length;i++)
   {
   System.out.println(k[i]);
   }
   if(k.length!=2)
   System.out.println("Enter the two value");
   else
   {
   int x=Integer.parseInt(k[0]);
   int y=Integer.parseInt(k[1]);
   int z=x/y;
   System.out.println("Division="+z);
   }
   }
}
```

Save as : The above program can be saved as:

```
CommandLineDiv.java
```

Compile as : The above program can be compiled as:

```
javac CommandLineSum.java
```

Run as : The above program will be run as:

```
java CommandLineSum
```

Output : The output of the program will be:

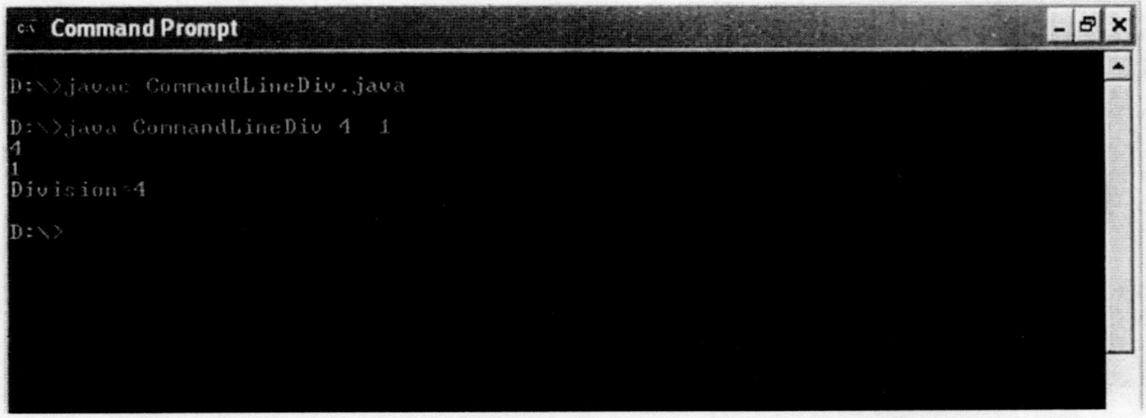

13.1.61. Program to understand the concept of abstract class

```
abstract class A
{
abstract void fun();

void fun1()
{
System.out.println("A-Fun");
}
}

class B extends A
{
void fun()
{

System.out.println("B-Fun");
}

void fun1()
{
super.fun1();
System.out.println("B-Fun1");
}
}
class Abstrct
{
public static void main(String arg[])
```

```
{
B b= new B();
b.fun();
b.fun1();

//A a=b;
//b.fun1();

}
}
```

Save as : The above program can be saved as:

Abstrct.java

Compile as : The above program can be compiled as:

javac Abstrct.java

Run as : The above program will be run as:

java Abstrct

Output : The output of the program will be:

13.1.62. Program to understand the concept of Packages

```
package p1;
public class A
{
int x;
A()
{
x=1;
}
public A(int p)
{
x=p;
}
```

```
public void show()
{
System.out.println(x);
}
}
package p1;
public class B
{
int y;
B()
{
y=1;
}
public B(int p)
{
y=p;
}
public void show()
{
System.out.println(y);
}
}
package p2;
import p1.A;
import p1.B;
public class Test
{
public static void main(String []k)
{
A a;
B b;
a=new A(15);
a.show();
b=new B(20);
b.show();
}
}
```

Save as : The above program can be saved as:

```
Test.java
```

Compile as : The above program can be compiled as:

```
javac Test.java
```

Run as : The above program will be run as:

```
java Test
```

13.1.63. Program to understand the concept of Interfaces in java

```
public class Main {

    public static void main(String[] args) {

        shape circleshape=new Circle();

            circleshape.Draw();
    }
}
 interface shape
 {
    public String baseclass="shape";

    public void Draw();

 }
 class Circle implements shape
 {

    public void Draw() {
       System.out.println("Drawing Circle here");
    }

 }
```

Save as : The above program can be saved as:

```
Main.java
```

Compile as : The above program can be compiled as:

```
javac Main.java
```

Run as : The above program will be run as:

```
java Main
```

Output : The output of the program will be:

```
Drawing Circle here
```

13.1.64. Program to understand the concept of Input/Output in java

```
import java.io.* ;
class InOut {
public static void main(String args[])
{
  InputStreamReader istream = new InputStreamReader(System.in);
  BufferedReader bufRead = new BufferedReader(istream) ;
```

```
        System.out.println("Welcome To My First Java Program");
          try {
          System.out.println("Please Enter In Your First Name: ");
          String firstName = bufRead.readLine();
                  }
          catch (IOException err) {
      System.out.println("Error reading line");
      }
      }
      }
```

Save as : The above program can be saved as:

```
InOut.java
```

Compile as : The above program can be compiled as:

```
javac InOut.java
```

Run as : The above program will be run as:

```
java InOut.java
```

Output: The Output of the program will be

```
Welcome to My First Java Program
Please Enter in Your First Name:
Vibha
```

13.1.65. Program to understand concept of Input Output in java

```
import java.io.* ;
class PrintName{
     public static void main(String args[])
      {
 InputStreamReader istream = new InputStreamReader(System.in) ;
        BufferedReader bufRead = new BufferedReader(istream) ;

         System.out.println("Welcome To My First Java Program");

           try {
         System.out.println("Please Enter In Your First Name: ");
                String firstName = bufRead.readLine();

 System.out.println("Please Enter In The Year You Were Born: ");
      String bornYear = bufRead.readLine();

      System.out.println("Please Enter In The Current Year: ");
                String thisYear = bufRead.readLine();

                int bYear = Integer.parseInt(bornYear);
```

```
                    int tYear = Integer.parseInt(thisYear);
                    int age = tYear-bYear;
                    System.out.println("Hello " + firstName + "You
    are " + age + "years old");
              }
              catch (IOException err) {
                  System.out.println("Error reading line");
              }
              catch(NumberFormatException err) {
              System.out.println("Error Converting Number");
              }
         }
    }
```

Save as : The above program can be saved as:

```
PrintName.java
```

Compile as : The above program can be compiled as:

```
javac PrintName.java
```

Run as : The above program will be run as:

```
java PrintName
```

Output : The output of the program will be:

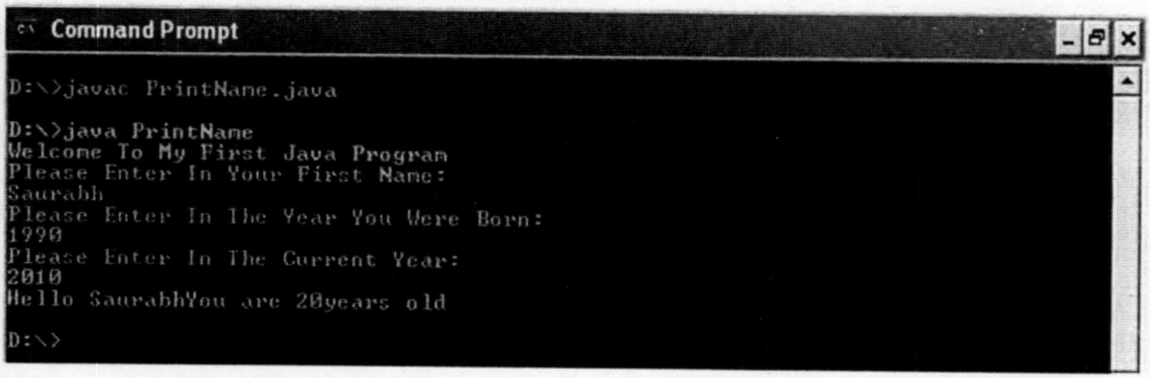

13.1.66. Program to show HelloJava using Java Applets

```
import java.awt.*;
import java.applet.*;
public class HelloJava extends Applet
{
   public void paint(Graphics g)
   {
      g.drawString("Hello Java",10,100);
   }
}
```

```
//Save as: HelloJava.java
<html>
<head>
<title>"Applet is running"</title>
</head>
<body>
<applet code = "HelloJava" width=500 height=500>
</applet>
</html>
```

Save as : The above program can be saved as:

```
HelloJava.html
```

Compile as : The above program will be compile as:

```
javac HelloJava.java
```

Run as : The above program will be run as:

```
appletviewer HelloJava.html
```

Output : The output of the above program will be:

13.1.67. Program to show life cycle of thread

```
class B extends Thread
{
   public void run()
   {
      String n=getName();
      System.out.println(n+"Started");
      for(int i=1;i<=10;i++)
      {
         System.out.println(n+"->"+i);
         System.out.println(n+"End");
      }
   }
}
class Test1
{
   public static void main(String args[])
   {
      System.out.println("Main Started");
      B a1=new B();
      B a2=new B();
      a1.start();
      a2.start();
      for(int i=1;i<=10;i++)
      {
         System.out.println("Main->"+i);
      }
      System.out.println("Main End");
   }
}}
```

Save As : The above program can be saved as:

```
Test1.java
```

Compile As : The above program can be compiled as

```
javac Test1
```

Run As : The above program can be run as:

```
java Test1
```

Output : The output of program will be:

```
Main Started
Main-->1
Main-->2
Main-->3
Thread-0Started
Thread-1Started
Thread-0-->1
Thread-1-->1
Thread-0End
Thread-1End
Thread-0-->2
Thread-1-->2
Thread-0End
Thread-1End
Thread-0-->3
Thread-1-->3
Main-->4
Thread-0End
Main-->5
Thread-0-->4
Main-->6
Thread-0End
Main-->7
Thread-0-->5
Main-->8
Thread-0End
Main-->9
Thread-0-->6
Main-->10
Thread-1End
Main End
Thread-1-->4
Thread-1End
Thread-1-->5
Thread-1End
Thread-1-->6
Thread-1End
Thread-0End
Thread-0-->7
Thread-0End
Thread-0-->8
Thread-0End
Thread-0-->9
Thread-0End
Thread-0-->10
Thread-0End
Thread-1-->7
Thread-1End
Thread-1-->8
Thread-1End
Thread-1-->9
Thread-1End
Thread-1-->10
Thread-1End
```

13.1.68. Program to show clock running with respect to system time

```
import java.applet.*;
import java.awt.*;
import java.util.*;
import java.text.*;
public class Clock1 extends Applet implements Runnable {

  int width, height;
```

```
    Thread t = null;
    boolean threadSuspended;
    int hours=0, minutes=0, seconds=0;
    String timeString = "";

    public void init() {
       width = getSize().width;
       height = getSize().height;
       setBackground( Color.black );
    }

    public void start() {
       if ( t == null ) {
          t = new Thread( this );
          t.setPriority( Thread.MIN_PRIORITY );
          threadSuspended = false;
          t.start();
       }
       else {
          if ( threadSuspended ) {
             threadSuspended = false;
             synchronized( this ) {
                notify();
             }
          }
       }
    }
    public void stop() {
       threadSuspended = true;
    }

    public void run() {
       try {
          while (true) {

             // Here's where the thread does some work
             Calendar cal = Calendar.getInstance();
             hours = cal.get( Calendar.HOUR_OF_DAY );
             if ( hours > 12 ) hours -= 12;
             minutes = cal.get( Calendar.MINUTE );
             seconds = cal.get( Calendar.SECOND );
```

```
            SimpleDateFormat formatter
                           = new SimpleDateFormat( "hh:mm:ss",
Locale.getDefault() );
            Date date = cal.getTime();
            timeString = formatter.format( date );

      // Now the thread checks to see if it should suspend itself
            if ( threadSuspended ) {
               synchronized( this ) {
                  while ( threadSuspended ) {
                     wait();
                  }
               }
            }
            repaint();
           t.sleep( 1000 );  // interval given in milliseconds
         }
      }
      catch (InterruptedException e) { }
   }

   void drawHand( double angle, int radius, Graphics g ) {
      angle -= 0.5 * Math.PI;
      int x = (int)( radius*Math.cos(angle) );
      int y = (int)( radius*Math.sin(angle) );
     g.drawLine( width/2, height/2, width/2 + x, height/2 + y );
   }
   void drawWedge( double angle, int radius, Graphics g ) {
      angle -= 0.5 * Math.PI;
      int x = (int)( radius*Math.cos(angle) );
      int y = (int)( radius*Math.sin(angle) );
      angle += 2*Math.PI/3;
      int x2 = (int)( 5*Math.cos(angle) );
      int y2 = (int)( 5*Math.sin(angle) );
      angle += 2*Math.PI/3;
      int x3 = (int)( 5*Math.cos(angle) );
      int y3 = (int)( 5*Math.sin(angle) );
     g.drawLine( width/2+x2, height/2+y2, width/2 + x, height/
2 + y );
```

```
g.drawLine( width/2+x3, height/2+y3, width/2 + x, height/2 + y );
g.drawLine( width/2+x2, height/2+y2, width/2 + x3, height/2 + y3 );
  }

  public void paint( Graphics g ) {
     g.setColor( Color.gray );
     drawWedge( 2*Math.PI * hours / 12, width/5, g );
     drawWedge( 2*Math.PI * minutes / 60, width/3, g );
     drawHand( 2*Math.PI * seconds / 60, width/2, g );
     g.setColor( Color.white );
     g.drawString( timeString, 10, height-10 );
  }
}
```

Save as : The above program can be saved as:

```
Clock1.java
```

HTML Code for program:

```
<applet width=300 height=300 code="Clock1.class"> </applet>
```

Save as: The html code can be saved as:

```
Clock1.html
```

Compile as : The above program can be compiled as:

```
javac Clock1.java
```

Run as : The above program will be run as:

```
appletviewer Clock1.html
```

Output : The output of the program will be:

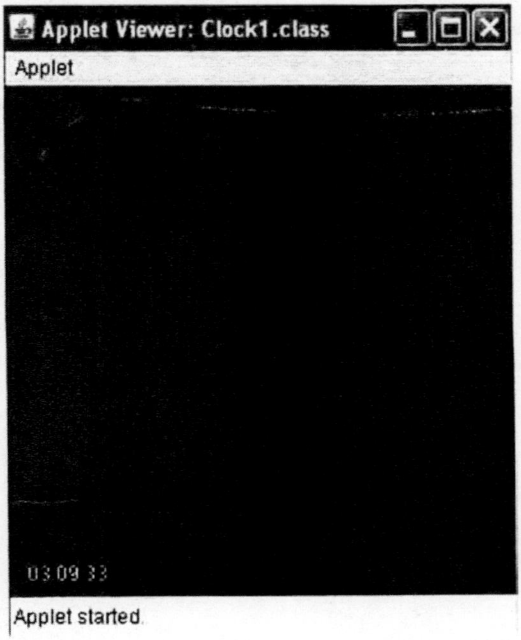

13.1.69. Program to show life cycle of thread using applet

```
import java.applet.*;
import java.awt.*;
public class Threads1 extends Applet implements Runnable {
   int width, height;
   int i = 0;
   Thread t = null;
   boolean threadSuspended;

   // Executed when the applet is first created.
   public void init() {
      System.out.println("init(): begin");
      width = getSize().width;
      height = getSize().height;
      setBackground( Color.black );
      System.out.println("init(): end");
   }

   // Executed when the applet is destroyed.
   public void destroy() {
      System.out.println("destroy()");
   }

   // Executed after the applet is created; and also whenever
   // the browser returns to the page containing the applet.
   public void start() {
      System.out.println("start(): begin");
      if ( t == null ) {
         System.out.println("start(): creating thread");
         t = new Thread( this );
         System.out.println("start(): starting thread");
         threadSuspended = false;
         t.start();
      }
      else {
         if ( threadSuspended ) {
            threadSuspended = false;
            System.out.println("start(): notifying thread");
            synchronized( this ) {
               notify();
            }
         }
      }
```

```
    System.out.println("start(): end");
  }

  // Executed whenever the browser leaves the page containing
the applet.
  public void stop() {
    System.out.println("stop(): begin");
     threadSuspended = true;
  }

  // Executed within the thread that this applet created.
  public void run() {
    System.out.println("run(): begin");
     try {
        while (true) {
          System.out.println("run(): awake");

          // Here's where the thread does some work
          ++i;  // this is shorthand for "i = i+1;"
          if ( i == 10 ) {
              i = 0;
          }
          showStatus( "i is " + i );

  // Now the thread checks to see if it should suspend itself
          if ( threadSuspended ) {
             synchronized( this ) {
                while ( threadSuspended ) {
                   System.out.println("run(): waiting");
                   wait();
                }
             }
          }
         System.out.println("run(): requesting repaint");
          repaint();
         System.out.println("run(): sleeping");
         t.sleep( 1000 );  // interval given in milliseconds
       }
     }
    catch (InterruptedException e) { }
   System.out.println("run(): end");
  }

  // Executed whenever the applet is asked to redraw itself.
```

```
    public void paint( Graphics g ) {
      System.out.println("paint()");
       g.setColor( Color.green );
       g.drawLine( width, height, i * width / 10, 0 );
    }
  }
```

Save as : The above program can be saved as:

```
Threads1.java
```

HTML Code for program :

```
<applet width=300 height=300 code="Threads1.class"> </applet>
```

Save as : The html code can be saved as:

```
Threads1.html
```

Compile as : The above program can be compiled as:

```
javac Threads1.java
```

Run as : The above program will be run as:

```
appletviewer Threads1.html
```

Output: The output of the program will be:

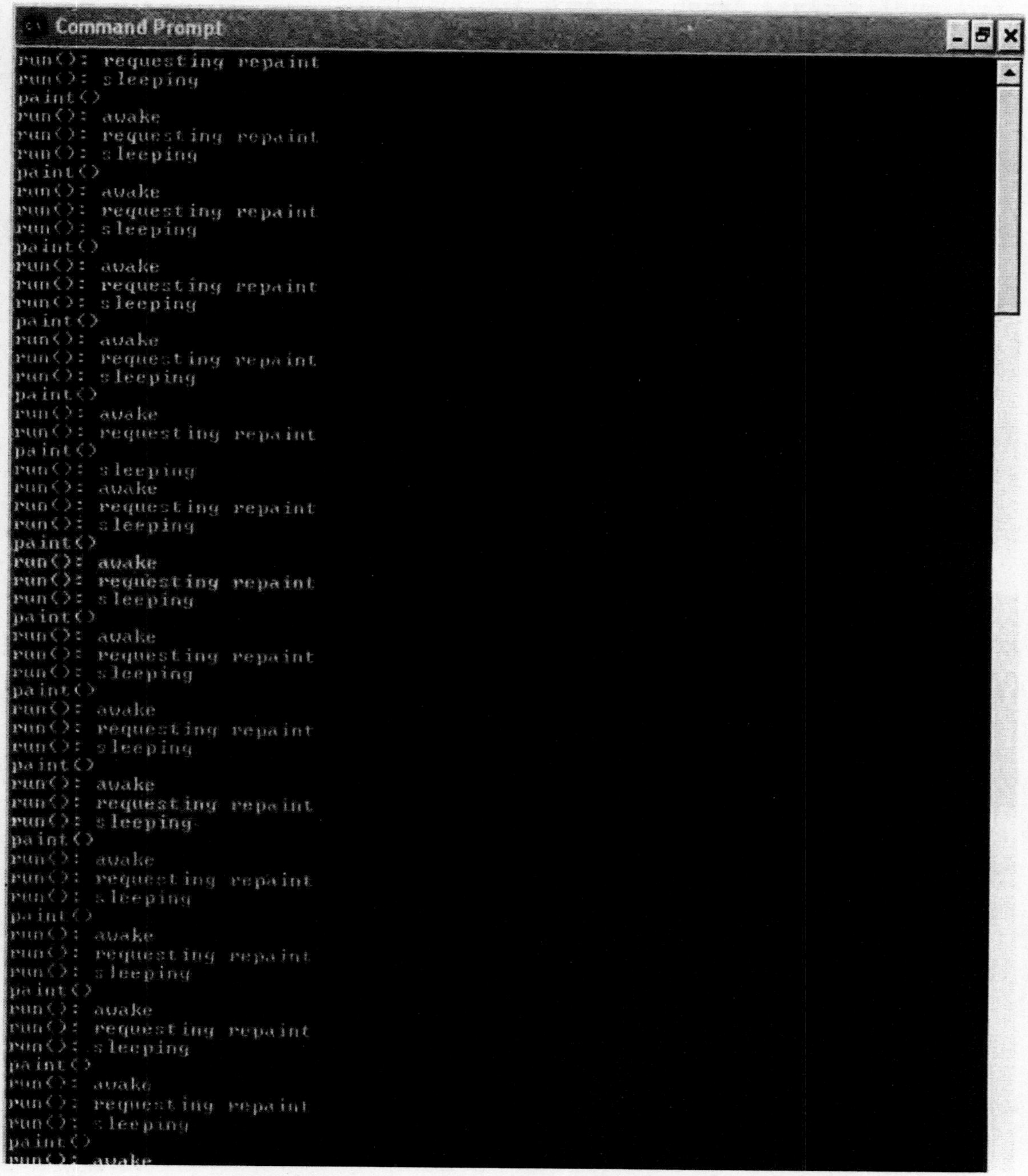

13.1.70. Program to use paint brush in applet using event handling.

```
import java.applet.*;
import java.awt.*;
import java.awt.event.*;
```

```
public class Brush1 extends Applet
   implements MouseMotionListener {

    int width, height;
    Image backbuffer;
    Graphics backg;

    public void init() {
       width = getSize().width;
       height = getSize().height;

       backbuffer = createImage( width, height );
       backg = backbuffer.getGraphics();
       backg.setColor( Color.black );
       backg.fillRect( 0, 0, width, height );
       backg.setColor( Color.white );

       addMouseMotionListener( this );
    }

    public void mouseMoved( MouseEvent e ) { }
    public void mouseDragged( MouseEvent e ) {
       int x = e.getX();
       int y = e.getY();
       backg.fillOval(x-5,y-5,10,10);
       repaint();
       e.consume();
    }

    public void update( Graphics g ) {
       g.drawImage( backbuffer, 0, 0, this );
    }

    public void paint( Graphics g ) {
       update( g );
    }
}
```

Save as : The above program can be saved as:

Brush1.java

HTML Code for program:

```
<applet width=300 height=300 code="Brush1.class"> </applet>
```

Save as : The html code can be saved as:

```
Brush1.html
```

Compile as : The above program can be compiled as:

```
javac Brush1.java
```

Run as : The above program will be run as:

```
appletviewer Brush1.html
```

Output : The output of the program will be:

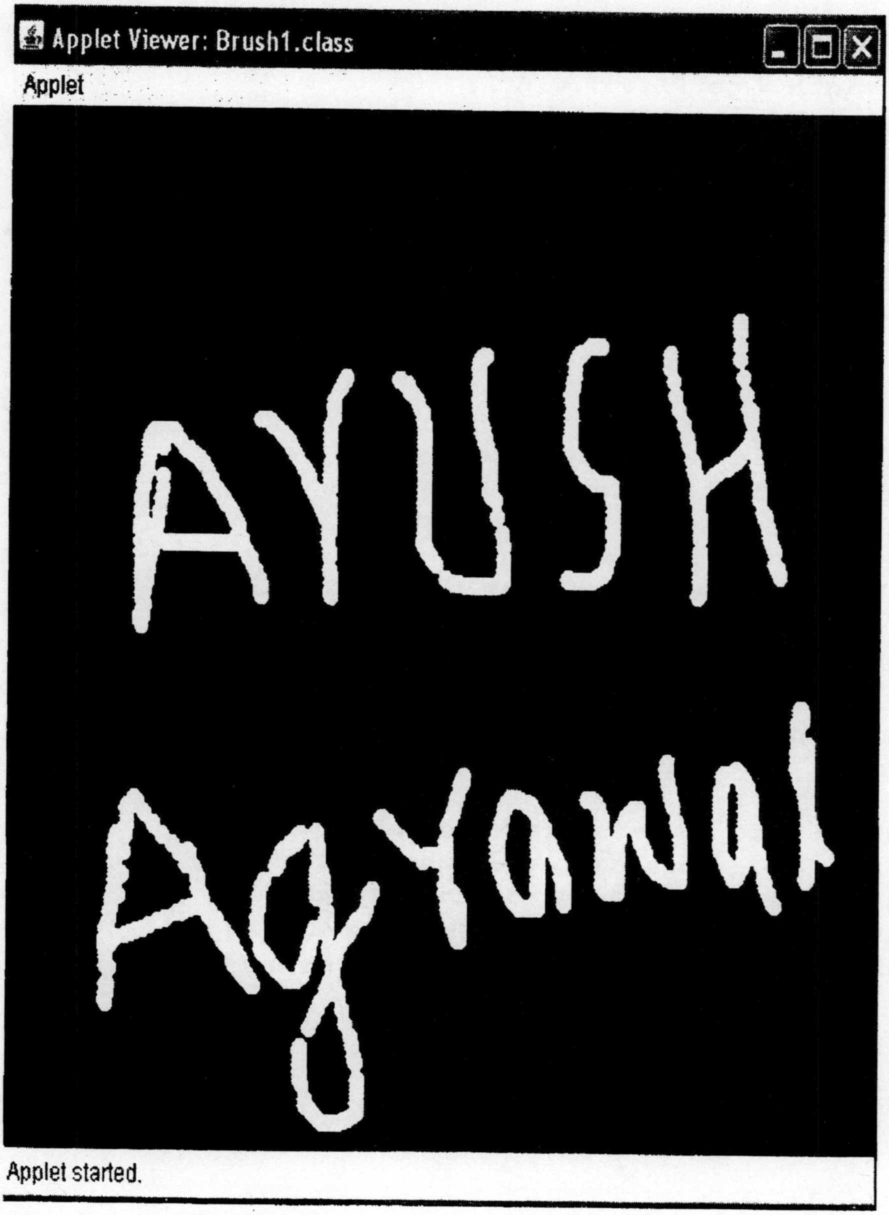

13.1.71. Program to take input through keyboard in applet using event handling.

```
import java.applet.*;
import java.awt.*;
import java.awt.event.*;

public class Keyboard1 extends Applet
  implements KeyListener, MouseListener {

   int width, height;
   int x, y;
   String s = "";

   public void init() {
      width = getSize().width;
      height = getSize().height;
      setBackground( Color.black );

      x = width/2;
      y = height/2;

      addKeyListener( this );
      addMouseListener( this );
   }

   public void keyPressed( KeyEvent e ) { }
   public void keyReleased( KeyEvent e ) { }
   public void keyTyped( KeyEvent e ) {
      char c = e.getKeyChar();
      if ( c != KeyEvent.CHAR_UNDEFINED ) {
         s = s + c;
         repaint();
         e.consume();
      }
   }

   public void mouseEntered( MouseEvent e ) { }
   public void mouseExited( MouseEvent e ) { }
   public void mousePressed( MouseEvent e ) { }
   public void mouseReleased( MouseEvent e ) { }
   public void mouseClicked( MouseEvent e ) {
      x = e.getX();
      y = e.getY();
      s = "";
      repaint();
      e.consume();
   }
```

```
      public void paint( Graphics g ) {
         g.setColor( Color.gray );
         g.drawLine( x, y, x, y-10 );
         g.drawLine( x, y, x+10, y );
         g.setColor( Color.green );
         g.drawString( s, x, y );
      }
   }
```

Save as : The above program can be saved as:

```
Keyboard1.java
```

HTML Code for program:

```
<applet width=300 height=300 code="Keyboard1.class"> </applet>
```

Save as : The html code can be saved as:

```
Keyboard1.html
```

Compile as : The above program can be compiled as:

```
javac Keyboard1.java
```

Run as : The above program will be run as:

```
appletviewer Keyboard1.html
```

Output : The output of the program will be:

13.1.72. Program to take input through Mouse in applet using event handling.

```
import java.applet.*;
import java.awt.*;
import java.awt.event.*;

public class Mouse1 extends Applet
   implements MouseListener, MouseMotionListener {

   int width, height;
   int mx, my;  // the mouse coordinates
   boolean isButtonPressed = false;

   public void init() {
      width = getSize().width;
      height = getSize().height;
      setBackground( Color.black );

      mx = width/2;
      my = height/2;

      addMouseListener( this );
      addMouseMotionListener( this );
   }

   public void mouseEntered( MouseEvent e ) {
      // called when the pointer enters the applet's rectangular
area
   }
   public void mouseExited( MouseEvent e ) {
      // called when the pointer leaves the applet's rectangular
area
   }
   public void mouseClicked( MouseEvent e ) {
      // called after a press and release of a mouse button
      // with no motion in between
      // (If the user presses, drags, and then releases, there
will be
      // no click event generated.)
   }
   public void mousePressed( MouseEvent e ) {  // called after a
button is pressed down
```

```
        isButtonPressed = true;
        setBackground( Color.gray );
        repaint();
        // "Consume" the event so it won't be processed in the
        // default manner by the source which generated it.
        e.consume();
    }
   public void mouseReleased( MouseEvent e ) {  // called after
a button is released
        isButtonPressed = false;
        setBackground( Color.black );
        repaint();
        e.consume();
    }
   public void mouseMoved( MouseEvent e ) {  // called during
motion when no buttons are down
        mx = e.getX();
        my = e.getY();
        showStatus( "Mouse at (" + mx + "," + my + ")" );
        repaint();
        e.consume();
    }
   public void mouseDragged( MouseEvent e ) {  // called during
motion with buttons down
        mx = e.getX();
        my = e.getY();
        showStatus( "Mouse at (" + mx + "," + my + ")" );
        repaint();
        e.consume();
    }

   public void paint( Graphics g ) {
        if ( isButtonPressed ) {
           g.setColor( Color.black );
        }
        else {
           g.setColor( Color.gray );
        }
        g.fillRect( mx-20, my-20, 40, 40 );
    }
}
```

Save as : The above program can be saved as:

```
Mouse1.java
```

HTML Code for program:

```
<applet width=300 height=300 code="Mouse1.class"> </applet>
```

Save as : The html code can be saved as:

```
Mouse1.html
```

Compile as : The above program can be compiled as:

```
javac Mouse1.java
```

Run as : The above program will be run as:

```
appletviewer Mouse1.html
```

Output : The output of the program will be:

13.1.73. Program to take input through Mouse in applet using event handling.

```
import javax.swing.*;
import java.awt.event.*;

public class MasterForm extends JFrame
{
   public MasterForm()
   {
      super("Master Form");

   JButton btnInsert= new JButton("Insert");
   JButton btnUpdate= new JButton("Update");
   JButton btnDelete= new JButton("Delete");
   JButton btnView= new JButton("View");
   JButton btnPrevious= new JButton("Previous");
   JButton btnNext= new JButton("Next");

   JPanel pnlMenu=new JPanel();
   pnlMenu.add(btnInsert);
   pnlMenu.add(btnUpdate);
   pnlMenu.add(btnDelete);
   pnlMenu.add(btnView);
   pnlMenu.add(btnPrevious);
   pnlMenu.add(btnNext);

   btnInsert.setMnemonic('i');
   btnUpdate.setMnemonic('u');
   btnDelete.setMnemonic('d');
   btnView.setMnemonic('v');
   btnPrevious.setMnemonic('p');
   btnNext.setMnemonic('n');

   btnInsert.setToolTipText("To Insert New Records");
   btnUpdate.setToolTipText("To Update New Records");
   btnDelete.setToolTipText("To Delete New Records");
   btnView.setToolTipText("To View Existing Records");
   btnPrevious.setToolTipText("Go to Previous Record");
   btnNext.setToolTipText("Go to Next Record");
   setContentPane(pnlMenu);
   }
```

```
        public static void main(String args[])
        {
            MasterForm frmMaster=new MasterForm();
            frmMaster.setSize(500,300);
            frmMaster.setVisible(true);

            WindowListener listener= new WindowAdapter()
            {
                public void windowClosing(WindowEvent winEvt)
                {
                    System.exit(0);
                }
            };

            frmMaster.addWindowListener(listener);
        }
    }
```

Save as : The above program can be saved as:

```
MasterForm.java
```

Compile as : The above program can be compiled as:

```
javac MasterForm.java
```

Run as : The above program will be run as:

```
java MasterForm
```

Output : The output of the program will be:

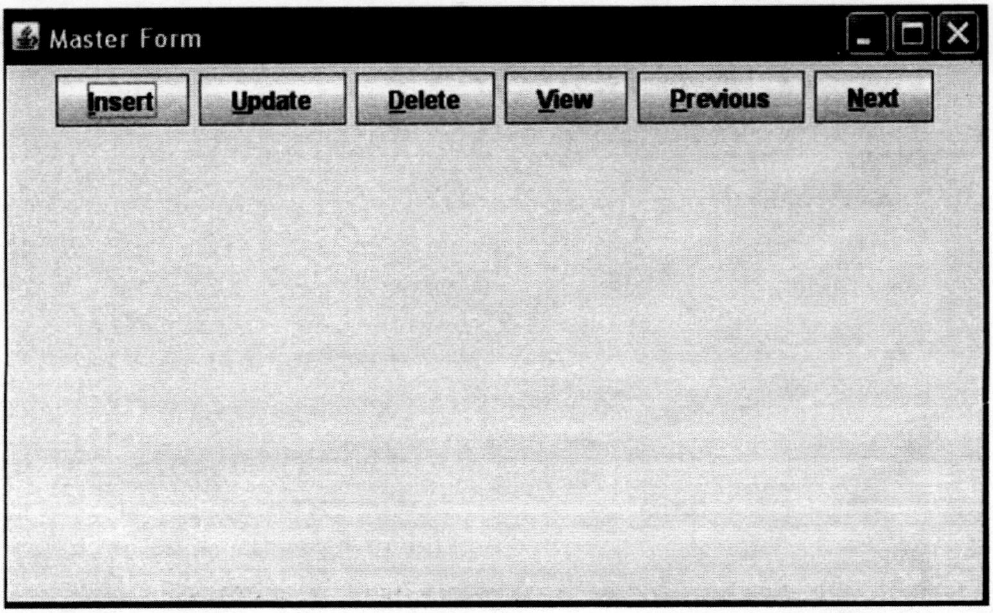

13.1.74. Program to print your name and address in text box with the button submit. On clicking submit the entered information should be shown.

```
import javax.swing.*;
import java.awt.event.*;

public class TextAreaDemo extends JPanel implements ActionListener
{
   JLabel lblName, lblAdd;
   JTextField txtName,txtAdd;
   JTextArea taRemarks;
   JButton btnIcon;

   public TextAreaDemo()
   {

   setLayout(null);

   lblName  = new JLabel("Enter Your Name");
   lblAdd   = new JLabel("Enter Your Address");
   txtName  = new JTextField(15);
   txtAdd   = new JTextField(25);
   taRemarks= new JTextArea(10,10);
   btnIcon  = new JButton("Submit");

   btnIcon.addActionListener(this);

   lblName.setBounds(10,20,120,25);
   txtName.setBounds(150,20,150,25);
   lblAdd.setBounds(10,60,120,25);
   txtAdd.setBounds(150,60,200,25);
   btnIcon.setBounds(120,100,150,30);
   taRemarks.setBounds(30,140,330,100);

   add(lblName);
   add(txtName);
   add(lblAdd);
   add(txtAdd);
   add(btnIcon);
   add(taRemarks);
   }
   public void actionPerformed(ActionEvent actEvt)
   {
      if(actEvt.getSource()==btnIcon)
      {
         taRemarks.append("Name:" +txtName.getText()+"\n");
         taRemarks.append("Address:"+txtAdd.getText()+"\n");
      }
```

```
    }

    public static void main(String args[])
    {
        TextAreaDemo tademo= new TextAreaDemo();
        JFrame frm=new JFrame("Text Area Demo");
        frm.setContentPane(tademo);
        frm.setSize(400,300);
        frm.setVisible(true);
        WindowListener listener=new WindowAdapter()
        {
            public void windowClosing(WindowEvent winEvt)
            {
                    System.exit(0);
            }
        };
        frm.addWindowListener(listener);
    }

}
```

Save as : The above program can be saved as:

```
TextAreaDemo.java
```

Compile as : The above program can be compiled as:

```
javac TextAreaDemo.java
```

Run as : The above program will be run as:

```
java TextArea
```

Output : The output of the program will be:

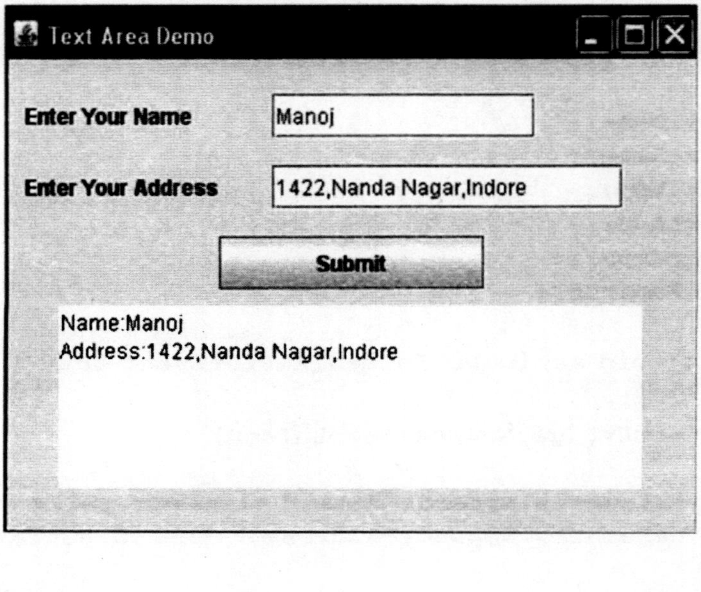

13.1.75. Program to understand the concept of try and catch clause

```
class NumFormExcp
{
    public static void main(String args[])
    {
        try
{
    String str1= new String("text12");
    int num1= Integer.parseInt(str1);
    System.out.println(num1);

        }catch(NumberFormatException e)
{
    System.out.println("##Wrong Number##");
}
}
}
```

Save as : The above program can be saved as:

```
NumFormExcp.java
```

Compile as : The above program can be compiled as:

```
javac NumFormExcp.java
```

Run as : The above program will be run as:

```
java NumFormExcp
```

Output : The output of the program will be:

```
##Wrong Number##
```

13.1.76. Program to understand the concept of Throw clause

```
class Throw_clause
{
Public static void main(String args[])
{
try
{
   throw new NullPointerException();
}catch(NullPointerException e)
{
System.out.println("Invalid Reference Use ");
}}}
```

Save as : The above program can be saved as :

`Throw_Clause.java`

Compile as : The above program will be compile as:

`javac Throw_Clause.java`

Run as : The above program will be run as:

`java Throw_Clause`

Output : In the above program, output will be:

```
Invalid reference use
```

Here, the throw clause throws an object of a system defined exception NullPointerException, which is actually thrown when an object storing a null-pointer is referenced.

13.1.77. Program to understand the concept of Throws clause

```
Class Throws_clause
{
   static void throwExcp() throws IllegalAccessException
{
Throw new IllegalAccessException();

}

public static void main(String arg[])
{
   Try
{
   throwExcp();
}catch(IllegalAccessException e)
{
   System.out.println("Exception Caught");
}}}
```

Save as : The above program can be saved as:

`Throws_clause.java`

Compile as : The above program can be compiled as:

`javac Throws_clause.java`

Run as : The above program will be run as:

`java Throws_clause`

Output : The output of the above program is :

```
Exception Caught
```

13.1.78. Program to understand the concept of threads

```
public class DisplayMessage implements Runnable
{
   private String message;
   public DisplayMessage(String message)
    {
       this.message = message;
    }
   public void run()
    {
       while(true)
        {
          System.out.println(message);
        }
    }
}
public class GuessANumber extends Thread
{
   private int number;
   public GuessANumber(int number)
    {
       this.number = number;
    }
   public void run()
    {
       int counter = 0;
       int guess = 0;
       do
        {
           guess = (int) (Math.random() * 100 + 1);
          System.out.println(this.getName()
                        + " guesses " + guess);
           counter++;
      }while(guess != number);
      System.out.println("** Correct! " + this.getName()
                        + " in " + counter + " guesses.**");
   }
}
public class ThreadClassDemo
{
```

```
    public static void main(String [] args)
    {
      Runnable hello = new DisplayMessage("Hello");
      Thread thread1 = new Thread(hello);
      thread1.setDaemon(true);
      thread1.setName("hello");
      System.out.println("Starting hello thread...");
      thread1.start();

      Runnable bye = new DisplayMessage("Goodbye");
      Thread thread2 = new Thread(hello);
      thread2.setPriority(Thread.MIN_PRIORITY);
      thread2.setDaemon(true);
      System.out.println("Starting goodbye thread...");
      thread2.start();

      System.out.println("Starting thread3...");
      Thread thread3 = new GuessANumber(27);
      thread3.start();
      try
      {
        thread3.join();
      }catch(InterruptedException e)
      {
        System.out.println("Thread interrupted.");
      }
      System.out.println("Starting thread4...");
      Thread thread4 = new GuessANumber(75);

      thread4.start();
      System.out.println("main() is ending...");
    }
}
Starting hello thread...
Starting goodbye thread...
Hello
Hello
Hello
Hello
Hello
Hello
```

```
Hello
Hello
Hello
Thread-2 guesses 27
Hello
** Correct! Thread-2 in 102 guesses.**
Hello
Starting thread4...
Hello
Hello and more...
```

13.2. WEB APPLICATION DEVELOPMENT USING JSP

Well Friends, till now we have learned the theoretical as well as programming approach of Java programming. Now we are going to use both the approaches for developing web application using JSP. So friends have fun with web application of your own.

13.2.1. Prerequisite

Students should have deep knowledge of Java programming and some basic knowledge of html. JSP, *i.e.*, Java Server Pages is a combination of Java and HTML. So friends if you do not read the above mentioned chapters please do it first.

13.2.2. Software Requirement Specification

For developing this web application we need to have the following software install on our computer. The list of software to be installed is given below in table:

S.No.	Name of Software	Version
1.	Java	JDK 1.5/1.6
2.	Microsoft frontpage or Dreamweaver	Comes with office 2000
3.	My Sql	5.0
4.	Sql yog	-
5.	Apache Tomcat	5.5

Well friends please ensure that all the above mentioned software are installed on your computer.

13.2.3. Student Entry System

Student entry system is a web application that keeps the record of student entering into the college. This application is useful in the areas where we need to keep record of the students into the database. We are just digitalizing the registration form that student enters to keep their record into the file system.

13.2.4. Objective

The objective of student entry system is to digitalize the registration scheme of the students.

13.2.5. Scope

The scope of the project is very wide. We can use the application into any of the college system where we need to keep the record of each student. We can also use the same application into the school system to handle the laborious task of file maintenance. After further modifications the same application is useful for maintaining record into the universities.

13.2.6. Goal

Our goal is to make the application as shown in the illustration below:

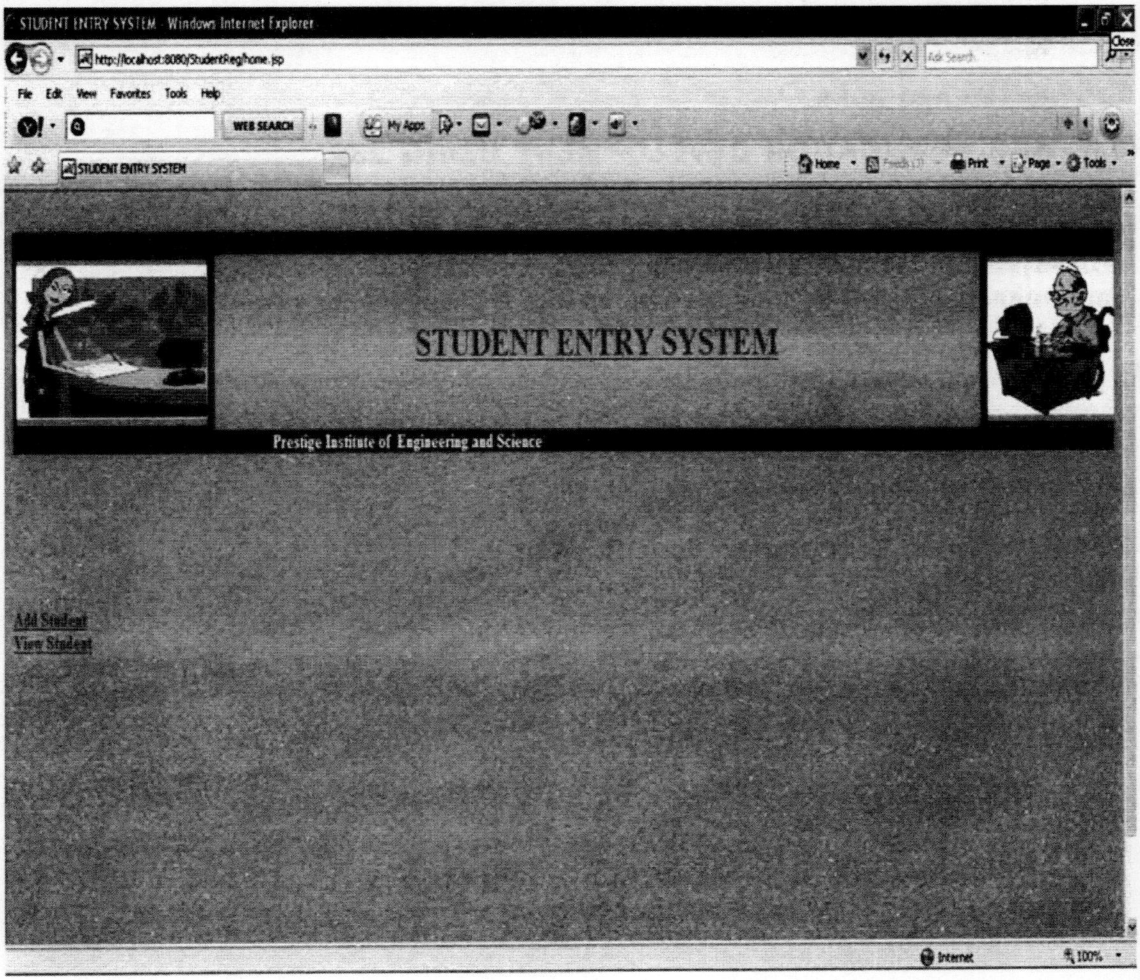

13.2.7. Steps for Creating Web Application

Well friends, now we are going to follow some steps for creating web application which makes the process of creating web application easy to use.

Step 1: Creation of the database: In the first step we are going to develop a database which is used to keep record of the student. For that we need to install mysql and sqlyog to make the task easier. Now, we can create the database as mentioned in illustration below.

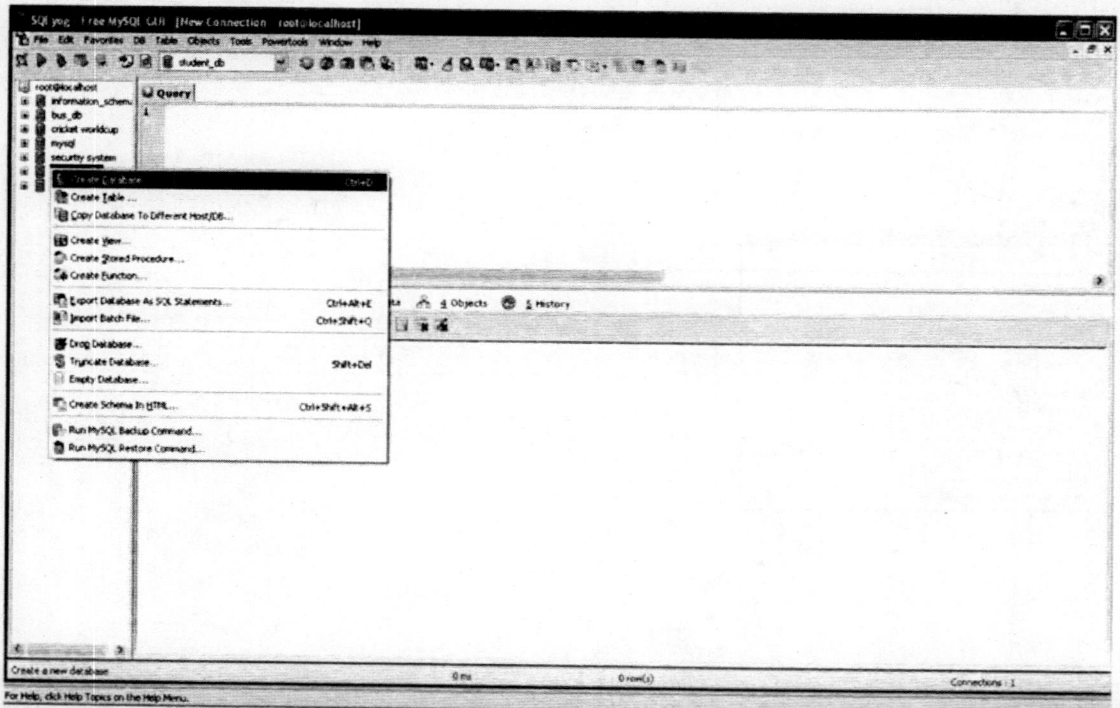

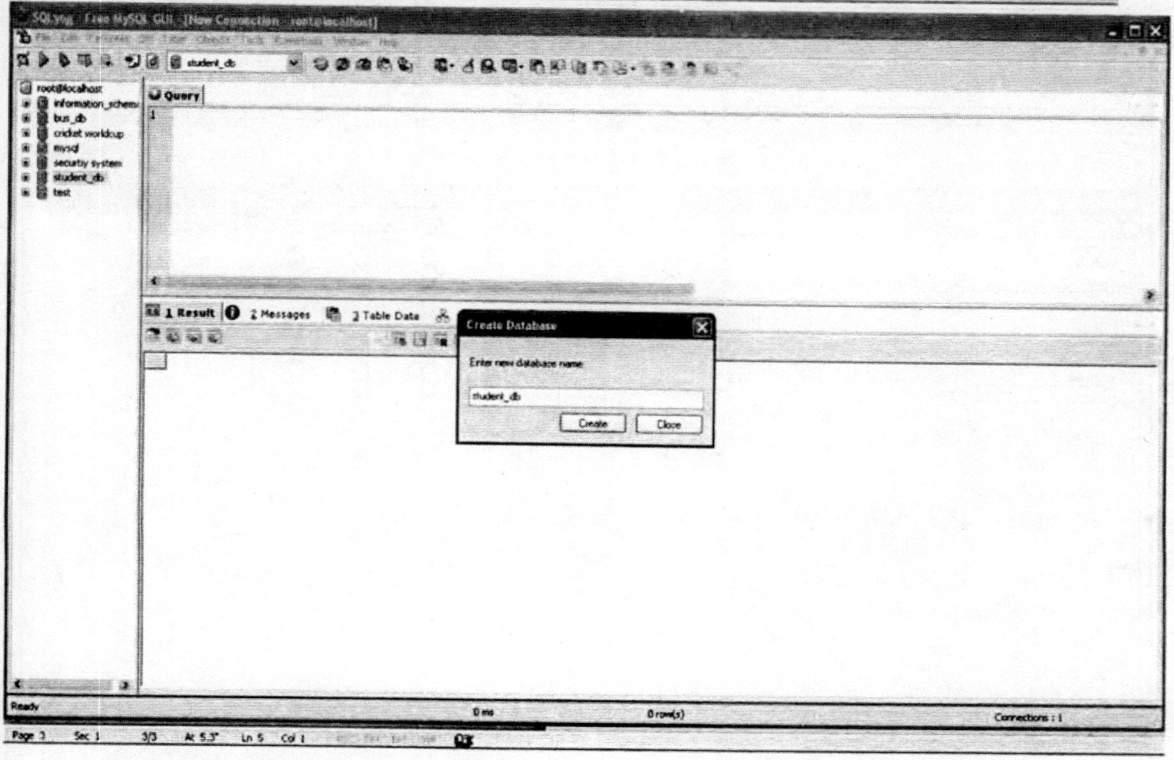

Step 2 : Create table into the database: Now friends, the next step is to create table into the database. This is shown below into the illustration.

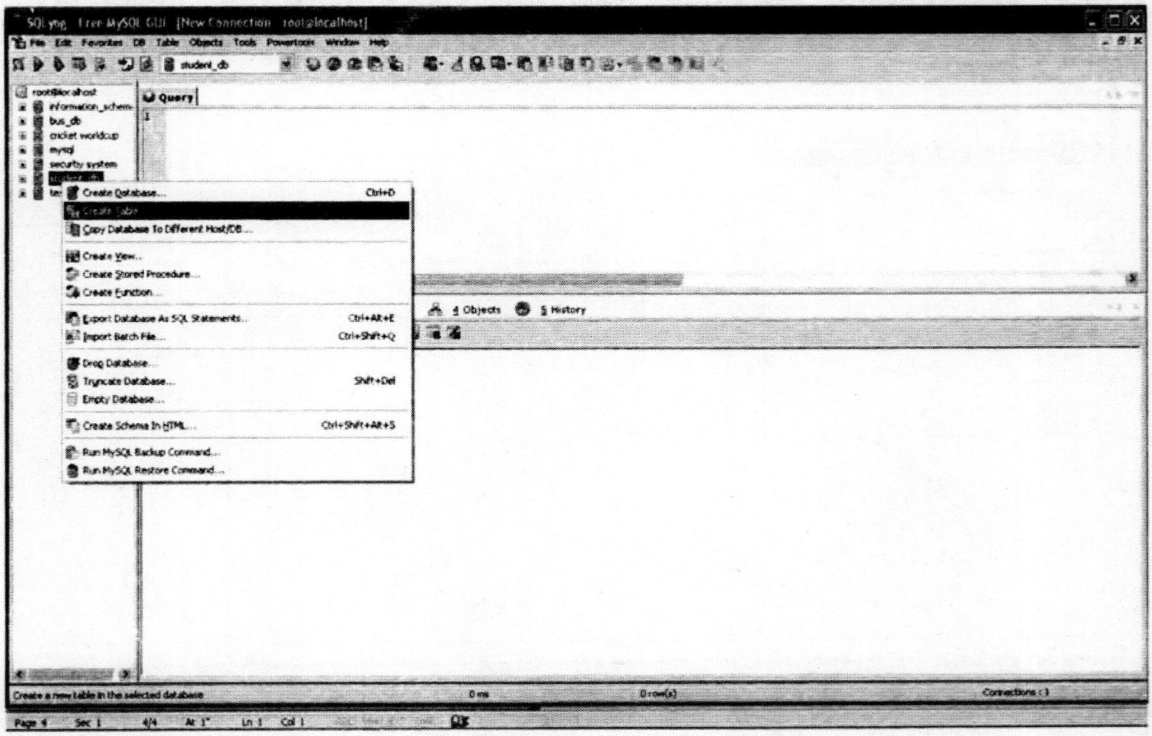
Create Database...
Create Table
Copy Database To Different Host/DB...
Create View...
Create Stored Procedure...
Create Function...
Export Database As SQL Statements...
Import Batch File...
Drop Database...
Truncate Database...
Empty Database...
Create Schema In HTML...
Run MySQL Backup Command...
Run MySQL Restore Command...

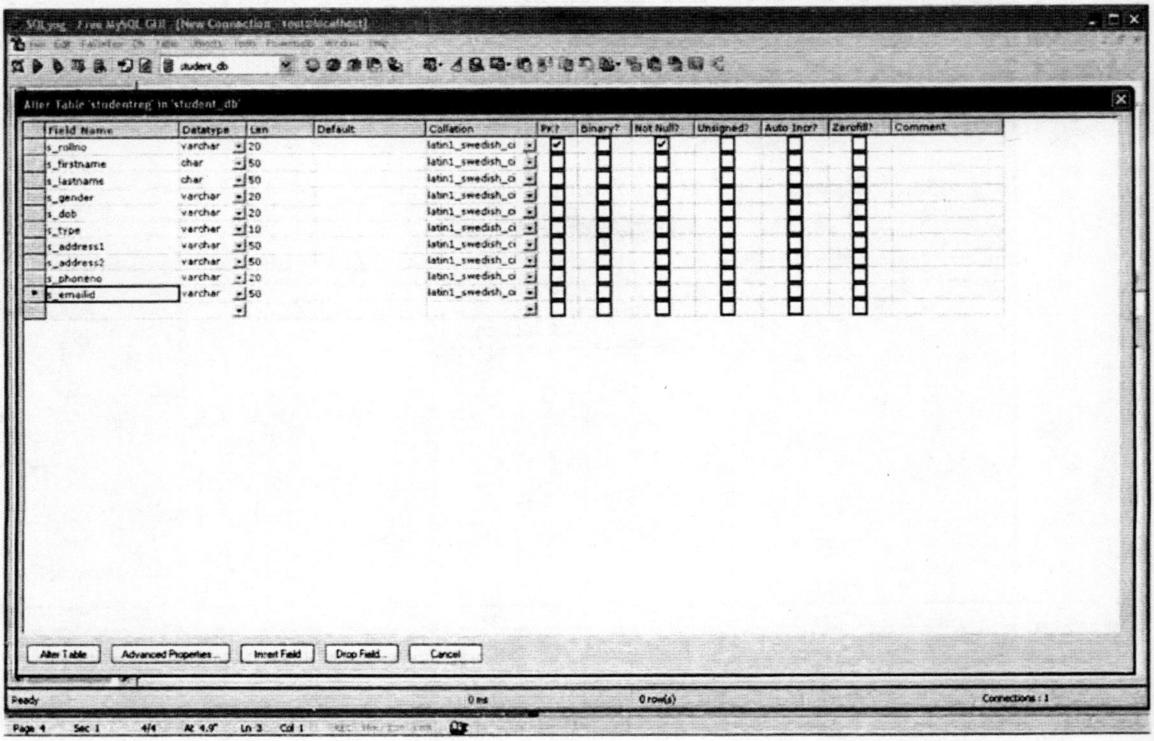
Alter Table 'studentreg' in 'student_db'
Field Name
Datatype
Len
Default
Collation
s_rollno
s_firstname
s_lastname
s_gender
s_dob
s_type
s_address1
s_address2
s_phoneno
s_emailid
Alter Table
Advanced Properties...
Insert Field
Drop Field...
Cancel

The above mentioned database will look like:

S.No	Name	Data Type	Length	Remark
1.	s_rollno	varchar	20	Primary key
2.	s_firstname	varchar	50	Not Null
3.	s_lastname	varchar	50	Not Null
4.	s_gender	varchar	20	Not Null
5.	s_dob	varchar	20	Not Null
6.	s_type	varchar	10	Not Null
7.	s_address1	varchar	50	Not Null
8.	s_address2	varchar	50	Not Null
9.	s_phoneno	varchar	20	Not Null
10	s_emailid	varchar	50	Not Null

Step 3: Create folder into apache tomcat folder: Well friends, after completing the development of database the next step is to create a folder named as "**StudentReg**" into the location given below:

```
C:\Program Files\Apache Software Foundation\Tomcat 5.5\webapps
```

Step 4 : Paste the Web-Inf folder from inbuilt folder: Well friends, after creating the **"StudentReg"** folder, the next step is to copy the Web-Inf folder from the folder named as "Root"(Root is autogenerated folder in the location **C:\Program Files\Apache Software Foundation\Tomcat 5.5\webapps**). After copy the Web-Inf folder from the above mentioned location lets paste the folder into the "**StudentReg**" folder.

Step 5 : Creation of web pages: Well friends, now the time has come to create the web pages. For creating the web pages we first create a layout page using Microsoft frontpage or dreamweaver.

(*a*) Open the Microsoft frontpage, create new file and save the file in our created folder StudentReg as "Layout.jsp". Inside this file, first create a table with 8 row and then right click and go to table properties and set table size to 0. This will show the table without boundaries. Now, select the fourth row of the table and divide this row into three columns and inside the same row press enter button thrice. Now select the whole table and set the background colour to sky blue as shown below in illustration.

(*b*) Now friends after creating the layout page now create new Microsoft frontpage file and save the webpage as mycon.jsp. Inside the page, open the html code and delete the code written there. Now write there a new code as:

```
<%@ page import="java.sql.*" %>
<%Class.forName("com.mysql.jdbc.Driver");
Connection con=DriverManager.getConnection("jdbc:mysql://
localhost:3306/securtiy system","root","root");
%>
```

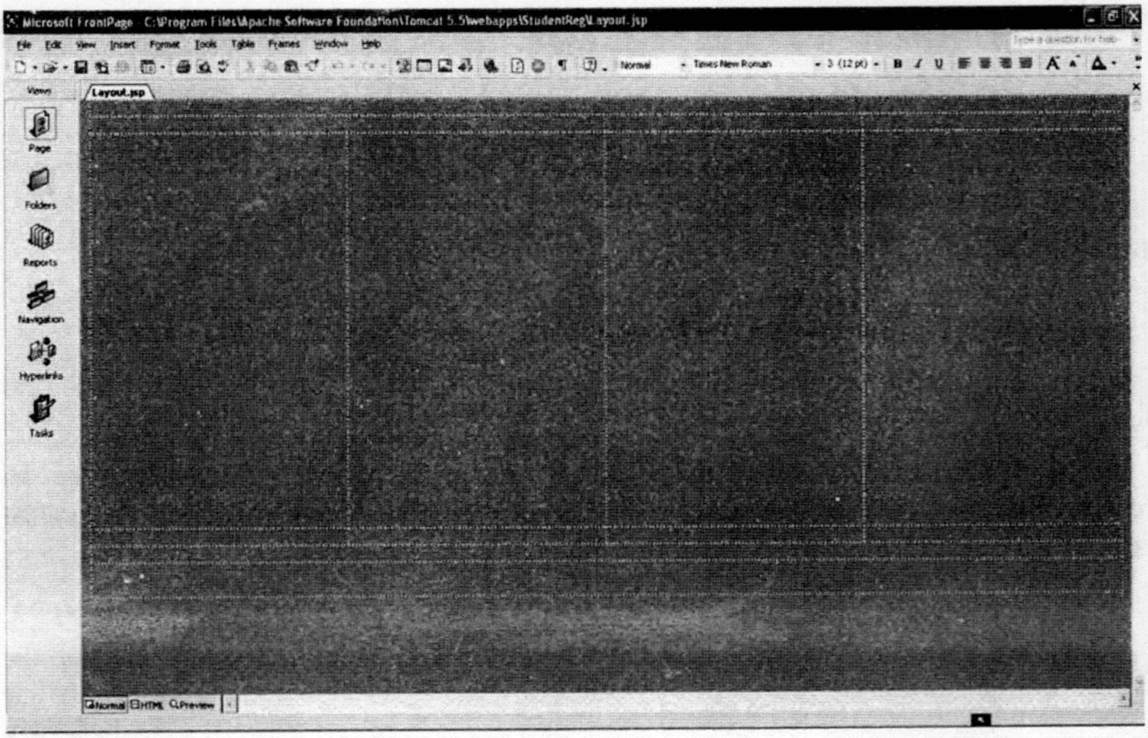
Microsoft FrontPage - C:\Program Files\Apache Software Foundation\Tomcat 5.5\webapps\StudentReg\Layout.jsp
File Edit View Insert Format Tools Table Frames Window Help
Views
Layout.jsp
Page
Folders
Reports
Navigation
Hyperlinks
Tasks
Normal HTML Preview

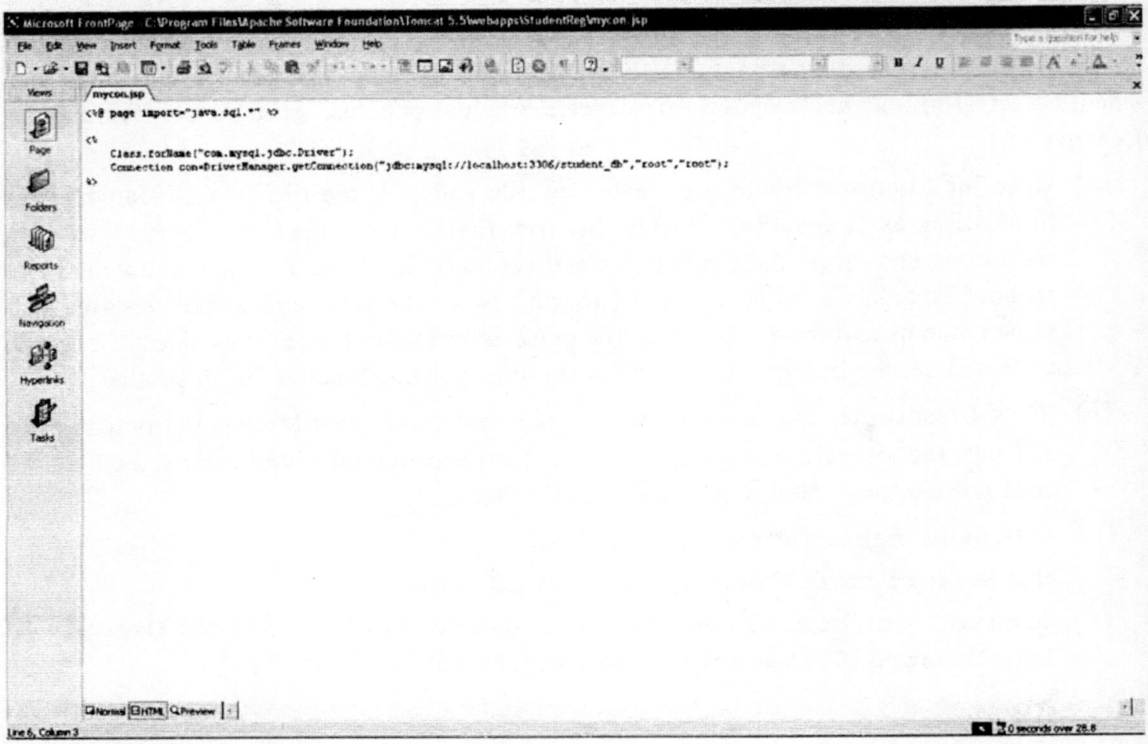
Microsoft FrontPage - C:\Program Files\Apache Software Foundation\Tomcat 5.5\webapps\StudentReg\mycon.jsp
File Edit View Insert Format Tools Table Frames Window Help
Views
mycon.jsp
<%@ page import="java.sql.*" %>
<%
Class.forName("com.mysql.jdbc.Driver");
Connection con=DriverManager.getConnection("jdbc:mysql://localhost:3306/student_db","root","root");
%>
Page
Folders
Reports
Navigation
Hyperlinks
Tasks
Normal HTML Preview
Line 6, Column 3
0 seconds over 28.8

(*c*) Now friends, we can create a head page as shown below:

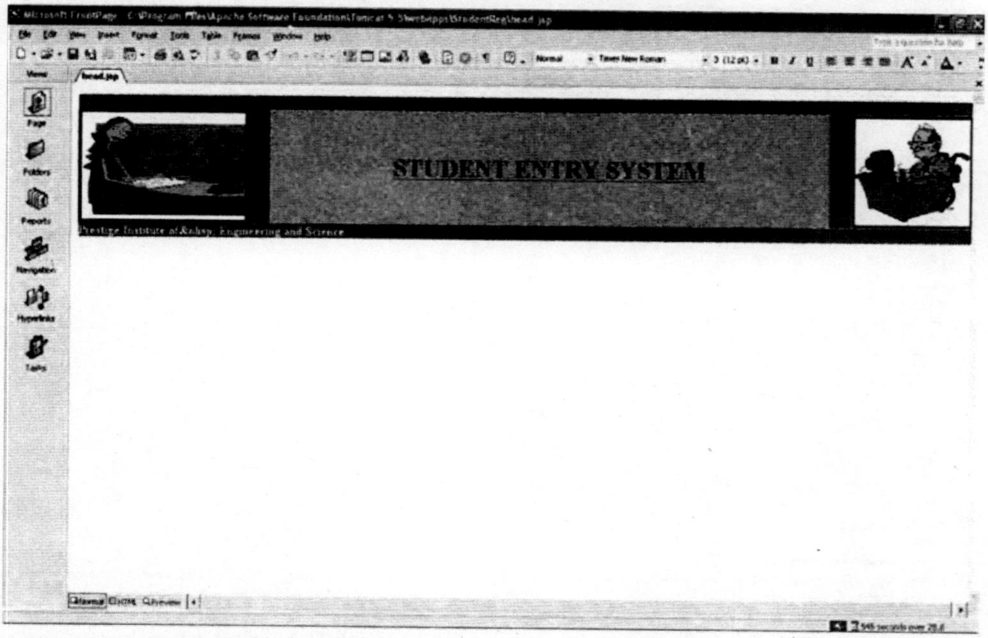

Now friends, select onto the college name that you had written onto the web page and then write around it as:

<marquee>Prestige Institute of Engineering and Science</marquee>

This will move the text from one end to another.

(*d*) Similarly friends lets create the foot page save as foot.jsp. Insert a table inside it with one row and set the table size to 0. In this page we will write the the text as:

<marquee>@developed by Piyush Choudhary</marquee>

This will look like as:

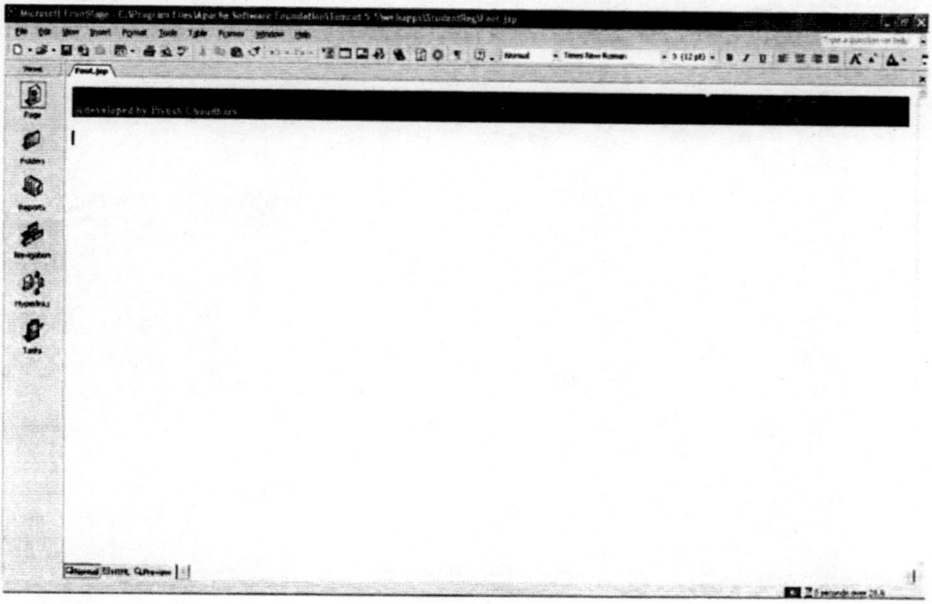

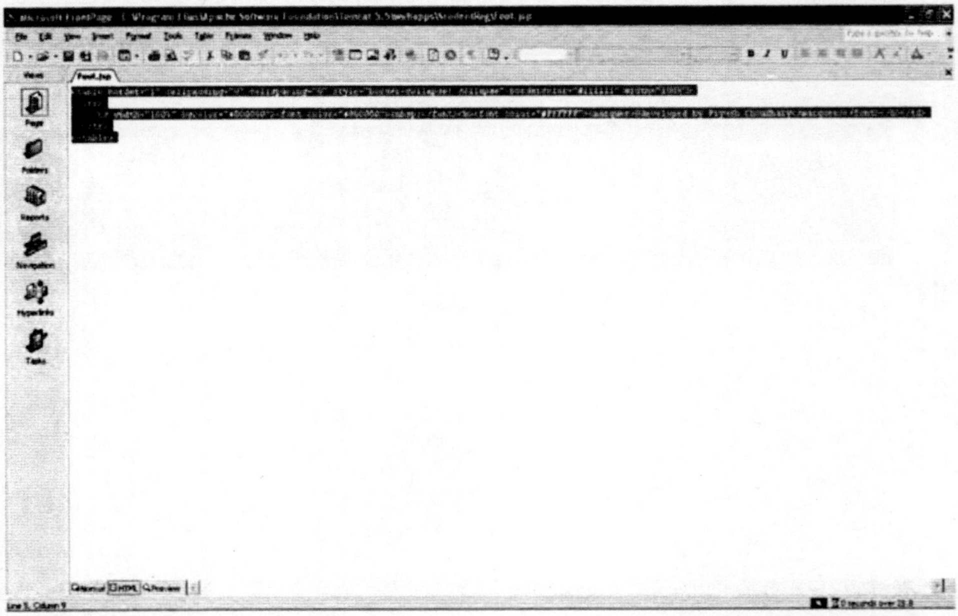

(*e*) Now friends, lets open the layout page which we had created earlier. Now save as the page as "home.jsp". In home.jsp, the table was shown with 0 borders as in layout page. Select the first row of the table click on the html tag press the arrow key and write code there as:

```
<%@ include file="head.jsp" %>
```

Similarly, select the last row of the table, click on the html tag press the arrow key and write code there as:

```
<%@ include file="Foot.jsp" %>
```

In the first column of the third row lets enter a table of size two rows with size 0.

In the first row of the new table created enter AddStudent and in the next row enter ViewStudent. Now create new webpages by saving layout page as the AddStudent.jsp and ViewStudent.jsp. Create a link to both the statements to the pages mentioned above.

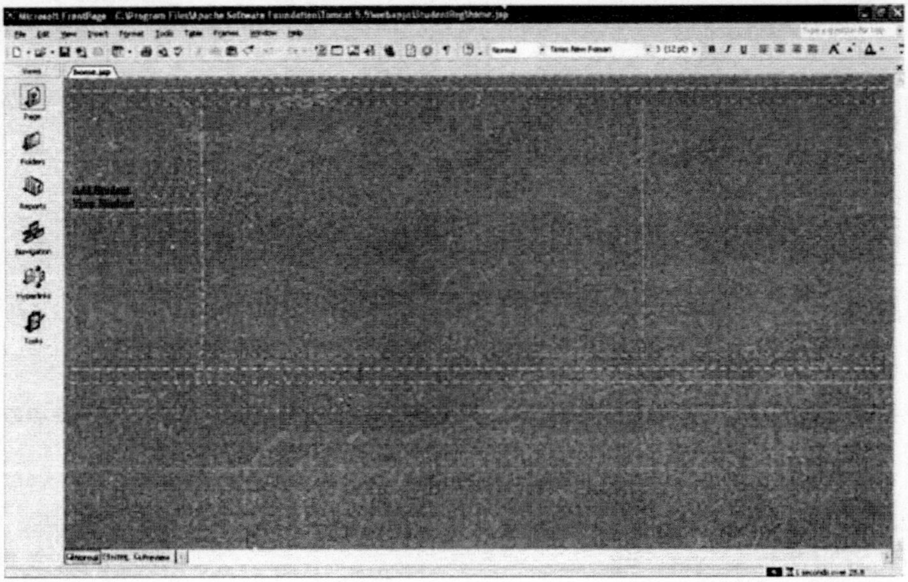

(*f*) Now open the AddStudent.jsp and make the registration form as shown below with the fields as mentioned into the database.

Note: The name of the text box, dropdown box etc. should be same as in the database. For example: The name for textfield accepting rollno should be s_rollno.

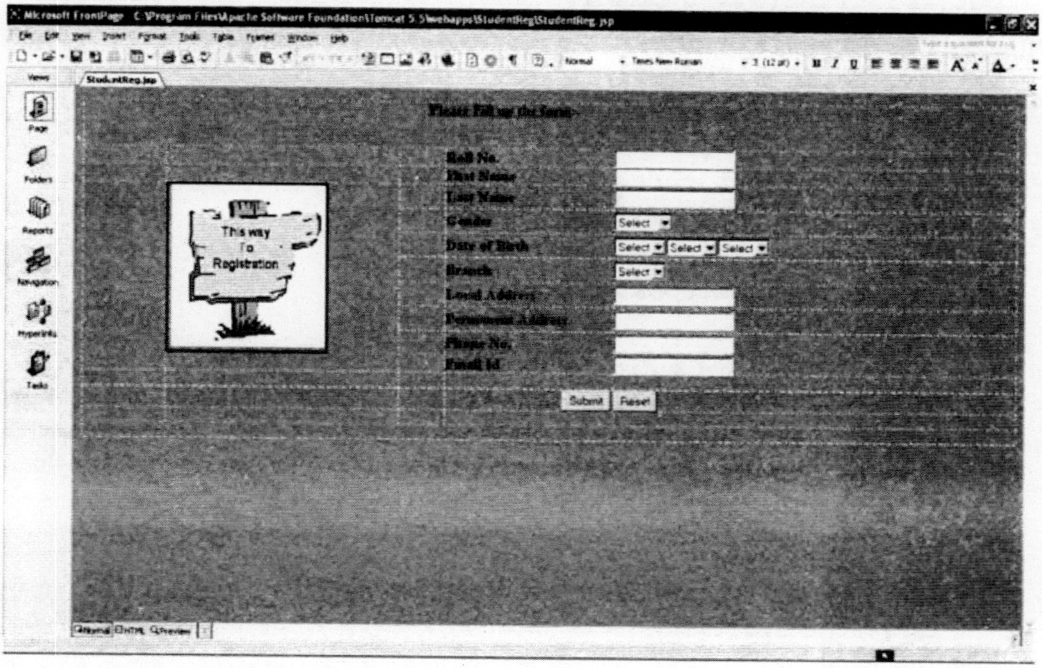

(*g*) Now create a new web page entitled as addstudentreg.jsp and clear all the html tag of this and put the following code inside that.

```
<%@ include file="mycon.jsp" %>
<%
String s_rollno=request.getParameter("s_rollno");
String s_firstname=request.getParameter("s_firstname");
String s_lastname=request.getParameter("s_lastname");
String s_gender=request.getParameter("s_gender");
String d1=request.getParameter("dd");
String d2=request.getParameter("mm");
String d3=request.getParameter("yy");
String s_dob=d1+"/"+d2+"/"+d3;
String s_type=request.getParameter("s_type");
String s_address1=request.getParameter("s_address1");
String s_address2=request.getParameter("s_address2");
String s_phoneno=request.getParameter("s_phoneno");
String s_emailid=request.getParameter("s_emailid");

PreparedStatement pst=con.prepareStatement("insert into
studentreg(s_rollno,s_firstname,s_lastname,s_gender,s_dob,
s_type,s_ address1,s_address2,s_phoneno,s_emailid) values
```

```
(?,?,?,?,?,?,?,?,?,?)");
pst.setString(1,s_rollno);
pst.setString(2,s_firstname);
pst.setString(3,s_lastname);
pst.setString(4,s_gender);
pst.setString(5,s_dob);
pst.setString(6,s_type);
pst.setString(7,s_address1);
pst.setString(8,s_address2);
pst.setString(9,s_phoneno);
pst.setString(10,s_emailid);

int r1=pst.executeUpdate();
%>
{
%> </font> <font size="4"><font face="Times New Roman"
color="#800000">Data Inserted Successfully</font><font face="Times
New Roman" color="#000080">
<%
}
else
%><%
pst.close();
con.close();
%>
```

Now, again open the Addstudent.jsp and its html code enter the information as:

```
<form method="POST" action="insertstudentreg.jsp">
```

(*h*) Now friends create a View page as shown below:

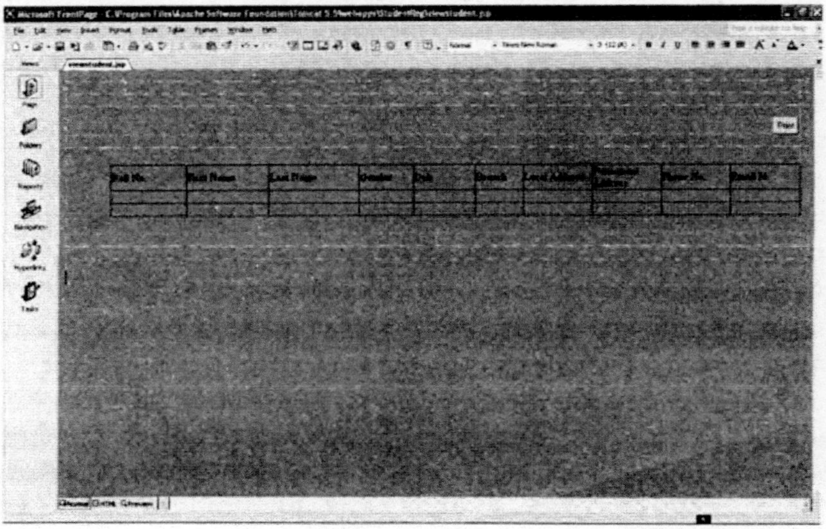

And its html code look like as:

```
<body bgcolor="#CC99FF">
<%@ include file ="mycon.jsp" %>
<%
PreparedStatement pst=con.prepareStatement("select * from studentreg");
ResultSet rs=pst.executeQuery();
%>

<form method="POST" action="—WEBBOT-SELF—">
  </form>
  <!—webbot bot="SaveResults" u-file="C:\Program Files\Apache
Software  Foundation\Tomcat  5.5\webapps\StudentReg\_private\
form_results.csv" s-format="TEXT/CSV" s-label-fields="TRUE" —
><form method="POST" action="—WEBBOT-SELF—">
  <!—webbot bot="SaveResults" u-file="C:\Program Files\Apache
Software Foundation\Tomcat 5.5\webapps\StudentReg\_private\form_
results.csv" s-format="TEXT/CSV" s-label-fields="TRUE" —><table
border="0" cellpadding="0" cellspacing="0" style="border-collapse:
collapse" bordercolor="#111111" width="100%">
    <tr>
   <td width="100%" colspan="4"> <%@ include file="head.jsp"
%>
</td>
    </tr>
    <tr>
     <td width="6%"> </td>
     <td width="44%"> </td>
     <td width="49%"> </td>
     <td width="1%"> </td>
    </tr>
    <tr>
     <td width="6%"> </td>
     <td width="44%"> </td>
     <td width="49%"> </td>
     <td width="1%"> </td>
    </tr>
    <tr>
     <td width="6%"> </td>
     <td width="93%" colspan="2"> </td>
     <td width="1%"> </td>
```

```
        </tr>
        <tr>
         <td width="6%"> </td>
         <td width="93%" colspan="2">
          <p align="left">
           <b>
        <input type="button" value="Print" onClick="window.print()"
name="B1" style="float: right"></b></td>
         <td width="1%"> </td>
        </tr>
        <tr>
         <td width="6%"> </td>
         <td width="93%" colspan="2"> </td>
         <td width="1%"> </td>
        </tr>
        <tr>
          <td width="6%">
          <p> </p>
          <p> </p>
          <p> </p>
          <p> </td>
         <td width="93%" colspan="2">
              <table border="1" cellpadding="0" cellspacing="0"
style="border-collapse: collapse" bordercolor="#111111"
width="100%">
            <tr>
             <td width="11%"><b>Roll No.</b></td>
             <td width="12%"><b>First Name</b></td>
             <td width="13%"><b>Last Name</b></td>
             <td width="8%"><b>Gender</b></td>
             <td width="9%"><b>Dob</b></td>
             <td width="7%"><b>Branch</b></td>
             <td width="10%"><b>Local Address</b></td>
             <td width="10%"><b>Permanent Address</b></td>
             <td width="10%"><b>Phone No.</b></td>
             <td width="10%"><b>Email Id</b></td>
            </tr>

              <% if(rs.next())

          {
```

```
 do{
String s_rollno=rs.getString("s_rollno");
String s_firstname=rs.getString("s_firstname");
String s_lastname=rs.getString("s_lastname");
String s_gender=rs.getString("s_gender");
String s_dob=rs.getString("s_dob");
String s_type=rs.getString("s_type");
String s_address1=rs.getString("s_address1");
String s_address2=rs.getString("s_address2");
String s_phoneno=rs.getString("s_phoneno");
String s_emailid=rs.getString("s_emailid");
 %>
   <tr>
    <td width="11%"> <%=s_rollno%></td>
    <td width="12%"> <%=s_firstname%></td>
    <td width="13%"> <%=s_lastname%></td>
    <td width="8%"> <%=s_gender%></td>
    <td width="9%"> <%=s_dob%></td>
    <td width="7%"> <%=s_type%></td>
    <td width="10%"> <%=s_address1%></td>
    <td width="10%"> <%=s_address2%></td>
    <td width="10%"> <%=s_phoneno%></td>
    <td width="10%"> <%=s_emailid%></td>
   </tr>

 <%
}while(rs.next());
 }
rs.close();
pst.close();
con.close();
 %>
   <tr>
    <td width="11%"> </td>
    <td width="12%"> </td>
    <td width="13%"> </td>
    <td width="8%"> </td>
    <td width="9%"> </td>
    <td width="7%"> </td>
    <td width="10%"> </td>
    <td width="10%"> </td>
    <td width="10%"> </td>
    <td width="10%"> </td>
```

```
          </tr>
         </table>
         </td>
        <td width="1%"> </td>
       </tr>
       <tr>
        <td width="6%"> </td>
        <td width="44%"> </td>
        <td width="49%"> </td>
        <td width="1%"> </td>
       </tr>
       <tr>
             <td  width="100%"  colspan="4"> <%@  include
  file="Foot.jsp" %>
  </td>
       </tr>
     </table>
     <p> </p>
  </form>
```

(*i*) Now friends, from the start menu open the apache tomcat and configure it to start. After that open internet explorer and in the address bar as:

```
http://localhost:8080
```

Now enter the id and password given at the time of installation. Select in tomcat manager Studentreg and open the home page. The complete application will look like as:

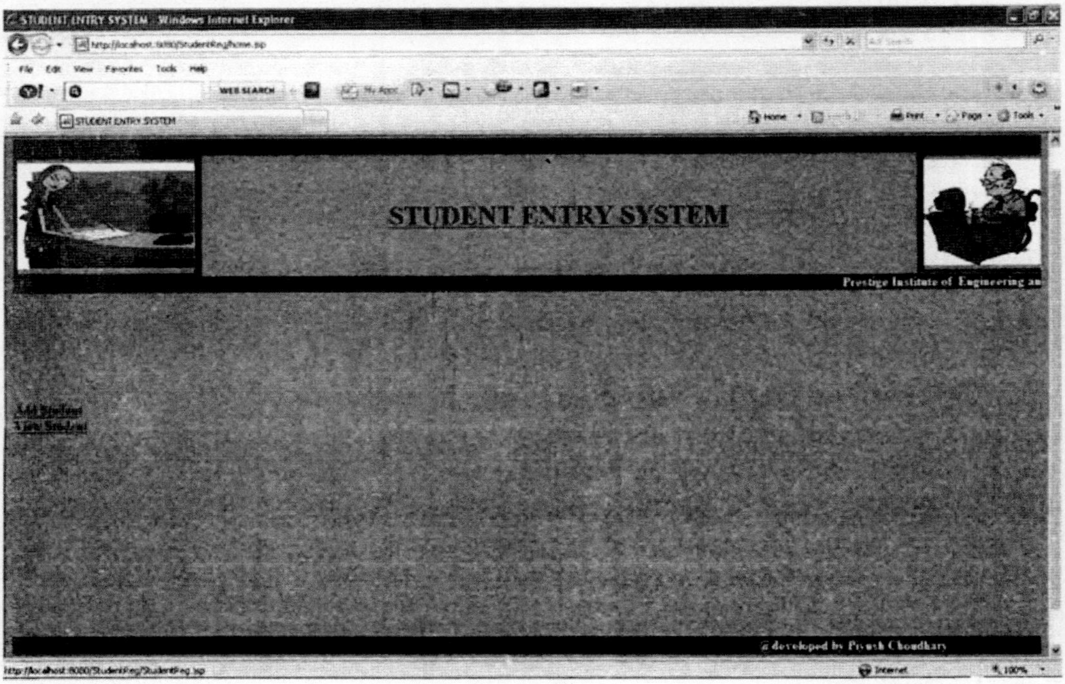

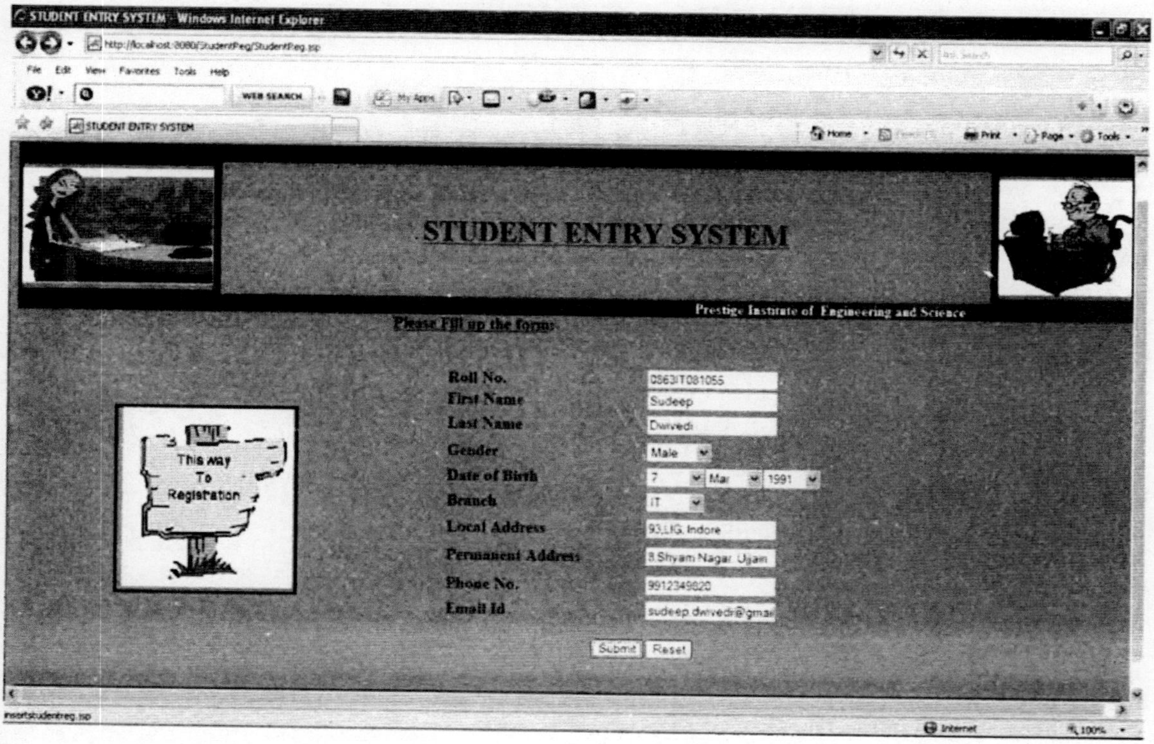
STUDENT ENTRY SYSTEM - Windows Internet Explorer
STUDENT ENTRY SYSTEM
Prestige Institute of Engineering and Science
Please Fill up the form:
This way To Registration
Roll No.
0863IT081055
First Name
Sudeep
Last Name
Dwivedi
Gender
Male
Date of Birth
7
Mar
1991
Branch
IT
Local Address
93,LIG, Indore
Permanent Address
8 Shyam Nagar, Ujjain
Phone No.
9912349820
Email Id
Submit
Reset

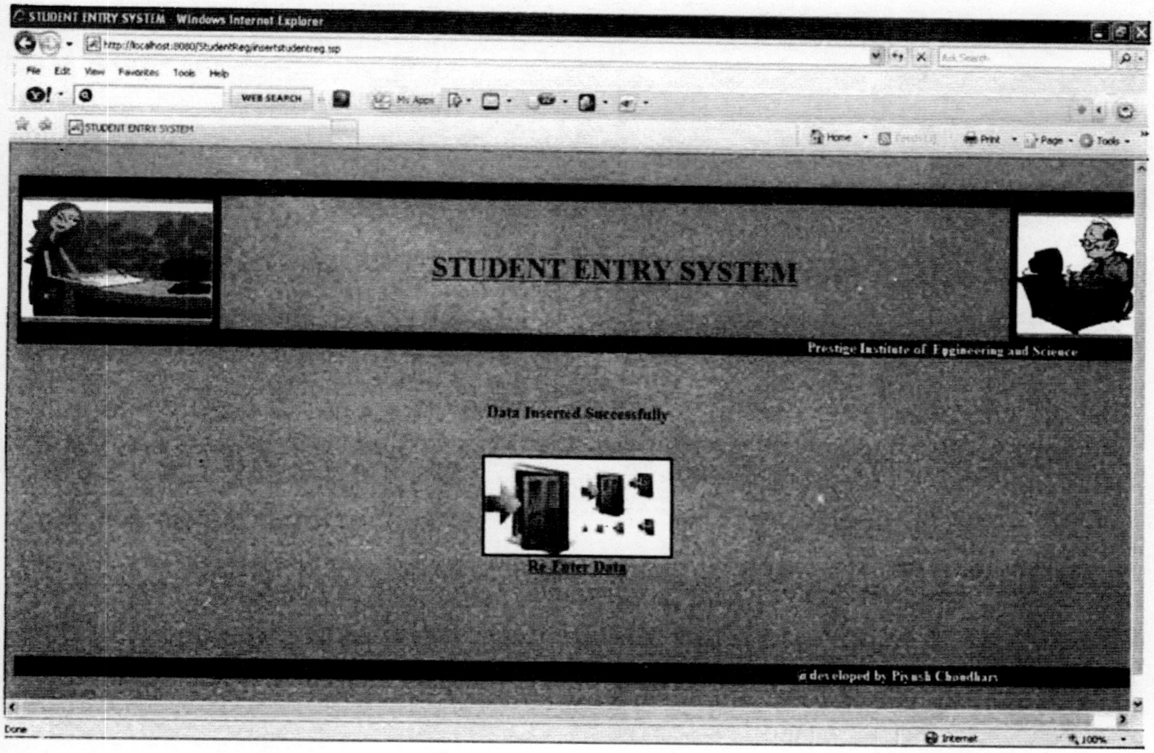
STUDENT ENTRY SYSTEM - Windows Internet Explorer
STUDENT ENTRY SYSTEM
Prestige Institute of Engineering and Science
Data Inserted Successfully
Re Enter Data

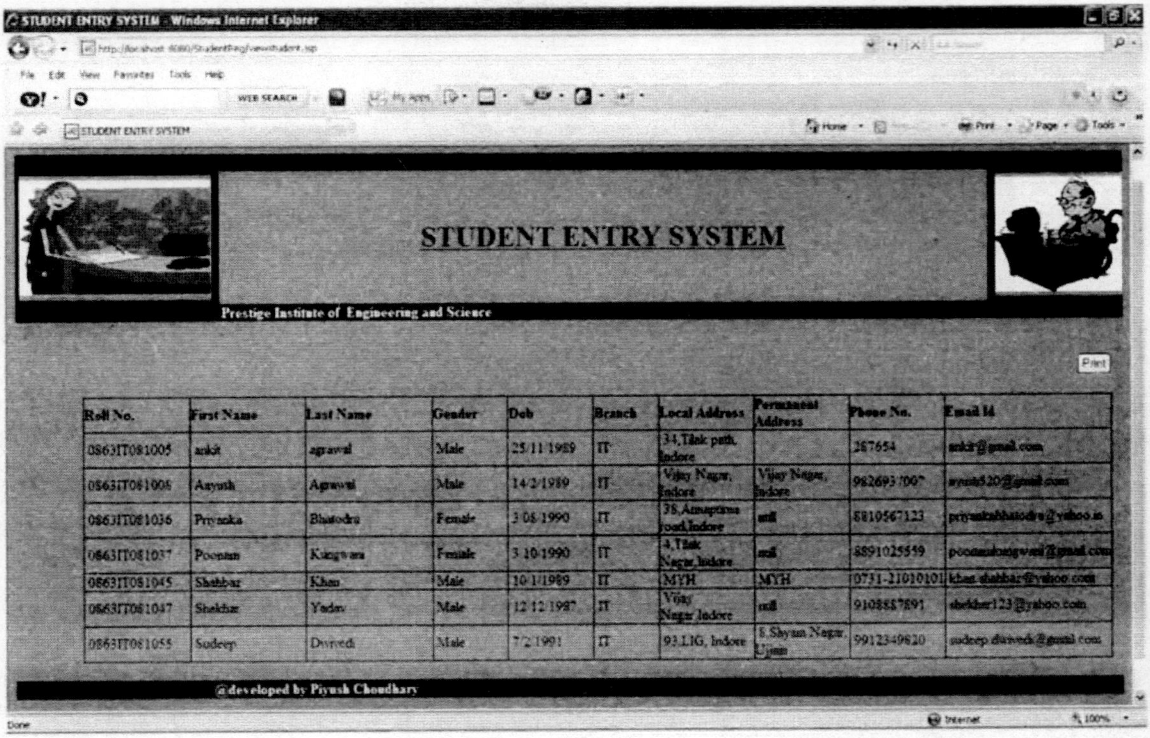
STUDENT ENTRY SYSTEM - Windows Internet Explorer
STUDENT ENTRY SYSTEM
Prestige Institute of Engineering and Science
Print
Roll No.
First Name
Last Name
Gender
Dob
Branch
Local Address
Permanent Address
Phone No.
Email Id
@developed by Piyush Choudhary

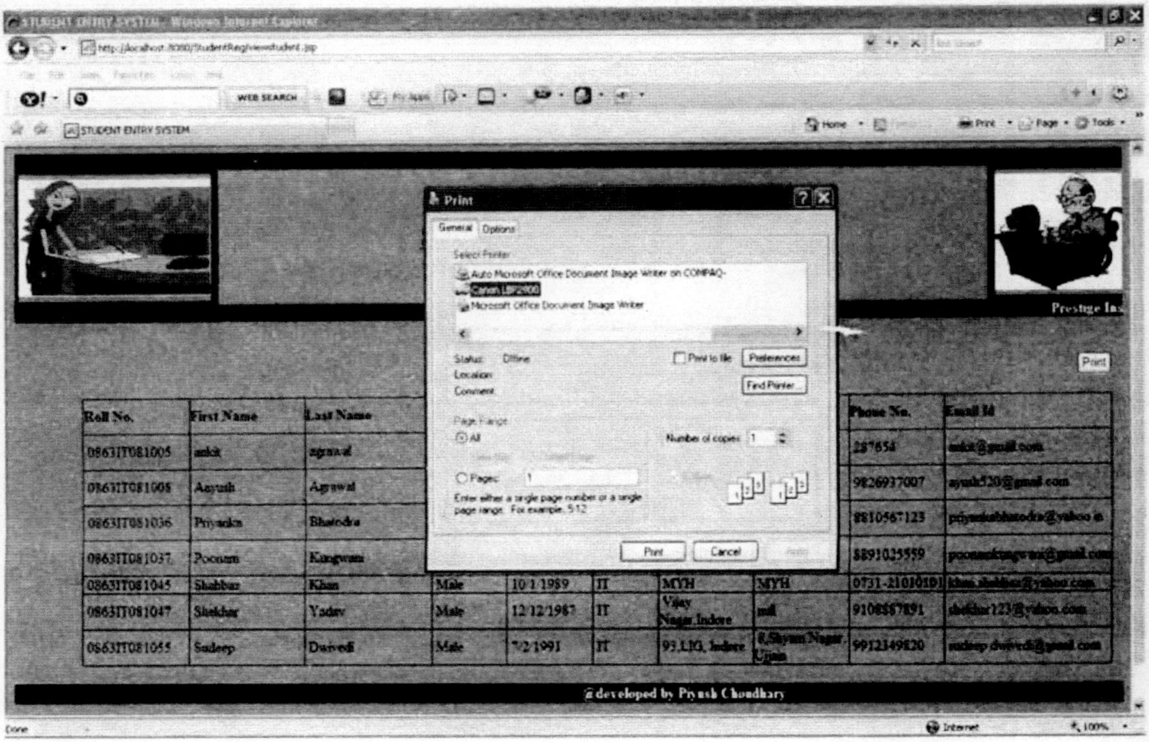
Print
General
Options
Select Printer
Status:
Location:
Comment:
Print to file
Preferences
Find Printer...
Page Range
All
Pages:
Number of copies:
Print
Cancel
Apply
@developed by Piyush Choudhary

APPENDIX I

Viva-Voce Questions

Q. 1. What is JAVA?

Ans. Java is a platform independent, object oriented programming language developed by Sun Microsystems in 1991.

Q. 2. What are the basic features of Java ?

Ans. There are various features of Java:

1. Java is Platform Independent and Portable
2. Object Oriented
3. Freeware
4. Compile and Interpreted
5. Robust
6. Secure
7. Distributed
8. Simple
9. Multithreaded and interactive
10. High performance
11. Dynamic and extensible

Q. 3. What is Platform Independency?

Ans. In Java, after compilation, the **source code** is converted to **Byte code (.class file).** The Byte code is not machine specific code. Java compiles with the help of JRE (Java Run Time Environment) and JRE doesn't require operating system during compilation and hence Java is Platform Independent language.

Q. 4. What is JDK (Java Development Tool Kit) ?

Ans. JDK comes with a collection of tools that are used for developing and running java program. They include:

1. Applet Viewer — for viewing java applet

2. Javac — Java Compile
3. Java — Java Interpreter
4. Javadoc — for creating HTML documents
5. Javah — for c header files
6. Javap — Java disassembler
7. jdb — Java debugger

Q. 5. What is JSL (Java Standard Libraries) or Application Programming Interface (API) ?

Ans. Java Standard Libraries or API includes several or hundreds of methods grouped into several functional packages like—

1. Language Support Packages
2. Utilities Packages
3. Input/Output Packages
4. Networking Packages
5. Awt Packages
6. Applet Packages

Q. 6. What is Java Environments ?

Ans. Java Environment includes

1. JDK
2. API or JSL

Q. 7. Define the keywords.

Ans.
1. **Public Keyword :** The keyword public is given which is an **access specifier** that declares main method as unprotected and therefore making it accessible to all other classes.
2. **Static :** Next appears the keyword **static**, which declares this method as one that belongs to entire class and not the part of any object of the class. The **main** must be declared as **static** since the interpreter uses this method before any objects are created.
3. **Void :** The type modifier **void** states that the main method does not return any value (but simply prints some text to the screen).
4. **Final :** A keyword that makes variable constant.
5. **Break :** The break statement is used to permanently out current loop.
6. **Continue :** The continue statement is used to terminate the current iteration only and resumes the loop.

Q. 8. What is JVM (Java Virtual Machine) ?

Ans. All language compilers translate source code into machine code for a specific computer. Java compiler produces an intermediate code known as **Byte code** for a machine that doesn't exist. This machine is called **JAVA VIRTUAL MACHINE** and it exists only inside computer memory. It is simulated computer and does all major function of real computer.

Q. 9. Difference between C++ and JAVA?

Ans.

S.No.	C++	Java
1.	C++ was developed by Bjarne Stroutsup in 1970's.	Java was developed by James Gosling in 1995.
2.	C++ support classes, Structure and Unions.	Java Support Classes but doesn't support Structure or Unions.
3.	Global Function and Global data is allowed in C++	Global Function and Global data are not allowed in Java.
4.	C++ supports multiple inheritance.	Java doesn't support Multiple inheritance.
5.	C++ supports the concept of Pointers.	Java doesn't support the concept of Pointers. This make Java program to be very safe.
6.	C++ supports all data types like integer, character, float etc., but it doesn't support Boolean type.	Java supports all data types including Boolean type which provide true or false value.
7.	C++ requires that classes and functions be declared before they are used.	It is not necessary in Java to declare classes and functions before they used.
8.	C++ support Constructor as well as Destructor.	Java support Constructor, but there is no destructor in Java.
9.	Data Structure classes are not their.	Several "data structure" classes are contained in the "standard" version of Java. More specifically, they are contained in the standard class library that is distributed with the Java Development Kit (JDK).
10.	It doesn't support concept of Multithreading.	Multithreading is a standard feature of the Java language.
11.	It doesn't support concept of Exception Handling.	It support concept of Exception handling.
12.	C++ support operator overloading	Java does not support operator overloading.
13.	C++ doesn't have built-in support for program documentation.	Java has built-in support for program documentation.

Q. 10. Define the keywords.

Ans. 1. **Objects:** The basic runtime entity in a object oriented system is known as **Object**.

2. **Classes:** The collection of objects of similar type is known as **Class**.

3. **Data Abstraction: Abstraction** refers to the act of representing essential features without including the background details or explanation.

4. **Data Encapsulation**: The wrapping up of data into a single unit is known as **Encapsulation**. It means that data is not accessible to the outside world and only those functions which are wrapped in the class can access it.
5. **Inheritance**: The process by which object of one class acquire the properties of object of another class is known as **Inheritance**. For inheriting the class we use the keyword **extends**.
6. **Polymorphism**: Polymorphism is another OOP concept. It may be defined as "Ability to take more than one form is known as **Polymorphism**."
7. **Dynamic Binding**: Binding refers to the linking of a procedure call to be executed in response to the call. **Dynamic Binding** means that the code associated with a given procedure call is not known until the time of the call at runtime.
8. **Message Passing**: One object communicates with other object by passing messages to one another.
9. **Constructor**: A method that is used to create an instantiation of class is known as **Constructor**.
10. **Methods**: Small functions that we use inside the class are known as **Methods**.
11. **Arrays:** An Array is a group of data items of similar data types. It is defined as- "**Collection of data Items of Similar data types is known as Array**."
12. **String:** String represents sequence of character.

Q. 11. What is Wrapper Class?

Ans. The Primitive data types like int, float, long, char and double may be converted into object types by using the **Wrapper classes** contained in the **java.lang** packages.

Q. 12. What is Type Casting?

Ans. The process of converting one data type into another is known as **Type Casting**.

Q. 13. What is Abstract Class?

Ans. A class that cannot be instantiated directly is known as **Abstract class**. Abstract classes exist so that subclasses can inherit variables and methods from them.

Q. 14. What do you mean by Operator Precedence?

Ans. **Operator Precedence** determines the order in which mathematical operations are performed.

Q. 15. What do you mean by Multithreading?

Ans. **Multithreading** is a conceptual programming paradigm where a program(process) is divided into two or more sub-programs(process) which can be implemented in same time in parallel.

Q. 16. What is Threads?

Ans. Program in execution is known as **Process.** A small process is known as **Thread**.

Q. 17. What do you mean by Generics in Java ?

Ans. **Generics** are a facility of generic programming that was added to the Java programming language in 2004 as part of J2SE 5.0. They allow "a type or method to operate on objects of various types while providing compile-time type safety."

Q. 18. What do you mean by Packages in Java?

Ans. The way of grouping of varieties of classes and/or interfaces together is known as **Packages**. The grouping is done according to functionality.

For example, java.lang, java.util, java.io, java.awt, java.net etc.

Q. 19. Explain Exception Handling in Java?

Ans. **Exception Handling** allows to detect errors easily. The term "Exception" means Error and the term "**Exception Handling**" stands for handling the error.

Q. 20. What do you mean by Method Overloading?

Ans. In java, it is possible to create methods that have the same name, but different parameter lists and different definitions. This is called **Method Overloading**.

Q. 21. Explain the following Data Structures.

Ans. 1. **Linked List:** The Linked List or one way list is a linear collection of data items called nodes, linked to one another. The logical ordering is represented by having each element pointing to the next element.

2. **Stack:** The Stack is a non-primitive linear data structure. It is defined as the list in which addition of new data item and deletion of already existing data item is done from only one end called **Top** of the stack. The stack means **Last in First Out**.

3. **Queue:** A Queue is a non-primitive linear data structure. It is an ordered group of elements in which element is are added at one end called **Rear End** and the existing elements are removed from the other end called **Front end**.

4. **Trees:** A Tree is nonlinear non-primitive data structure mainly used to represent data containing hierarchical relationship between elements.

Q. 22. What do you mean by Socket and Socket Programming?

Ans. **Sockets** were originally developed at the University of California at Berkeley as a tool to easily accomplish network programming.

Q. 23. What do you mean by Servlets?

Ans. A Servlet is a small program that runs on the server.

Q. 24. What is JDBC and ODBC?

Ans. **JDBC** stands for **Java Database Connectivity**.

ODBC stands for **Open database Connectivity**.

Q. 25. What are Applets?

Ans. A java program that is embedded in an HTML document and run in context of a Java-capable browser.

Q. 26. What is JSP?

Ans. **Java Server Pages (JSP)** is a server side Java technology that allows software developers to create dynamically generated web pages.

Q. 27. What is J2ME?

Ans. **Java Platform, Micro Edition**, or **Java ME**, is a Java platform designed for mobile devices and embedded systems.

Q. 28. What is J2EE?

Ans. **Java Platform, Enterprise Edition** or **Java EE** is a widely used platform for server programming in the Java programming language. The Java platform (Enterprise Edition) differs from the Java Standard Edition Platform (Java SE) in that it adds libraries which provide functionality to deploy fault-tolerant, distributed, multi-tier Java software, based largely on modular components running on an application server.

Q. 29. What is EJB?

Ans. **Enterprise JavaBeans (EJB)** is a managed, server-side component architecture for modular construction of enterprise applications.

Q. 30. What is XML?

Ans. **XML (Extensible Markup Language)** is a set of rules for encoding documents electronically. It is defined in the XML 1.0 Specification produced by the W3C and several other related specifications; all are fee-free open standards.

Notes :

1. Java does not support the concept of pointers
2. Java does not support the concept of multiple inheritances but it supports the concepts of interfaces.
3. Access specifiers means Public, Private and Protected.

❑❑❑

APPENDIX II

Java Keywords

Keyword	Meaning
Abstract	an abstract class or method
Assert	used to locate internal program errors
Boolean	the Boolean type
Break	breaks out of a switch or loop
Byte	the 8-bit integer type
case	a case of a switch
catch	The clause of a try block catching an exception
char	the Unicode character type
class	defines a class type
const	not used
continue	continues at the end of a loop
default	the default clause of a switch
Do	the top of a do/while loop
double	the double-precision floating-number type
else	the else clause of an if statement
extends	defines the parent class of a class
final	a constant, or a class or method that cannot be overridden
finally	the part of a try block that is always executed
float	the single-precision floating-point type
For	a loop type
goto	not used

Keyword	Meaning
If	a conditional statement
implements	defines the interface(s) that a class implements
import	imports a package
instanceof	tests if an object is an instance of a class
Int	the 32-bit integer type
interface	an abstract type with methods that a class can implement
long	the 64-bit long integer type
native	A method implemented by the host system
new	allocates a new object or array
null	a null reference
package	a package of classes
private	a feature that is accessible only by methods of this class
protected	a feature that is accessible only by methods of this class, its children, and other classes in the same package
public	a feature that is accessible by methods of all classes
return	returns from a method
short	the 16-bit integer type
static	a feature that is unique to its class, not to objects of its class
strictfp	Use strict rules for floating-point computations
super	the superclass object or constructor
switch	a selection statement
synchronized	a method or code block that is atomic to a thread
this	the implicit argument of a method, or a constructor of this class
throw	throws an exception
throws	the exceptions that a method can throw
transient	marks data that should not be persistent
Try	a block of code that traps exceptions
void	denotes a method that returns no value
volatile	ensures that a field is coherently accessed by multiple threads
while	a loop

❑❑❑

B.E. (FIFTH SEMESTER) EXAMINATION, MAY-DEC., 2009
IT-505(N) (NEW SCHEME)
(INFORMATION TECHNOLOGY ENGG. BRANCH)
JAVA PROGRAMMING

Time : *Three Hours*

Maximum Marks:100

Minimum Marks:35

Note : *Attempt any five questions. All question carry equal marks.*

1. (*a*) How many interface can a class inherit and can a same interface be inherited by two different classes? Explain it.

(*b*) Explain abstract classes with an example program. Also describe the properties of abstract classes.

OR

2. (*a*) What is multiple inheritance and how to perform it in java?

(*b*) Write a program which will read a string and rewrite it in the alphabetical order. For example, String should be written as GNIRTS.

3. (*a*) What is an Event Delegation model and what are event classes and event interfaces?

(*b*) Create applet in which one string moves from left to right.

OR

4. (*a*) What is the difference between AWT and Swing?

(*b*) Write an AWT application with check box such that all cable TV channels will be displayed from the selected category.

5. (*a*) Explain the following term briefly.

(*i*) Multithreading

(*ii*) Daemon thread

(*iii*) Thread Synchronization

(*b*) Write a program to demonstrate "IndexOutOfBounds-Exception".

OR

6. (*a*) List ten different exception defined in Java.

(*b*) Write a program which contains three threads.

7. (*a*) Write a program to illustrate reading data with the help of StringTokenizer.

(*b*) Why do we need stream objects?

OR

8. (*a*) Explain the architecture of JDBC.

(*b*) How to establish connection with database in Java? Write a code for connection.

9. (*a*) What is the difference between TCP/IP programming and datagram programming?

(*b*) Explain TCP/IP programming with example.

OR

10. (*a*) Explain the client server architecture.

(*b*) Write the steps of creating RMI application with example.

B.E. (FIFTH SEMESTER) EXAMINATION, JUNE, 2010
IT-505(N) (NEW SCHEME)
(INFORMATION TECHNOLOGY ENGG. BRANCH)
JAVA PROGRAMMING

Time *: Three Hours* *Maximum Marks:100*

Minimum Marks:35

Note : *Attempt any five questions. All question carry equal marks.*

1. (*a*) What is Java Virtual Machine (JVM) and its role in Java Programming environment ? Explain.

(*b*) Explain Application Programming Interface (API) and what do you mean by Interface.

2. (*a*) Differentiate between the following :

(*i*) Application and Applet in Java.

(*ii*) Compiler and Interpreter in Java.

(*b*) Explain abstract class and abstract method in java with example.

3. (*a*) How many layout are available in AWT package in Java? Explain each layout in brief.

(*b*) Explain in brief container and component in AWT package.

4. (*a*) What is Applet? Explain its life cycle.

(*b*) Explain swing package in Java.

5. (*a*) What are the basic idea of multithreaded programming and its synchronization?

(*b*) Explain the term try, catch and throw with respect to exception handling in Java.

6. (*a*) Explain java input and output stream.

(*b*) Explain JDBC and ODBC bridge and role of driver manager.

7. (*a*) Why do you need Java.net package to write Java networking program? Explain.

(*b*) Explain Remote Method Invocation (RMI) and its client-server architecture.

8. Write short notes on the following:

(*a*) Byte code in java

(*b*) Security

(*c*) Garbage collection

(*d*) Adapter classes

B.E. (FIFTH SEMESTER) EXAMINATION, DEC., 2010
IT-505(N) (NEW SCHEME)
(INFORMATION TECHNOLOGY ENGG. BRANCH)
JAVA PROGRAMMING

Time : Three Hours

Maximum Marks:100

Minimum Marks:35

Note : *Attempt any five questions. All question carry equal marks.*

UNIT-I

1. (*a*) What are the advantages of platform independent languages? Also explain how java is platform independent.

   (*b*) What is method overloading? What are important points which should be taken care of while overloading methods? Write a Java program to explain the working of overloaded methods.

OR

2. (*a*) What is Constructor? Write a Java Program to explain the need of a constructor.

   (*b*) Discuss the requirement of each keyword in the following Java program statement.
   "public static void main(String args[])"

UNIT-II

3. (*a*) Using AWT classes,create a closeable window to receive the following inputs:
   (*i*) User name
   (*ii*) Sex
   (*iii*) Qualification
   (*iv*) Address
   Submit and reset button.

   (*b*) Explain in detail:
   (*i*) Advantages of swing over AWT
   (*ii*) Life cycle of applet.

OR

4. (*a*) Receive two values as command line argument and display their sum.

   (*b*) What is event? Explain different components of an event.

UNIT-III

5. (*a*) Explain the following terms briefly:
   (*i*) Multithreading
   (*ii*) Daemon Thread
   (*iii*) Thread Synchronization

(*b*) What is an exception? Explain with an example how exceptions are handled in Java.

OR

6. (*a*) Create a try block that is likely to generate three types of exception and then incorporate necessary catch blocks to catch and handle them appropriately.

   (*b*) What is 'Super' in Java? Explain at least two different uses of 'Super' in the Java program with an example.

UNIT-IV

7. (*a*) Using file input stream write the contents of a Text Area in C:\\My Documents folder.

   (*b*) What are the differences between DataOutput Stream and PrintStream.

OR

8. (*a*) How are the data input and output streams used to read and write data?

   (*b*) Write the procedure to establish connection with the remote database.

UNIT-V

9. (*a*) Explain the steps of creating RMI applications with an example.

   (*b*) How do you create a server socket? What port numbers can be used ? What happens if a requested socket number is already in use? Can a port connect to multiple clients?

OR

10. (*a*) How does a client program imitate a connection?

    (*b*) Explain client/server architecture. What is RMI registry services?

❑❑❑

INDEX

A

B

C

D

E

F

G

H

I

J

K

L

U

V

W

❑❑❑

Win Prizes

ATTENTION READERS

Win Prizes

We request for your frank assessment regarding various aspects of the book as given below:

JAVA PROGRAMMING

(RGTU)

By : PIYUSH CHOUDHARY

Please Fill up the Sheet in Neat and Clean Writing

(i) What topics of your syllabus, important for your examination point of view, are not covered in this book ?

....

....

....

....

(ii) What are the chapters wherein the treatment of the subject matter is not systematic or organised or updated?

....

....

....

....

(iii) Have you come across misprints/mistakes/factual inaccuracies in the book? Please specify the chapters and the page numbers.

....

....

....

....

(iv) What other books on the same subject have you found/heard better than the present book? Please specify in terms of price and quality

....

....

....

....

(v) Further suggestions and comments for the improvement of this book.

....

....

....

....

(PS: If need be please attach a separate sheet to write your views)

OTHER DETAILS

(i) Who recommended you this book? (Please tick (✓) in the box near the option relevant to you.

Teacher ☐ ☐ Friends ☐ Bookseller

....

....

....

....

(ii) Name of the recommending teacher, his designation and address:

....

....

....

....

(iii) Name and address of the bookseller you purchased the book from :

....

....

....

....

(iv) Name and address of your institution (Please mention the University or Board as the case may be)

....

....

....

....

(v) Your name and complete postal address:

....

....

....

....

(vi) Course you are enrolled in:

....

....

....

....

The best assessment will be awarded each month: The award will be in the form of our publications as decided by the Editorial Board.

Please mail the filled up coupon at your earliest to:

S.K. KATARIA & SONS®
4885/109, Prakash Mahal, Dr. Subhash Bhargav Lane,
Opposite Delhi Medical Association, Daryaganj, New Delhi–110002 (INDIA)
Phone: +91-11-43551243; Mobile: +91-9871775858, 7678425209
e-mail: katariabook@gmail.com, katariabooks@yahoo.com
Website: www.skkatariaandsons.com